Visual Usability

Visual Usability

Principles and Practices for Designing Digital Applications

Tania Schlatter
and Deborah Levinson

AMSTERDAM • BOSTON • HEIDELBERG • LONDON
NEW YORK • OXFORD • PARIS • SAN DIEGO
SAN FRANCISCO • SINGAPORE • SYDNEY • TOKYO

Morgan Kaufmann is an imprint of Elsevier

Acquiring Editor: *Meg Dunkerley*
Development Editor: *Heather Scherer*
Project Manager: *Malathi Samayan*
Designer: *Russell Purdy*

Morgan Kaufmann is an imprint of Elsevier
225 Wyman Street, Waltham, MA 02451, USA

Notices
Knowledge and best practice in this field are constantly changing. As new research and experience broaden
our understanding, changes in research methods or professional practices, may become necessary. Practitioners
and researchers must always rely on their own experience and knowledge in evaluating and using any information
or methods described herein. In using such information or methods they should be mindful of their own safety
and the safety of others, including parties for whom they have a professional responsibility.

To the fullest extent of the law, neither the Publisher nor the authors, contributors, or editors, assume any
liability for any injury and/or damage to persons or property as a matter of products liability, negligence or
otherwise, or from any use or operation of any methods, products, instructions, or ideas contained in the
material herein.

Library of Congress Cataloging-in-Publication Data
Levinson, Deborah A.
   Visual usability : principles and practices for designing digital applications / Deborah Levinson and Tania Schlatter.
      pages cm
   Includes bibliographical references and index.
   ISBN 978-0-12-398536-1 (alk. paper)
   1. Computer software—Human factors. 2. Software engineering. 3. Software visualization. I. Schlatter, Tania.
   II. Title.
   QA76.76.H85L48 2013
   005.1—dc23

                                                                              2013001110

British Library Cataloguing-in-Publication Data
A catalogue record for this book is available from the British Library

ISBN: 978-0-12-398536-1

For information on all MK publications
visit our website at http://store.elsevier.com

Printed and bound by CPI Group (UK) Ltd, Croydon, CR0 4YY

Transferred to digital print 2012

Contents

Contents

Acknowledgments

It took far more than just two people to bring this book to life. We'd like to thank:

- Morgan-Kaufmann employees past and present: Meg Dunkerley, Robyn Day, Heather Scherer, and Steve Elliot, who took *Visual Usability* from concept to the printed and digital page; and Rachel Roumeliotis, who first contacted us about turning a Boston CHI seminar presentation into this book.

- Our reviewers for both the book proposal and the book itself, who sent invaluable comments about how to shape the final manuscript: Cynthia Baron, Ted Booth, Vanessa DiMauro, Antony Donovan, Frank Gruger, Chad Jennings, Jennifer McPhilimy, Aaron Oppenheimer, Sharon Poggenpohl, Louis Weitzman, and Blake Winton.

- Gretchen McClure, who worked tirelessly and cheerfully on the SuperTracker redesign.

- Kurt Fendt, Maz Kessler, Kara Parsons, and Matt Sigelman, for their additional support.

Tania would also like to thank her family, Tom, Luke, and Otelia, for their encouragement and enthusiasm; Debby, whose patience I tested on numerous occasions, but whose support and indulgence made the book possible; and our clients, who enable us to practice, learn, and further develop our skills and expertise.

Debby would like to thank her patient spouse, Todd Belton, for support, read-through, and martinis; Tania, for putting up with me and being the creative force behind this book; Stacey Becker, Bill Coderre, Francis Heaney, and Judy Keys for supplying screenshots, links, and editorial backup brains; and her family, friends, Twitter followers, LJ flist, and fellow Suspects for their assistance and encouragement.

About the Authors

Tania Schlatter is a visual designer equally interested in content, form, and people. She designs interfaces and communication systems that help people by combining user-centered and visual design techniques and applying them to complex applications.

Tania has been practicing design for more than 20 years. Her formal design study includes an M.Des. in human-centered communication design from the Institute of Design in Chicago; a summer with Paul Rand and Armin Hofmann in Brissago, Switzerland; and a BFA in graphic design from Boston University. She served as the first experience design chair for the AIGA at the local level. Tania currently teaches interactive information design to graduate students at Northeastern University in Boston. Tania can be reached on Twitter at @taniaschlatter.

Deborah A. Levinson is a user interface designer with over 16 years of expertise helping designers, engineers, and communications professionals find common ground and build successful digital applications. A former webmaster for the Massachusetts Institute of Technology, Debby is also a coauthor of *The MIT Guide to Teaching Website Design*, published by MIT Press in April 2001. She and Tania co-own Nimble Partners, a Boston-area user experience and user interface design firm. Debby can be reached on Twitter at @nimblepartners.

The year this book was written, Tania and Debby worked with the founder of Catapult.org to define the site's user experience and administrative interface; with researchers at MIT's HyperStudio on interfaces for social annotation; with CafePress.com; and with a software firm on a suite of applications utilizing artificial intelligence and labor data.

Introduction

"Visual communication of any kind, whether persuasive or informative ... should be seen as the embodiment of form and function: the integration of the beautiful and the useful."

—Paul Rand, *A Designer's Art, p. 3*

Digital applications are designed for use. They help people get things done, whether purchasing a gift, conducting research, processing patients, or managing systems. They're highly interactive. They display content pulled from databases. They communicate with other systems. They're dynamic, and change without our touching them. They often enable more than one type of activity, such as finding and managing patient records.

As designers who focus on user experience for complex applications, too often we see applications that either look great or are highly functional—but not both. As these applications become the primary tools for what we do at work, how we manage our lives, and how we socialize and entertain ourselves, we believe the gap in form and function can and must be closed.

We see a lot of potential. What makes these applications challenging to design is also what makes them compelling to use—real-time access to data. Compare managing household finances in a desktop spreadsheet program to managing them online with Mint.com: the spreadsheet provides a static view of your current status, and you must manually enter information about your bank accounts and spending. By contrast, Mint.com imports up-to-the-minute data about your finances and uses charts, projections, and recommendation tools to provide highly visual, interactive ways to explore not just where you are now, but how your spending and investments could affect you in the future.

The challenge

When designing applications, we know firsthand how challenging it is to focus both on aesthetics and functionality, even when everyone involved wants a great interface. Team members often come from different disciplines. Language and ideals differ and conflict. Roles overlap. Education hasn't kept up with the pace of change: graphic design training teaches how to create "beautiful" or "innovative" interactive designs, but that isn't enough to guide the design of complex, visual systems; and computer science usability courses don't yield competition-crushing, desirable interfaces.

The ubiquity of digital applications has diluted and washed away early conventions we depended on to help us design and use web-based systems. The number of technical platforms and devices that applications are developed on and for has resulted in a dizzying set of rapidly evolving standards and patterns. The days of relying on blue, underlined hyperlinks are gone. Today, there's no single pattern of use, and no unified visual language for application design. All this change makes designing applications a free-for-all, and using them an ad-hoc experience.

While we have no desire to return to the straightjacket of blue, underlined links, we want the applications we design and use to be more than merely usable. Clients come to us when they realize their functional applications need to look more professional or are expensive to support because they're hard to use—in short, when they realize that better-designed interfaces can improve customer satisfaction and set them apart from their competition. In the offline world, retail giant Target changed the discount big-box retailing model by using design to differentiate its products and stores. Most data-driven applications are a bit like standard big-box retailers: they aren't exciting, but they're part of life, and provide what's needed to a lot of people. They can be improved beyond the drab standard with design grounded in principles of aesthetics and an understanding of people—what we call *visual usability*.

Sending the right signals

Interfaces mediate communication and interaction through screens and networks. In this automated environment, there's a need for visual language made up of signs and symbols to inform and provide direction and feedback. Aaron Marcus called for a "visible language" in his ahead-of-its-time book, *Graphic Design for Electronic Documents and User Interfaces*, saying, "A primary technique to achieve improved visual communication is to use clear, distinct, consistent visible language. Visible language refers to all the verbal and visual signs that convey meaning to a viewer."[1]

Complex visual interfaces may have many messages to convey on a single screen. The challenge for design is to provide order, direction, and pattern to help people process and derive meaning from what they see. Communication involves a sender, a message, a signal that conveys the message, and a receiver or viewer who interprets the message. Thinking about these components sheds light on the fact that designers and developers don't control the entire process. In interface design, selecting elements with user expectations in mind, and combining those elements with visual signals people expect and understand, makes it more likely an audience will successfully interpret a message.

We don't need to be entertained when using applications to track packages or configure client accounts, but we do need interfaces that help us successfully manage increasing complexity, and keep our humanity in mind.

Approach and organization

This book focuses on presentation of what the user sees, and how to design that presentation for understanding. It aims to help anyone involved in creating digital interfaces define and defend a rationale for design decisions based on heuristics and best practices from a variety of languages and disciplines. It is grounded in usability research, perceptual psychology, web design, typographer's practices, visual design principles, and communication theory. Rather than pull together what has been well described elsewhere (e.g., user experience best practices), we refer to and reference these principles, and use them as design requirements. Our goal is to help you design complex application interfaces by providing a framework—what we call the *meta-principles*—to inform design decision-making that

[1] Marcus, A. *Graphic Design for Electronic Documents and User Interfaces*, p. 2.

bridges form and function, the beautiful and the useful. We outline the tools of interface design, show you how to use them successfully, and provide steps and tips to guide you throughout the design process.

Part I: The meta-principles

In the first section of the book, we introduce the three core meta-principles of consistency, hierarchy, and personality. There are many design principles—the second edition of *Universal Principles of Design* lists 125 of them!—but consistency, hierarchy, and personality are the ones we see that most strongly affect application design.

You can think of the meta-principles as if they're part of a language. *Consistency* and *hierarchy* are the grammar people learn while using your application: the basic elements that define how the language is spoken. The "words" you speak (i.e., the visual design characteristics you choose to convey your message) create your application's *personality*. While technology that affects interfaces changes, these underlying meta-principles hold true.

Beginning in Chapter 3, we use a case study—a sample redesign of the United States Department of Agriculture's food- and fitness-tracking application, SuperTracker[2]—to show how the meta-principles apply.

Chapter 1: Consistency

What does *consistency* mean in the context of visual design for applications, and how does it help people? Like spoken language, visual language needs to define conventions and use them consistently to be understandable. Chapter 1 includes a framework for understanding what people expect, and guidelines for how to apply visual design tools to create consistency.

---

[2] The USDA was not involved with our SuperTracker redesign, which was done purely as an example for this book.

Figure I.1 Related applications in a suite will be easier to use if they share conventions, such as consistent login/registration areas and positioning and treatment of primary buttons.

Chapter 2: Hierarchy

How do you make sure people notice what you need them to? Visual hierarchy is the perception and interpretation of the relative importance of elements on the screen. Chapter 2 explains the role of hierarchy in interface design, how to define it, and how to ensure your application uses hierarchy appropriately and informatively.

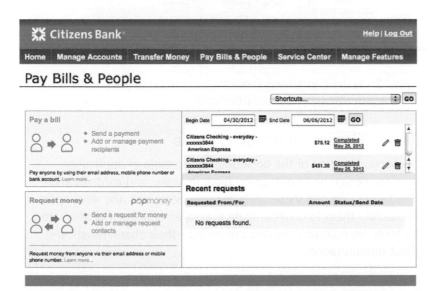

Figure I.2 Unclear hierarchy on a banking application screen. The eye is drawn to the tinted area at the top left, but pulled away by the strong use of contrast and greater real estate in the "Recent payments" area. Ideally, the "Pay a bill" and "Pay a person" sections would be more visually prominent, because that's what people have come here to do.

Chapter 3: Personality

John Maeda said, "Nobody wants objects or experiences that just do the job—they want something they *want* to do the job with."[3] Appeal affects perception of use.[4] An application's personality (i.e., the visual aspects that inform how people perceive it) helps build expectations about what the application does and who it's meant for. Chapter 3 discusses how to define personality and its attributes, and how to extend them throughout your application.

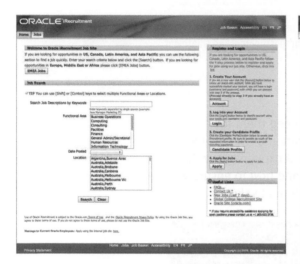

Figure I.3 The lack of personality on Oracle's online recruitment application is a missed opportunity to inspire potential candidates.

Part II: The visual usability tools

The second section of the book defines the tools of application interface design as layout, color, type, imagery, and controls and affordances. We call these *tools* because designers and developers manipulate them to communicate messages and functionality. How the tools are manipulated and presented—their characteristics—affect interpretation.

[3] Maeda, J. (2012, Sept. 21). If Design's No Longer the Killer Differentiator, What Is? *WIRED*. Retrieved Nov. 13, 2012, from *http://www.wired.com/opinion/2012/09/so-if-designs-no-longer-the-killer-differentiator-what-is/*.

[4] The more appealing users find a website, the more usable they perceive it to be. Trachinsky, N. Aesthetic and Apparent Usability: Empirically Assessing Cultural and Methodological Issues. *CHI 97 Proceedings*, Atlanta, 1997, pp. 115–123.

These topics are common, but addressing how to use them in complex applications to help people is not. Part II focuses on applying each tool strategically to help people understand your application. A section in each chapter shows the evolution of the SuperTracker case study project, which began with mobile application design and extended to redesigning for the web.

Chapter 4: Layout

Where should the button go? Chapter 4 addresses positioning, alignment, white space, and grids, which affect perception of what goes with what. It also addresses practical considerations of layout at all levels of new and redesigned applications.

Chapter 5: Type

How many fonts do you need? How do you choose? This chapter introduces typography basics, reviews how to select the right fonts for your application, and supplies rules of thumb for professional-looking type.

Chapter 6: Color

Isn't color subjective? Why not just use blue? There's logic to choosing and using color strategically. Chapter 6 shows how to use color to help people know where they are, what they can do, and associate appropriate attributes with your application. It also covers how to choose a color palette, and how to decide where to use different colors.

Chapter 7: Imagery

What kind of images, if any, are appropriate for your application? Chapter 7 reviews the types of imagery that apply to applications—logos, photography/video, illustration, icons, patterns—and outlines when each is useful. Examples show how to use imagery to create contrast, draw attention, and provide valuable information without overwhelming the user.

Chapter 8: Controls and affordances

How do people know what they can do? Controls are interface elements and methods people use to interact with your application, and affordances a control's perceived properties—whether a button feels clickable, a slider draggable, and so on. Chapter 8 outlines methods and considerations for styling controls to help them reveal what they do.

Design Checklists

Because there are so many interface design best practices to keep in mind, each chapter in this book concludes with a checklist of tips to review.

Avoid common mistakes

Much of avoiding usability and visual design mistakes is about establishing consistency. It sounds simple, but is actually challenging. Interfaces that avoid common mistakes have these characteristics:

- Elements are organized using alignment (see Chapter 4).
- Elements are placed where people expect (see Chapters 1 and 4).
- Similar elements are placed in groups (see Chapters 1 and 4).
- Fonts are appropriate for the situation of use (see Chapter 5).
- Consistent typographic standards (see Chapters 1 and 5).
- Colors are appropriate for the situation of use (see Chapters 3 and 6).
- Consistent use of colors (see Chapters 1 and 6).
- Consistent use and styling of controls (see Chapters 1 and 8).

Make informed decisions

Having a sound rationale for design decisions helps establish and maintain a visual hierarchy, and is especially relevant as goals shift, requirements change, and features are added. Informed decisions result in:

- Typographic standards that create or support a visual hierarchy (see Chapters 2 and 5).
- Use of colors to help direct the eye (see Chapter 6).
- Images, logos, and iconography that enhance content and understanding (see Chapter 7).
- Appropriate design of controls to reveal their affordances (see Chapter 8).

Elevate the ordinary

Elevating the ordinary is about going beyond the everyday to communicate meaningfully. It involves delivering more than the basics, and has a lot to do with establishing an appropriate personality that appeals to users. Applications that elevate the ordinary may include:

- Colors that convey appropriate personality (see Chapters 3 and 6).
- Fonts that convey personality without distracting from content and use (see Chapters 3 and 5).
- Images such as a logo, icons, and patterns that convey personality and enhance understanding without distracting users (see Chapters 3 and 7).
- Use of motion to reveal and provide effective feedback (see Chapter 8).

Embodying form and function

Designing applications without mastering color, type, layout, and use of imagery is like filling a house with purely utilitarian furnishings: it's functional, but it isn't necessarily enjoyable. Information architecture and technical development provide what you need to sleep, bathe, and cook, but not what you need to relax.

Similarly, a house built without a sound rationale may look good at first, but it might be hard to remodel, and its paint may chip and peel within months. Design and development must work hand-in-hand to create a solid structure with a beautiful, comfortable interior.

Regardless of the type of application you design or maintain, we hope *Visual Usability* inspires you to improve and push your interfaces in ways that highlight your content; help people work, find, learn and connect; and earn loyalty.

Part I
The Meta-Principles

Consistency

"If in doubt, do it consistently."
>—***A. Marcus,*** Graphic Documents for Electronic Documents
>and User Interfaces, p. 43

What do we mean by consistency?

How do you learn to use an application that looks different on every page? That uses icons for actions in some places, and links for the same actions in others? Or that applies colors and fonts unreliably, emphasizing content and features without any discernible rules?

You can, but it won't be easy. To help users—and avoid common interface design mistakes—designers and developers need to establish rules for placement and treatment of interface elements and then stick to them. Just as you can't speak in English, French, and German and expect to be clearly understood, you can't mix visual interface characteristics without causing confusion.

Visual language, like verbal language, requires rules applied consistently to be recognized and interpreted. You can learn to interpret inconsistent cues or you can guess, but in applications that help people get things done, guessing games aren't fun.

Consistency may sound boring. There are no awards for "most consistent" interface. Whether you're designing an application or cooking dinner, doing something exactly the same way over and over isn't exciting. What *is* exciting is watching people use your interface to do the things they want to do. Keep in mind that consistency isn't about pleasing yourself—it's about pleasing others by giving them what they understand and can rely on.

Consistency and the marketplace

This book focuses on the design of digital applications that help people get things done—everything from complex tasks like online banking or software download, to simple tasks like leaving yourself a reminder on your cell phone. Even the smallest changes, such as moving the location of a button, can make a big difference in perception and usability. Creating a consistent interface that people can quickly grasp and figure out how to interact with is critical for the success of this kind of application.

Some types of applications have changed more rapidly than others. At this time, consumer interfaces are breaking new ground in terms of combining evolving technical capabilities with interaction and visual design. (Pinterest, which uses endless scroll to display a rich variety of images, is one example of this.) Still, there are a lot of people using awful-looking and awkward applications every day. Frequent users create workarounds—sequences of actions that they repeat to do what they need to despite an interface that doesn't fit their goals or methods of working—or they simply give up, and place costly calls to tech support.

Establishing consistency

Establishing consistency means setting and maintaining expectations by using elements people are familiar with. Expectations are set by what people see onscreen, as well as what they've seen in the past. For example, someone filling in payment information on a checkout screen may interpret the flow of the form based on the fields and organization they see, as well as what they saw on the login screen they just left. What they expect is affected by what they've seen on other login and payment information screens. They're likely to look for the "Submit" button in the same place they've seen it on other screens within the application, or they may look where they've seen it on payment forms elsewhere.

Establishing consistency depends on awareness of user expectations (Figure 1.1). Part of it is the expectation you set via visible conventions on the current screen; another part is the expectation set on other screens in the same application. A third part is beyond our control—it's set by what users have seen on separate applications.

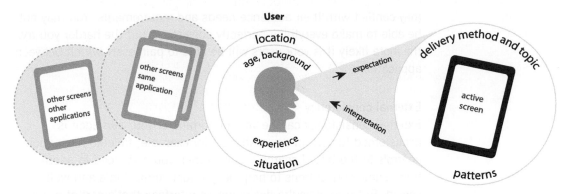

Figure 1.1 How people interpret what they see on a screen is affected by what they actively see, as well as what they've seen elsewhere in the same and in other applications.

If we're aware of what screens users perceive as related, we can *anticipate* their expectations. You're more likely to establish consistency successfully if you base design decisions on what users expect, discerning the patterns they've seen and incorporating what's relevant. You can, and in some cases must, adopt patterns used on related screens or applications into your interfaces to provide what people expect. (User-centered design methods like contextual inquiry and prototype tests can help you determine this; see Chapter 3 for more information.) Understanding user expectations is part of defining interface conventions—creating rules and a rationale for how your application's visual language will work.

Types of consistency: internal versus external

Consistency between screens within an application can be called *internal consistency*, while consistency between applications can be called *external consistency*. Put another way:

1. *External consistency*: Are the application's design, content, and behavior similar to other applications used by the same audience?

2. *Internal consistency*: Do the application's design, content, and behavior remain largely the same within screens and features, as well as within the boundaries of platform-specific limitations and requirements?

Internal and external consistency intersects when an application is part of a suite of related programs. In these circumstances, internally consistent elements of one application may apply to its suite-mates, or may conflict with their audience needs and requirements. You may not be able to make everything perfectly consistent, but the harder you try, the more likely it is your users will be able to painlessly switch between applications.

External consistency

External consistency can be very important. If your audience is accustomed to certain conventions—for example, faceted navigation controls to the left of search results—then you may need to adopt these same conventions to help people feel comfortable and well served. But unless you're designing an interface that's part of a suite or overall product line, external consistency for the sake of it is, frankly, ridiculous. Your audience may not have the same needs as the audience for the website or mobile application your CEO has fallen in love with, and the choices those designers made to help their users aren't necessarily the best choices for your users.

Thinking about and reviewing external consistency are great ways to start defining interface conventions for a new application started from scratch. If your users have strong expectations, then part of establishing consistency needs to include reviewing and possibly adopting patterns used in other applications. You can begin by researching and asking yourself what sort of layout and interface controls the audience might be familiar with based on demographics or known user characteristics, and you can inform assumptions by conducting surveys and contextual inquiries.

New applications for organizations with an existing product set can be started this way as well. For example, imagine you're developing an event registration application for a company that produces productivity software. The event registration application represents a new product line, will have its own name, and may be for a different set of users than the company's other products.

It makes sense to begin the design process by comparing features and looking for commonalities. If the applications share features, you may be able to reuse the underlying code. Even if the event registration application has a completely different brand name, it could be prudent from a corporate brand consistency standpoint to use the same general layout, controls and affordances, and cascading style sheet (CSS) code (or at least font characteristics) for the new application. This will help the parent company appear consistent and organized to users, as well as in marketing materials and campaigns.

Internal consistency

Internal consistency is when the application's design and behavior remain largely the same within screens and features. Having an internally consistent application is a big part of avoiding common mistakes and is also crucial to usability. No one wants to learn a new language on every screen. No one wants to guess whether they have to tap or swipe to see more information, and then have to guess again on the next screen. What they want is to use what they already know to get things done as quickly as possible.

Internal consistency is achieved when the visual usability tools in an application—that is, layout, type, color, imagery, treatments, and controls and affordances—are applied consistently at the screen and widget level. If the application is available across platforms (e.g., desktop/laptop, mobile phone, tablet), the tools should be applied as consistently as possible while still taking platform-specific user interface (UI) conventions into account. Internal consistency is why selecting appropriate paradigms is so important; ideally, once you decide on a convention, you can use it over and over again, and users won't think twice. If you choose a paradigm based on one case and then find it doesn't apply to others, it's time to rework it.

What role does consistency play in application design?

Successful application design requires juggling business goals, audience needs, design rationale, and technical capabilities, all while keeping in mind the basic usability principle popularized by Steve Krug: "Don't make me think." Not making people think requires understanding your audience: who they are, when and how they use your application, and why they use it. It also includes understanding their expectations: the basic knowledge you can expect them to have, their level of comfort with technology, and what similar applications they're using.

Assuming you have that understanding as part of a sound user-centered design process, the next step is using what you've learned to inform all aspects of the interface design:

- *Layout*: Have you positioned elements that perform the same function in the same place on every page?
- *Typography*: Do you treat similar elements the same way typographically?
- *Color*: Do you have a set of colors defined, and a system for applying color to emphasize and support your information hierarchy?
- *Imagery*: Do you use the same style of images to convey similar information?
- *Controls and affordances*: Do you use the same interface elements and design treatments to represent the same actions? Do you use the same motions for feedback and interactive controls?

Consistency in layout

In any application, you're going to have pages or screens that show similar types of information, and they'll include units of functionality (widgets, content blocks, etc.) that may perform similar tasks no matter where they appear. These two rules of thumb will help you create your layout:

1. Screens showing the same types of information should have all elements positioned (i.e., laid out) the same way every time.
2. Different elements that relate to one another should maintain their spatial relationship no matter where they appear. For example, in an e-commerce application, a product name should always be placed in a consistent position relative to the product image.

The best way to ensure this happens is by developing templates for your different widgets and screen types. If you're a developer, you're probably already very familiar with the concept of templates within the context of content management systems; if you're a designer, you've probably used them in print and website layouts. The basis of a template is a grid. Like a grid, a good template is flexible enough to accommodate change, but strong enough to support consistent placement from screen to screen. (We'll go into grids and template design more in Chapter 4.)

Let's take a look at some real-world examples: Google applications Gmail, Google News, and Google Drive (Figure 1.2). Although their layouts are different, they share structural similarities that make them feel like part of a single family. Because they are independent but may share users, we consider them to be externally consistent. However, these applications have also become increasingly internally consistent over time, likely as part of Google's efforts to improve cross-platform application usability and appearance. Their similarities include:

- Cross-application navigation bar at the top.
- Secondary bar containing logo on the left, a search feature in the center, and a user identification and sharing tool on the right.
- Left column to identify the application and provide internal navigation.
- Main content area in one or two columns to the right of the navigation bar.
- Application tools and configuration above the main content area.

Figure 1.2 (a) Gmail, (b) Google News, (c) Google Drive have evolved to use a consistent visual language.

If you were going to design another Google application, potentially for use by the same audience, you'd want to begin by reviewing these existing applications for similarities in content and features. You'd want to place the application name and navigation in the same position, and reuse elements as much as possible to make the new application familiar to people who use the other applications in the suite. The conventions you adopt become the starting point for the rules and rationale for the new application's layout.

Consistent use of typography

The fonts you choose and the way you apply them are vital parts of creating a strong information hierarchy. Applying a standard set of type specifications to your headers and content helps people quickly discern what's important; applying it inconsistently creates a muddle, where people have to scan an entire page or screen (or worse, several screens) to find what they want.

Although we've already discussed how Google uses a limited number of layouts across some applications to help create consistency, we can see in those same examples that their typography is consistent as well, at least for related types of data. The primary interface for Google Drive (Figure 1.2c) and Gmail (Figure 1.2a) is a tabular list of information. Both applications set this type in the same point size and font, and use a well-spaced navigation area on the left.

The two applications also use font weight and color choices to emphasize the hierarchy of information.

- Google Drive uses black, roman type for a document name, followed by the document's sharing status—less important information—in smaller, gray type.
- Gmail puts the most important information for new messages—the sender's name and message subject line—in bold, unmissable type, and begins to expose the message content in roman, gray type.
- Google Drive boldfaces the names of files with recent changes, indicating they're more important than the unchanged files in roman text.

Despite some of the outward differences between the applications, their shared typographic standards help people understand what they need to pay attention to and when, no matter which application they're using.

Consistency in color

When developing your application, you'll need a color palette with primary, secondary, and accent colors. Your color palette is another tool to help people "read" the interface. Color helps identify what's related by leading the brain to group elements of the same color. It also helps us know what's more important, drawing the eye to key elements if they're colored in a warm, saturated hue, and helping others recede into the background.

JetBlue's mobile application is externally consistent with the corporate website's color palette: dark blue, lighter shades of the same blue, and bright orange accents.

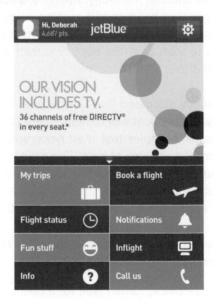

Figure 1.3 JetBlue mobile application's home screen.

The application's home screen introduces two of the main aspects of the color palette, and begins to shape the rules for how it's applied (Figure 1.3). There's a dark blue header area with bold, white type to identify where you are and who's logged in to the application, as well as a slightly paler, dimensional area for settings on the right. But the most important application of the color palette appears below the large promotional area: the tabular display for key actions that alternates dark blue and light blue to make it easier to distinguish different active areas. Related areas share the same row, but because they don't share the same color, you can quickly tell where to tap to get what you want (Figure 1.4).

JetBlue's rules for how to apply the color palette become clearer on the secondary screens. Again, large, dark blue areas with white type guide the eye to the header and content areas, but now bright orange is introduced to indicate active selections or buttons for key actions. In form fields, paler shades of the same blue for buttons, icons, and instructional text help identify points of interaction. Unselected items, the least important information on the page, appear in shades of gray that recede into the background.

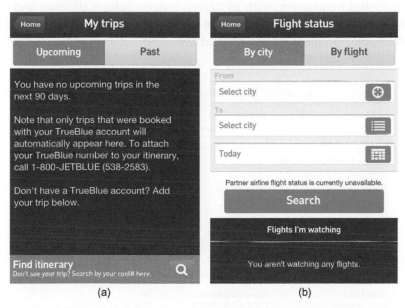

(a)   (b)

Figure 1.4 JetBlue adds orange as an accent to identify active selections and key actions.

Consistency in imagery

Imagery covers anything that isn't a typographic element or an interface control: charts, logos, video, photography, icons, background patterns, etc. Sticking to a unified style for your imagery—as well as understanding where and when to use imagery in the first place—is a crucial part of consistency.

Imagery is a strong conveyor of personality. Because of this, it's tempting for visual designers to want to start from scratch when defining imagery. While this is appropriate for most types of imagery, it doesn't work for icons.

Consistency in icons

Icons are like letters of the alphabet. We use them relying on the assumption that people will know what they mean—that is, how to "read" them. If you need to create a new icon, you won't be able to depend on people knowing what it means, and you may need to accompany it with words. If an icon design is very straightforward— for example, a question mark for help—or testing shows that it is easily interpreted, you may not need to use additional text.

JavaScript frameworks, such as jQuery, provide default UI icons and form elements, as do mobile device operating service (OS) developers like Apple, Google (Figure 1.5), and Microsoft.

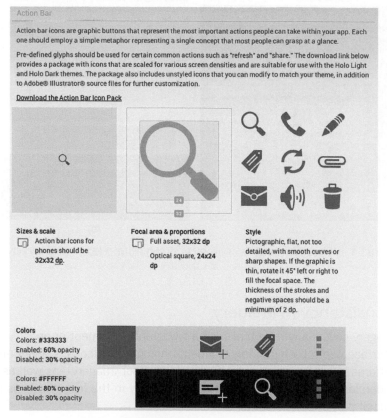

Figure 1.5 Google's Android OS Action Bar icons defined.[1]

---

[1] Portions of this image are reproduced from work created and shared by the Android Open Source Project and used according to terms described in the Creative Commons 2.5 Attribution License.

Relying on standard visual elements and UI paradigms limits the surprise factor by increasing the likelihood you're providing what people expect.

Consistency in logos

Unlike icons, logos rely on being unique, but several aspects of consistency still apply:

- *Design.* The logo should always look the same throughout the application (Figure 1.6), unless brand standards allow altering it noticeably (e.g., Google's doodles, *http://www.google.com/doodles/*).

- *Position.* The logo can appear in a different position or size on an application's main screen, but then should be shown at a consistent size and location on all other screens.

- *External consistency.* If maintaining external consistency with related applications (e.g., the Google applications), the logo should be treated the same way in all applications.

Figure 1.6 Logos for Yahoo! Movies, Finance, and Travel all integrate the parent identity consistently in the website name.

Consistency in charts

Charts should be represented consistently within applications. If some charts are more important than others, they can be considered "featured" charts and one or two characteristics could be treated differently, such as size and color. Otherwise, charts should be consistent in the following ways:

- *Consistent element placement.* Chart elements—text head, text labels, key, the chart itself—should be placed with consistent proximity between them in each instance.

- *Consistent treatment for all text used.* All chart heads should be the same, all chart labels should be the same, and all chart text should be the same. A featured chart may vary one or two characteristics, such as using a larger or different color headline.

- *Consistent colors, applied consistently.* For example, if you make chart bars blue and shaded, all bars in similar types of charts should be blue and shaded. Again, only the featured chart could stand out by using a different color.

Consistency in treatments

We use the word *treatments* to refer to graphic details such as corner radii, background patterns, and shading used in buttons or other shapes. The general rule of thumb for consistency in treatments is similar to that for other image elements: treat all like elements the same. If an element is more important than others, it can be treated differently to stand out, but within boundaries. No more than two characteristics (e.g., size and color) should be changed.

Consistency in controls and affordances

Although this book focuses on the visual aspects of interface design, because we are talking about functional applications, we need to address another important aspect of consistency: ensuring controls and their affordances are discoverable and learnable. Providing consistent visual design for controls wherever they appear in your application ensures people will recognize them, and will know that what they've learned about using them on one screen can be applied to other screens (Figure 1.7).

There are two issues we run into when it comes to controls and consistency. One is that different platforms have different visual interface standards for controls. Adopting standard controls for an application delivered across platforms means that its controls won't look consistent.

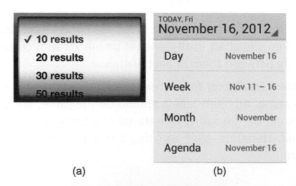

(a)   (b)

Figure 1.7 (a) Standard iOS picker, and (b) Android's spinner.

The second issue is that the design of standard controls may not be in keeping with the personality you want your interface to portray, or may throw off the visual hierarchy. Customizing the look of controls (discussed further in Chapters 3 and 8) can mitigate this problem.

Consistency in motion

In application design, use of motion is tied closely to control and affordance choice. At the most basic level, simple confirmation feedback, like providing rollover states for buttons and links in web applications to help users confirm their selection, should be handled the same way for similar elements. This may involve choosing the opposite state from the element's design—for example, switching a plain link to an underlined one on hover, switching all your green buttons to another color in your palette on rollover, or simply flipping the dimensional look of a button from one side to the other to make it look like it's been pressed.

Beyond simple buttons and links, once you've made the choice to include controls that feature motion, such as drag-and-drop selection, or accordions that open and shut to control information display, these items should be used consistently throughout the application. Similarly, transitions, or motions such as fades and flips that move people from screen to screen, should be applied consistently, which both teaches users what to expect and avoids overwhelming them visually.

Finally, standard platform controls may involve motion—for example, iOS's spinning date-selection tools, Windows 8's flipping tiles, and Android's skinny slider bars. We'll look at examples in Chapter 8.

Choosing the right paradigm

Sometimes, there's more than one paradigm that may help your interface be consistent, such as multiple methods of deleting information. When that happens, a solid rationale is to pick the convention that most closely matches the model your audience has already learned for that type of data.

A good rule of thumb is to look to your own application first. If you don't have an existing paradigm for what you need to design, use the research techniques covered in Chapter 3 to find out what applications and conventions your users are familiar with. Picking a convention and sticking to it can be really hard, especially when different parts of an application are developed by different people at different times, or when different types of data or situations of use suggest conflicting options. Your goal should be to serve your audience's needs while trying to be as consistent as possible.

The iOS Reminders application provides a good example of how to choose from multiple options (Figure 1.8). Reminders does exactly what you'd think: it allows you to create checklists of to-do items. These items can be assigned dates, times, and even locations so that your phone or iPad can remind you when you need to complete a task.

Figure 1.8 iOS Reminders application.

Sometimes, you'll need to delete a reminder, but iOS offers many different paradigms[2] for deletion. How do you pick the right one to use?

[2] *Note:* Screenshots in this section were taken on an iPhone. The iPad's deletion paradigms are essentially the same, although they sometimes use popovers for an operation the phone performs inline. Also, the voicemail deletion paradigm does not exist on the iPad, which has no built-in voicemail application.

There's the voicemail deletion interface, which offers two deletion paradigms: a large red "Delete" button shown if the user selects a call, and a smaller, inline "Delete" button shown if the user swipes to the right over a call (Figure 1.9).

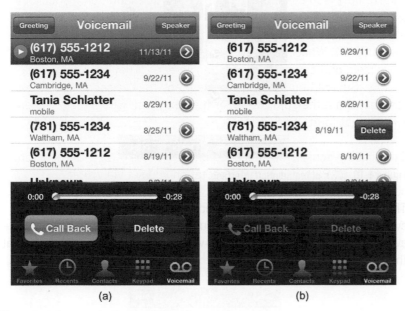

(a)   (b)

Figure 1.9 Two options for iOS "Delete" buttons.

The photo deletion interface only appears after you tap a sharing icon in the top right; after that, you tap on individual photos to select them, and then tap the small red "Delete" button in the bottom right (Figure 1.10).

Figure 1.10 iOS's photo deletion interface.

The calendar event deletion interface appears after you tap on an event and tap an "Edit" button. You then see a screen showing all the event details, followed by a screen-width red "Delete Event" button at the bottom (Figure 1.11).

Figure 1.11 iOS's calendar event deletion interface.

What role does consistency play in application design? **21**

There's also the table-based deletion interface, shown in Figure 1.12 in the iPhone's Messages application. Tap the "Edit" button at the top *left*—not right, this time!—and you'll reveal individual deletion icons for each message. Tapping that icon displays the same small "Delete" button we saw in one of the voicemail options.

Figure 1.12 iOS's table-based deletion interface.

Why does iOS include five different deletion conventions? What we're seeing is a library of paradigms for different types of information; they're patterns for solving specific design problems, and no single solution works for every problem. These aren't the only iOS deletion paradigms, either—for example, there's the trashcan display on individual photos—but we'll concentrate on these five for the purposes of this example.

Here's how we interpret what's going on.

- The first voicemail paradigm exists because it's a quick way to address the most common tasks with voicemail: playing a message, then deciding whether to delete it or return the call. Putting all the controls next to each other minimizes the finger motion necessary to complete all tasks.

- The second voicemail paradigm is a hidden "power user" feature available anywhere an iOS application uses this type of table view. Once advanced users learn this shortcut, they can use it in multiple places, like Messages and Mail.

- The photo grid paradigm works by layering a selection UI on top of a dense but parseable stream of information, enabling users to swiftly and easily identify multiple elements to act on at once. This is an extension of the same interface for selecting photos to email or copy into a folder.

- The event paradigm works because even though there are multiple ways to display an event (e.g., as a list, within a weekly view), having different ways to delete an event depending on your current display would be too confusing. It's better to drive people into the event to delete it than force them to perform the same task multiple ways within the application.

- The table view paradigm works for identifying and deleting entire rows of compactly displayed information.

So, after reviewing these paradigms, which makes the most sense? Let's look at Reminders again (Figure 1.13).

Figure 1.13 iOS Reminders application.

Its type and display of information are very different from what voicemail and photos need to support, so it's safe to eliminate those patterns from consideration. That leaves us with a tabular view of information, as well as the calendar-style list and date views—and, ultimately, it's the latter that dictates how the Reminders application should behave.

You can get to the next detail view of an event by tapping on it from either the list or the date view, so the calendar interface's model of a single, large "Delete" button instead of multiple approaches to deletion depending on the view makes the most sense (Figure 1.14). Besides, applying the tabular deletion convention would require overwriting Reminders' checkboxes with an iOS "Delete" button control, potentially confusing people. Using the calendar interface's paradigm not only makes for a cleaner display than table-style deletion, it mimics the behavior of what the audience perceives as similar types of information (events and to-dos).

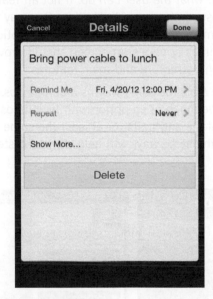

Figure 1.14 iOS Reminders app detail view.

As for the pink "Delete" button instead of the calendar interface's glossy red one? That's because Reminders applies skeuomorphic design—a design that mimics the look and feel of a physical object, here a datebook—to create its visual personality, and the standard iOS "Delete" button would be too visually prominent on the pale datebook entries. We'll cover this approach more in Chapter 7.

Consistent aesthetics across platforms

Desktop systems, mobile phones, and tablets all have different capabilities, and creating a unified experience across a myriad of devices can be very challenging. Some of this is part of defining the overall user experience—what features and content should be available on each platform. Some of it is presenting the interface elements as consistently as possible, and having a rationale to support decisions when trade-offs are necessary (Figure 1.15).

Understanding that you probably can't make everything look 100% the same everywhere, your primary goals for consistency should be:

- *Be sure the identity is represented clearly*. There should be no question about what application is being used.

- *Be clear about what the user can do*. If not all features are available across platforms, indicate this. One way to do this is through primary navigation. The navigation options that are visible at all times or on a start screen should provide cues about the application's structure and main features.

- *Use the same tools the same way as much as possible*. While this may not be much of an option with layout/position, using the same color palette and fonts (or at least the same typographic hierarchy) in the same ways will help with consistency.

(a)   (b)

Figure 1.15 The Epicurious applications for (a) iPhone and (b) iPad don't look exactly alike, but they share the same elements and visual aesthetic. Consistent logo placement, navigation style, icons, and colors create a unified experience across devices.

One way designers and developers are starting to address consistency issues across platforms is through *responsive web design*, a term coined by designer/developer Ethan Marcotte to describe applying CSS, HTML5, and JavaScript to deliver the same content in different layouts depending on platform and screen dimension. By carefully coding websites to rearrange themselves and present features in the most advantageous way for a specific device, designers can provide online experiences that consistently feel like they're part of a single application, even if they don't always look the same.

Other ways to provide consistent aesthetics across platforms include developing mobile-specific websites, mobile web applications, or native mobile applications. All three approaches have their pros and cons. Developing a mobile-specific website or mobile-specific CSS is probably the fastest of the three approaches, but may feel like the least rich experience; mobile web applications provide some functionality, but not the seamless OS integration of a native mobile application; and a native mobile application can require significant engineering effort, particularly if you need to develop for multiple devices. But whatever approach you choose, the three primary goals for consistency still apply.

What if you can't be consistent?

It's easier to design and expand your application if you have a rationale, but you can't account for every possible circumstance. Sometimes, you may need new paradigms for new features, or you may find that being consistent makes the application harder to use.

In the case of new content or features, review your template system. For features, break down individual elements and compare them to what you've already designed; there are bound to be some similarities, and that's your starting point. Similarly, with new types of text—say, detailed tables or charts when you hadn't expected to have to show either—look to your color palette and type specifications to see how they might apply or need to be extended.

A brief aside about accessibility

Although this book won't go into depth about accessibility issues, consistency is especially relevant to making applications usable for people with disabilities or cognitive limitations. The World Wide Web Consortium's Web Accessibility Initiative (WAI) guidelines for web content accessibility (content, in this case, includes text, images, form elements, and any other items displayed onscreen) recommend making "web pages appear in and operate in predictable ways"[3]:

> *It is difficult for some users to form an overview of the Web page: screen readers present content as a one-dimensional stream of synthetic speech that makes it difficult to understand spatial relationships. Users with cognitive limitations may become confused if components appear in different places on different pages.*
>
> *For example, people who use screen magnifiers see only part of the screen at any point in time; a consistent layout makes it easier for them to find navigation bars and other components. Placing repeated components in the same relative order within a set of Web pages allows users with reading disabilities to focus on an area of the screen rather than spending additional time decoding the text of each link. Users with limited use of their hands can more easily determine how to complete their tasks using the fewest keystrokes.*[4]

While accessibility focuses on providing resources to ensure usable, functional websites and applications for the disabled, these principles apply just as well for *all* users. Everyone benefits from consistently placed navigation, form fields that behave the same way throughout, and a limited set of interaction tools that operate the way people expect. Following WAI guidelines for predictability and consistency make a better experience for every person your application serves.

---

[3] Vanderheiden, G., Reid, L., Caldwell, B., and Henry, S. (2012, Jan. 3). How to Meet WCAG 2.0. World Wide Web Consortium. Retrieved May 24, 2012, from *http://www.w3.org/WAI/WCAG20/quickref/*.

[4] Cooper, M., Reid, L., and Vanderheiden, G. (2012, Jan. 3). Predictable: Understanding Guideline 3.2. Understanding WCAG 2.0: A Guide to Understanding and Implementing Web Content Accessibility Guidelines 2.0. World Wide Web Consortium. Retrieved May 24, 2012, from *http://www.w3.org/TR/UNDERSTANDING-WCAG20/consistent-behavior.html*.

Avoid common mistakes

Inconsistency introduces an element of surprise. And while surprise is a great concept when you're trying to delight an audience with an unexpectedly pleasant and useful feature, it's a lot less great when someone's trying to get work done. Easter eggs are fun; "guess what I am and how I work" isn't.

Design content and imagery consistently

- Present similar types of text (e.g., headers) consistently from screen to screen.
- Design or source icons as a family, so they all feel related.

Set consistent rules for color use

- Don't use color arbitrarily; for example, applying color to some headers but not to others at the same hierarchical level. See Chapter 6 for more on how to use color to communicate consistently.

Design controls consistently to reveal affordances

- Whenever possible, use the same control for the same type of action.
- Place submission buttons consistently across screens.

Make informed decisions

Informed decisions require a rationale. By establishing rules that incorporate consistency as a key part of your rationale, you provide yourself with a strong basis for decision-making.

Review existing rules and conventions

- Review platform and technical interface conventions to determine which are best suited for your users and your application's content and goals.
- Review any parent organization standards for logo, type, and color usage to understand how these influence or directly affect your application's visual design.

- Determine whether a new application needs to feel like anything the parent brand has previously created, and if so, consider adopting one of the parent identity's colors and/or typefaces to help things feel related.

Document decisions about consistency

- Log your decisions in a style guide that's easily accessible to everyone on your team as well as other teams (Figure 1.16). Detail the rules for all aspects of the application's design—screen templates, color palette, typographical specifications, and imagery—and provide a brief explanation of the rationale behind the rules. Expect to maintain the style guide; things will change. Decisions and specifications will need to be revisited as an application evolves.

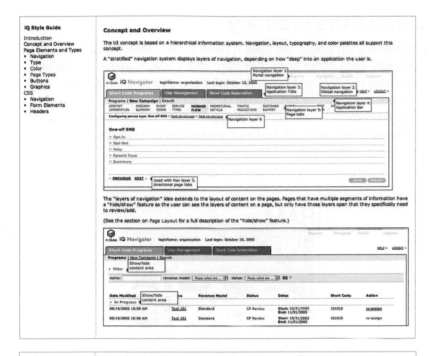

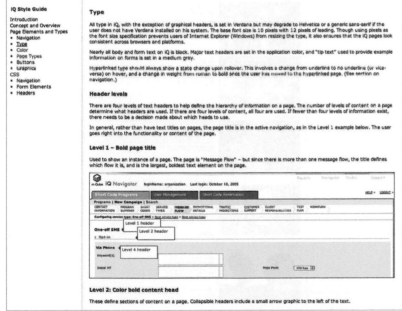

Figure 1.16 These sample pages from a web-based style guide show how examples, specifications, and rationale can be presented in a simple, yet useful way. There are many ways to document style; choose a format and delivery method that's easy to update and accessible to everyone.

Elevate the ordinary

Consistency isn't sexy, nor does it need to be. Trained graphic designers learn about grids, but they aren't taught about templates. Templates can feel restrictive to designers, and to a large extent they are—but you can still be creative while being consistent. Defining some content as "featured" is an opportunity to treat some elements differently than others. A featured area could change frequently, displaying a rotating set of images as shown in the email template for the Brooklyn Academy of Music in Figure 1.17.

Figure 1.17 Brooklyn Academy of Music email template.

Providing customization options is another way to push beyond ordinary design while still retaining consistency. For example, Twitter uses the same layout for all its members, but every person can configure their page background and header to make it uniquely theirs (Figure 1.18).

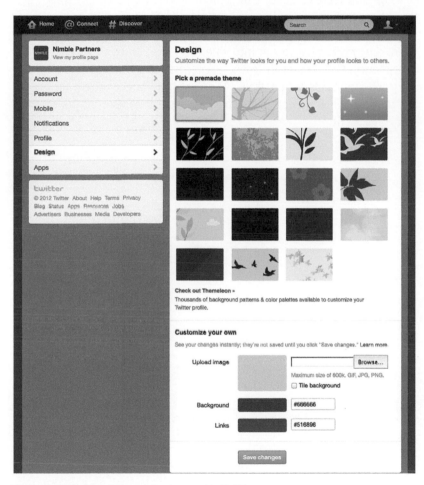

Figure 1.18 Options for page background in Twitter.

Similarly, Gmail, Yahoo! Mail, and Mozilla Firefox all offer ways to change the look and feel of their software while retaining the same layout and tools.

Hierarchy

"Hierarchical organization is the simplest structure for visualizing and understanding complexity."

—W. Lidwell, K. Holden, J. Butler,
Universal Principles of Design, p. 104

Visual hierarchy is the perception and interpretation of the relative importance of objects. In application design, these objects are elements presented on a screen. After consistency, visual hierarchy is the biggest factor we see in creating effective application interfaces.

Perception of hierarchy is affected by position, size, color, interface control type (e.g., a button versus a link), and treatment of elements. It is also affected by the way individual elements and groups of elements relate to each other. Regardless of whether interface elements are deliberately "designed," their characteristics and juxtapositions communicate information about their priority.

Hierarchy helps people know what to do, how to do it, and what to expect. A visual system based on hierarchy consists of decisions about where to place elements in an interface, what to place them with, how big to make them, what color they should be, and how to represent their behavior or interactivity based on each element's relative importance. To increase the likelihood that the audience will interpret these decisions as intended, we need to apply them consistently, as discussed in Chapter 1.

Creating hierarchy is a balancing act, because it's almost never the case that size, color, or placement are the only differences between objects on a screen. To create a visual hierarchy, you must develop a rationale for differentiation supported by an understanding of your audience, and then use that rationale to apply the visual usability tools effectively (Figure 2.1). The visual system that communicates hierarchy comprises the templates, images, characteristics, and rules for display, typically documented in a style guide. While most

(a)   (b)

Figure 2.1 (a) Presenting and treating all elements equally misses an opportunity to help people focus on what's most important. (b) Variation in relative size, placement, and treatment start to indicate a hierarchy.

designers and developers are familiar with style guides, they're often not aware of how important it is to incorporate hierarchy and rationale in the design process and documentation.

What do we mean by hierarchy?

Before we go into how to create visual hierarchy, let's look at its most basic aspects.

In practice, a lack of hierarchy exists when objects all attract the eye equally—that is, when nothing stands out more than any other thing. In concept, visual hierarchy is very similar to organizational hierarchy. It's an order based on ranks defined as part of a system. Military organizations have a rank system, martial arts have a rank system, and traditional business organizations have a rank system. With the exception of business ranks, hierarchical systems usually have a corresponding visual system that signifies an individual's status.

Figure 2.2 As with organizational structures in which one person or group is more important than others, rank is hierarchy's key concept. In interface design, rank is expressed through size, color, position, and treatment.

In the military or martial arts, visual systems that indicate rank—colored belts or insignia—are meaningful for people with direct knowledge of the organization. For them, rank is the basis for all behaviors and interactions. Individuals within a rank system have roles and responsibilities based on where they stand in that system. Similarly, successful interface designs depend on a visual ranking system to help people using it identify the importance and role of the elements they interact with.

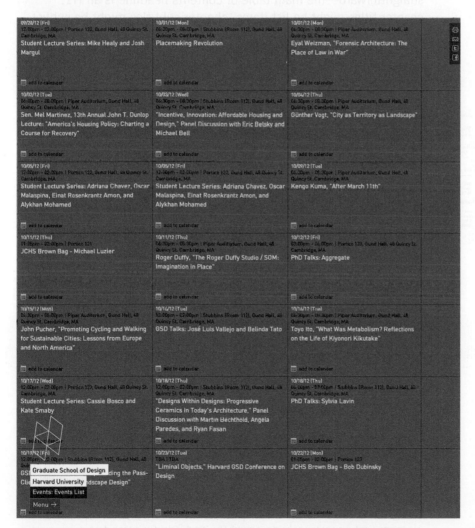

Figure 2.3 Unclear visual hierarchy. The reader must focus on and compare dates in more than one part of the screen to figure out the sequence in this dynamic display of events for Harvard University's Graduate School of Design. An indication of order would greatly improve use, and could be an opportunity for expression.

For example, in a web-based application, type styles are usually controlled by CSS, a hierarchical system in which visual aspects of parent items "cascade" down to their children. CSS creates direct links between the hierarchy of text and interface elements and the code controlling their appearance and placement.

If you consider a table of contents, which has an inherent, implied hierarchy people are familiar with, applying CSS styles is pretty straightforward—the main table of contents headline is an H1, chapter titles might be list items, chapter subtitles might be sublist items in the main list, and so on (Figure 2.4a). As long as your visual treatments mirror that same hierarchy, you can be fairly confident your table of contents will be understood.

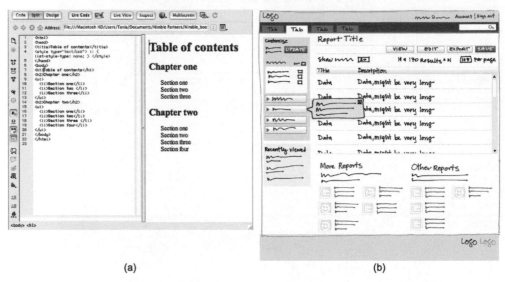

(a)   (b)

Figure 2.4 (a) Simple, hierarchical, text-based visual system and logical corresponding HTML tags. (b) Complex interface sketch with multiple levels of text and controls. There are too many element types and varying positions to apply a straightforward top-to-bottom system. Decisions about where things go and how they look should be based on a hierarchy that corresponds to what people need to do.

Hierarchy in complex application interfaces is seldom straightforward. Designers and developers manipulate the tools—layout, type, imagery, color, and controls—and their characteristics to express an application's purpose and convey use. Making decisions about where an element should go, what elements it should appear with, and how it should appear is part of defining a strategic visual system. A sound hierarchy that accounts for user priorities helps people know where they are, what they can do, and where they can go next.

Characteristics of hierarchy

As with consistency, people interpret interfaces based on what they see and expect. The characteristics of what they see also affect interpretation. To represent a hierarchy, elements need to be presented so that more important things have more visual weight or prominence than less important things. Perceived visual weight is a key component of visual hierarchy—generally, something with more visual prominence, or weight, draws the eye, and is therefore seen as more important.

Contrast

Colin Ware says in his book *Visual Thinking for Design*, "If you want to make something easy to find, make it different from its surroundings... ."[1] Contrast is about creating visible differences between elements and is the essential ingredient in visual hierarchy. It is what makes something appear different from—and potentially more important than—other things. Contrast is created in many ways.

Position

There are several aspects of positioning elements on a screen that affect contrast and perception of hierarchy. Some of these—grouping, proximity, and similarity—are defined in gestalt psychology "laws" that apply to visual interpretation, and inform these examples.[2]

- *Placement and proximity to frame*: Basic principles about placement apply no matter what's onscreen. Even the simplest possible placement, such as a dot in a frame (Figure 2.5), creates a relationship between the element and its background.

[1] Ware, C. *Visual Thinking for Design*, page 33.
[2] *Gestalt psychology* is a theory introduced in the first half of the 20th century that describes how people perceive visual objects. There are many sources for more about gestalt laws, one of which is Jeff Johnson's *Designing with the Mind in Mind*.

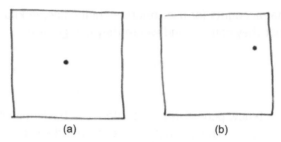

(a)   (b)

Figure 2.5 (a) Stable, static placement. (b) Unstable, active placement. The proximity of the dot to the frame affects its perceived importance.[3] The stable dot in the center looks important; its position tells us the illustration is about the dot. The position of the dot in (b) is tentative: Is it coming or going? It doesn't look as important as the centered dot. The illustration on the right is about the white space more than the dot.

- *Placement and proximity of elements*: Perception of hierarchy is affected by how close elements are to one another. Elements placed close together are seen as a group (Figure 2.6). If an element or group of elements is isolated from the others by having more space around it, the space will create contrast and draw the eye to the isolated element, giving it more visual prominence.

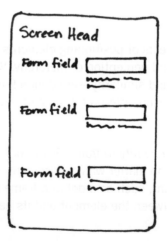

Figure 2.6 Elements placed in close proximity to one another create the appearance of groups. White space above the bottom group makes it different from the others.

[3] Hofmann, A. *Graphic Design Manual: Principles and Practice*, p. 13.

- *Eye behavior*: Tracking studies[4] conducted on websites show that people look the most at the top left portion of a web page when reading. The "inverted pyramid" principle—presenting information in descending order of importance—supports the top location as more important as well (Figure 2.7).[5]

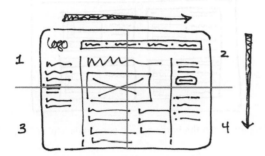

Figure 2.7 Since people look in quadrant 1 the most, and for the longest period of time on the web, elements in the top left position may be interpreted as more important than elements placed in other quadrants of a screen.

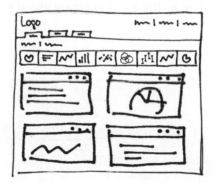

Figure 2.8 In a horizontal row of icons, all icons are seen as related if they're rendered and presented the same way. Position can affect visibility, however. The first one or two icons on the left are likely to be seen more than others in the row.

- *Nesting*: Placing some elements within others makes the "parent" elements seem to exist at a higher, more important level (Figure 2.9).

[4] Nielsen, J. (2006, April 17). F-Shaped Pattern for Reading Web Content, *Alertbox*. Retrieved from *http://www.useit.com/alertbox/reading_pattern.html*. Submitted date: November 19, 2012.

[5] Lidwell, W., Holden, K., & Butler, J. (2010). *Universal Principles of Design*. Beverly, MA: Rockport Publishers, p. 116.

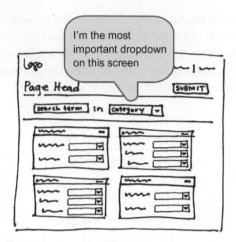

Figure 2.9 The dropdowns in the boxes appear subservient to, or "nested" under, the elements above.

- *Overlap*: Elements placed "on top of" other elements are more prominent. Lightboxes and popups are common examples of using overlap to draw the eye and create visual hierarchy (Figure 2.10).

Figure 2.10 The lightbox convention interrupts people and requires them to focus on something layered above what they were looking at. Overlapping tells people the thing on top is most important.

Treatment

The visual style or treatment applied to elements affects their perceived importance through creation of contrast. Although Chapters 5–8 address this in more depth, following are four common ways it affects hierarchy:

- *Size*: Bigger elements, or large groups of elements, appear more important than similar smaller elements (Figure 2.11).

Figure 2.11 Apple's website uses a large, central element with smaller ones—a simple and obvious way to use contrast in size to establish hierarchy.

- *Color*: On a light background, darker elements have more visual weight than similar, lighter elements, and may be interpreted as more important. Warm colors, such as red, yellow, and orange, appear to come forward compared to blues and greens; thus, elements shown in warm colors may feel more prominent than similar cool-colored items. Finally, saturated, or purer colors, draw the eye more than dull ones.

- *Ornament*: Think of a traditional wedding invitation: an ornate font is one cue that the invitation is special. An ornament is a type of decoration that can create contrast with plain elements and signal that something is important. Although ornament is typically used in marketing or advertising to differentiate and draw attention, it may also come into play in defining the personality of an application (Figure 2.12).

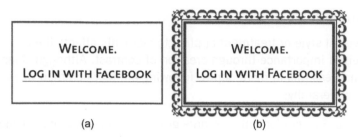

Figure 2.12 The ornamental border treatment makes the box in (b) seem more important than the box in (a).

- *Finish*: Gradation, or the illusion of dimensional depth, is a common *finish* applied to buttons and bars. Finishes are textures that can be applied to interface elements. Visually complex elements draw the eye more than plain elements (Figure 2.13), increasing their perceived importance. While effective in drawing the eye, finishes can send the wrong message if the style is inappropriate for the content, such as a metallic effect in an application for processing patients. They can also be distracting if they're too strong, and can incorrectly signal something is important when it isn't. As such, they should be used sparingly (if at all), and only if they help communicate appropriately and successfully.

Figure 2.13 Which treatment should you choose, solid or gradation? The button with the gradation is more visually complex, and draws the eye compared to the plain button. This causes the button on the right to be perceived as more important. The answer is contextual, however, and depends on the other methods of contrast you're using, as well as desired personality.

While treatments are effective ways to draw the eye, they should be used sparingly. When it comes to treatments, less really is more.

Interplay of characteristics

There are often several kinds of elements in complex, highly functional applications: buttons at one or more levels of importance, multiple levels and types of text, and form items like dropdown menus and text entry fields. When there are many options for what users can do on a screen, designers can't simply manipulate one characteristic and make all the options clear. Providing one big red button doesn't suffice when there are a half-dozen possible actions to click. While simple visual hierarchies can be established with one tool, such as text, and one characteristic, such as position, in complex interfaces, multiple characteristics need to be manipulated to communicate what the user can do.

When manipulating multiple characteristics, things get complicated fast. The simple dots in the frames in Figure 2.14 help show the effects of manipulating multiple variables, and the results on perceived importance.

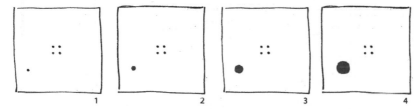

Figure 2.14 How much emphasis do we need to subvert a visual hierarchy? This illustration adds color and size to shift attention from the dots in the center in frame 1. In frame 2, the four dots still look more important than the red dot. In frame 3, the hierarchy isn't clear. Only in frame 4 is the dot emphasized enough to look more important.

The dot and frame examples show how small differences affect perception of importance. When dissimilar elements, such as buttons, tables, dropdown menus, and icons, are presented together, it becomes more difficult to establish visual hierarchy. That's why we first consider convention—what the user expects—and then manipulation of characteristics to establish hierarchy.

The elements presented in the Salesforce.com dashboard in Figure 2.15 are treated with some consistency—red rules and bold heads above content in equal columns. Not all content is of the same type; there are graphs, a gauge graphic, and lists.

In this example, the shading behind the graphics draws the eye, but are those content items the most important? Should the number of users logged in be in the top left, the most prominent spot in the main content area? When there's interplay between characteristics

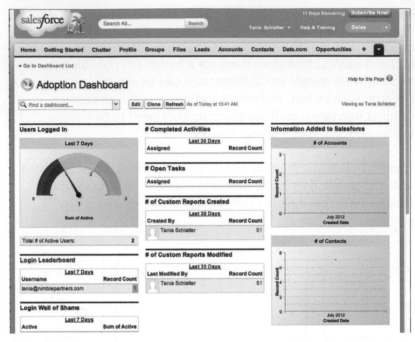

Figure 2.15 Salesforce.com dashboard. Graphic treatments (gradation, illustrated gauge) and position appear to be used randomly, not to indicate what's most important.

and conventions—for example, between treatment and position, or between position and expectation—presentation can work against meaning and understanding. Consider testing complex designs to determine if you've made valid assumptions about visual hierarchy, or if changes could help people make sense of your screens.

Defining a hierarchy

Regardless of your end product—e-commerce, productivity, mobile service application—the approach to establishing hierarchy is the same. Depending on the size of your team, you may need a formal process with documented decisions, or an informal one done in your head. Either way, decisions about hierarchy require a rationale that you can explain.

Identify the elements

After determining what conventions exist for your content and functionality, you'll have an idea of what users expect and what paradigms to keep in mind. The next question to address is what most people need to do (or what an organization might want them to do), and the priority of those interactions; for example, "we want everyone to sign up or log in, but if they don't want to, we at least want them to complete the checkout process." This effort should be informed by user personas defined with as much knowledge of user behavior as possible.

User personas

User personas, or stories about what people will ideally do with your application, are an important tool for defining hierarchy. Personas incorporate situations (why, when, and where people are using the application) and motivations (what your audience hopes to do) to help understand the user's perspective of which features and content are most important. Personas inform the flow at the levels you need to design for: application, screen, and widget. They describe where the user's attention is likely to be focused and why. The more you know about the people who use what you're designing, the more informed your hierarchy, its rationale, and its presentation will be. *About Face 3: The Essentials of Interaction Design*, by Alan Cooper, Robert Reimann, and David Cronin, is a good source for learning about user personas in detail.

List elements

List the screen elements you need based on the personas. An element is a unit of content or functionality. For a productivity application, your initial list might be something like this:

- Logo/identity
- Search box
- Filters to refine results
- Instructional text or help links
- Results list or table

- Actions that can be taken with the results
- Pagination
- "Submit" button
- Success/error messaging
- Footer
- Global navigation
- Local navigation
- Login/logout area

Number the items on the list from most to least important based on the use implied in the scenario. The scenario serves as your rationale for prioritizing. There can be more than one element with the same number, and they'll need to be treated in a way that visually represents their equal importance. This prioritized list, along with knowledge of what users expect, serves as a starting point for defining visual hierarchy—making decisions about placement, size, color, and treatment that support use or flow for the devices you are designing for.

Flow

If you have an idea about what people need to do when—that is, a flow of steps—based on people's goals and needs, you can make decisions about element characteristics and hierarchy. Understanding a scenario's flow can help you place elements in a wireframe or directly into page code based on expected priority and sequence.

For example, imagine you're redesigning an application that involves managing medical patient records. You know that users get requests to create a new record, or to delete, edit, or close an existing record. You also know that the most common task (about 85% of requests) is editing existing records. Users need to find a record before they can manage it. Between a search feature and a "Create New Record" button or feature, the search feature should be more visually prominent because it is used more frequently.

Next, you wonder if the "Create New Record" button should go in the global navigation at the top right or on the main screen with the search feature, but less prominent (Figure 2.16).

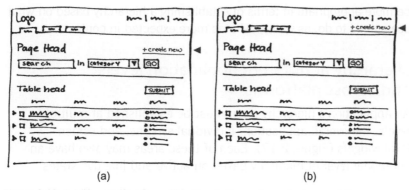

Figure 2.16 (a) "Create New Record" button in the main content area of the screen, versus (b) in the header area.

If you know that most users' flow involves going to the global navigation when they're between tasks, and that they expect to manage requests in the main part of the application, you can make an educated guess about placement: putting "Create New Record" near the search feature, but in a less prominent position, is a reasonable decision based on sound rationale, and is likely to hold up well. You can then evaluate your educated guesses by prototyping and testing your interface designs.

Patterns

UI patterns need to be taken into account when establishing hierarchy, as they may influence what users expect. Some UI patterns, such as a search feature, are integrated with hierarchy. Locating the search feature at either the top right (web application) or top center (e-commerce, mobile) is a placement-based pattern that implies hierarchy. In this pattern, content and features often appear below or nested under a search bar, implying that the search feature is important and applies to everything that falls below it.

Before applying patterns, evaluate if they apply both in terms of hierarchy and user expectations. For example, an infinite scroll, while expected in social media, might not work in the context of displaying text-based results. Depending on the scenario, users might want pagination instead of the ability to review all results. This is an example of how patterns and hierarchy can collide. Placing arrow and page number pagination controls above results, also a common pattern, may be more appropriate in terms of establishing a hierarchy based on what users need to do, as well as what is more expected in context.

Hierarchy at different application levels and across platforms

An application's hierarchy often must be established at multiple levels: the overall application, individual screens, and screen-level widgets (Figure 2.17). Each of these areas may also have an additional layer of hierarchy based on active and inactive states.

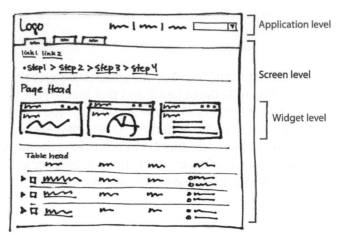

Figure 2.17 Visual hierarchy often needs to be established at different levels within a single screen of a highly functional application.

Building on the process of numbering screen elements, groups of elements need to be established and prioritized as well. After identifying as many elements as possible:

1. Define groups of elements based on level: application, screen, widget.
2. Define priority of the groups. Think about and evaluate conventions.
3. Define priority of the elements within the groups.
4. Place the groups in the screen frame based on these rankings.

The amount of design work necessary to define a visual hierarchy varies depending on the platform type. For example, if you're designing for mobile phones, there may be fewer elements visible onscreen at the same time and fewer visual relationships to juggle.

Navigation conventions dictated by the platform need to be evaluated and adopted or adapted, not created from scratch. However, because accomplishing a task may require several screens, there may be more work to do to define hierarchy in terms of getting the flow right, or the presentation order of features.

Prototyping and testing considerations

When establishing hierarchy, it's important to move elements around and try different relationships. Whether you're prototyping with software or sketching with a pencil, you'll need to try different options to see which best support the goals.

When prototyping, stick to representing hierarchy with position and size, leaving all other characteristics undesigned. Simple black-and-white wireframes with a single, plain font used in varying weights are perfect for defining and evaluating content, functionality, and hierarchy. Begin by placing elements according to device conventions. Consider if and how conventions affect hierarchy, and if they conflict with your personas and flow. Try alternates and evaluate them. Interface designer Aaron Marcus said, "[S]ketches are logical abstractions of the form that indicate probable content elements, their approximate size, and their approximate location. At this stage, it is easier to manipulate broad differences in the form's groupings and hierarchy. It is important not to be too precise or detailed early in the design process. It is more important to explore possible variations."[6]

When your prototypes reflect the desired content, functionality, and hierarchy, it's time to test them and iterate again. Assumptions you make about flow, patterns, positioning, and other characteristics need to be tested, even if they're grounded in user observation and/or data. Testing can take many forms, from paper prototyping to releasing products and asking for feedback from users. Regardless of the method, no rationale is bulletproof. Expect to continually evolve your visual system to accommodate new information and change.

Avoid common mistakes

When it comes to hierarchy, you should think logically and critically about people, placement, and treatment of all elements.

---

[6] Marcus, A. *Graphic Design for Electronic Documents and User Interfaces*, p. 39.

Use contrast, including position and treatment, to define a strong hierarchy

- Present an obvious "lead" element or group of elements.
- Clearly represent active and inactive states.
- If your screen includes a lot of actions, present them in groups if possible. Place and treat the groups differently to help people know the groups are separate and which group is most important.
- Don't overdifferentiate. Review Chapter 3, as well as the individual tools chapters, for more specific guidelines about designing to create personality and understanding without cluttering the screen and misleading users.
- Show people where they are in an application structure at all times.

Make informed decisions

- Use personas, prototypes, and testing to make decisions about what's important based on data and known behavior, not assumptions.
- Review and analyze related applications to research conventions and patterns relevant for your situation.
- Avoid allowing the visual design of out-of-the-box patterns to dictate a confusing hierarchy.
- Apply what you know about your core user base to position elements to support their most common tasks and flows.

Elevate the ordinary

The best way to elevate the ordinary terms of hierarchy is to edit the features presented, which is easier said than done. Deep understanding of users, their behaviors, and their expectations is required to present just the right controls and affordances at the right time.

For example, in the product pages in Figure 2.18, if the system behind the application knew about the user's preferences from past behavior, profile information, and what they'd viewed this session, fewer, more targeted options could be presented to the user. The fewer elements presented, the easier it is to define a clear and successful hierarchy.

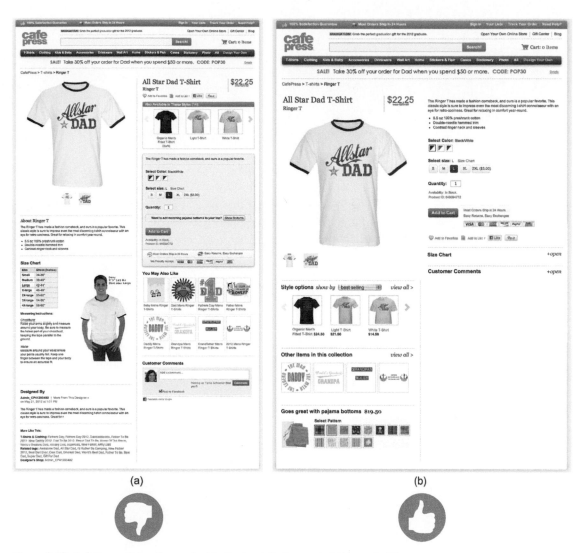

(a)   (b)

Figure 2.18 CafePress places the product in the top left, the most visible part of the screen, and makes it big, a good choice. The original product template (a) shows too many options, however, which undermines the product's importance. The redesigned version, (b) highlights the main product.

Personality

"The trick is to be practical at the same time that you are being impractical."

—Paul Rand[1]

Just as people react to other people, people react to applications. First impressions happen automatically, consciously and unconsciously. Other impressions are the result of interactions over time. *Personality* refers to impressions formed based on appearance and behavior, a concept that applies to applications as well as people.

Appearance, behavior, and satisfaction all come into play in how people judge an application. While each interaction affects how people interpret and evaluate an application, this chapter focuses on the visual aspects of an application's personality. What people see conveyed through layout, color, type, imagery, and controls and affordances affects not only their first impression, but also how they use and consider an application.

Don Norman provides a framework for product personality in his book *Emotional Design: Why We Love (or Hate) Everyday Things*, defining three aspects of design:

- *Visceral design* maps to appearance.
- *Behavioral design* represents the pleasure and effectiveness of use.
- *Reflective design* relates to self-image, personal satisfaction, and memories.[2]

[1] Rand, P. (1991). Interview [video file]. Retrieved from *http://www.youtube.com/watch?v=Ta4ef1xBeMA*.

[2] Norman, D. A. *Emotional Design: Why We Love (or Hate) Everyday Things*, pp. 38–39.

Though Norman focuses on all kinds of consumer products, his design aspects apply to the personality of application interfaces as well (Figure 3.1).

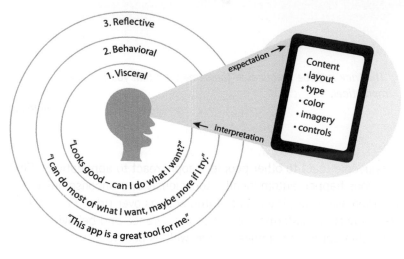

User interpretation forms over time   Content and delivery characteristics

Figure 3.1 Not all aspects of an application's personality can be determined at a glance (visceral). They are revealed through use (behavioral) and time (reflective).

Norman's framework fits our experiences designing applications and understanding how people use them. Interpretation of how an application looks happens instantly and viscerally, as Norman states, and interpretation of the pleasure or effectiveness of use happens over time. The sum of these interactions is overall interpretation, to the point of reflection.

While this framework applies to products at the conceptual level, we need more practical frameworks for establishing appropriate and desirable impressions of personality for application interfaces. This chapter outlines the elements of application personality, and dives into how to convey desirable and appropriate characteristics of personality in an interface.

First, we need to state that you cannot "create" personality. People determine personality based on characteristics interpreted from patterns they've detected through perception and experience. Interpretations vary based on norms and expectations—what people expect and are used to—and can be subjective. Just as diners can have different impressions of the same meal served by the same waiter at the same restaurant on the same night, application users will interpret what they see differently. People's frames of reference affect interpretation. Designers and developers cannot *know* how visual cues and attributes will be interpreted, but they can select and create visual cues and attributes that are likely to give the desired impression of personality. The likelihood that their selections and designs are successful increases with the amount of research they are part of and have access to.

Research for visual interface design

Research—watching people in situations similar to those you are designing for, learning about the culture you are designing for, and testing prototypes—helps you understand people and their expectations in context. Understanding how people use an application, their situations, and their interpretation of what they see and experience helps you select visual cues and attributes that improve ease of use and give the desired impression of an application's personality.

Methods of research are often combined. Demographic data is merely a source of information, and doesn't help you understand what motivates people; it needs to be combined with knowledge of how people behave in similar or proxy situations, as well as what they value, inferred from observation or testing. But all of these methods and results can be used to help inform design decisions.

Research methods
Contextual inquiry/observation

Contextual inquiry is a term coined by Hugh Breyer and Karen Holtzblatt to refer to a method of learning what people do for the purposes of designing better applications.[3] It involves sitting with, observing, and questioning people in the relevant situation of use (e.g., home, office, or car) rather than a lab setting.

[3] Beyer, H., and Holtzblatt, K. *Contextual Design: Defining Customer-Centered Systems (Interactive Technologies)*.

It's useful early on in a project, so designers can get to know the users, content, context, affinities, and behavior they will be designing or redesigning for. This method can stand alone, but is also effective for determining design goals that can be measured with other methods later on.

A/B testing

This research method, also known as split testing, shows two variations of a screen to users and assesses differences in how people respond to each option. Typically, this method is used to test a specific, desired response, such as purchase conversion or list signup. A/B testing can stand alone as a research method for determining the effectiveness of design options.

Conceptual prototype

A conceptual prototype can take many forms. For visual interface design, prototypes are concepts of screens that are flat or clickable, on paper or onscreen, black and white or full-color. They should represent some content, features, and elements that start to convey a personality, and are used to help designers and stakeholders understand user perceptions and preferences (Figure 3.2). They are for qualitative purposes only, and the context of testing must be taken into account in designing and evaluating the prototype.

Semantic differential

Semantic differentials involve rating via pairs of words that are opposites, such as *like* and *dislike*, with positions to select between them. Results are quantifiable, since the number of responses for each position can be counted. The scales can be used with any type of interface—conceptual, or live and functional—and are especially effective when used to compare participant perceptions with qualities stated in initial requirements or goals.

The semantic differential is especially useful for gaining insight into perceptions—how people interpret something and value it. It helps quantify subjective opinions.

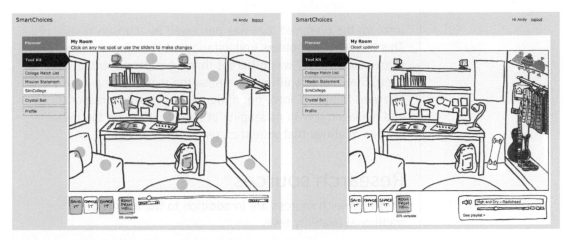

Figure 3.2 Example of two screens from a conceptual paper prototype tested with target users to determine interest and get early input.

	very	somewhat	neither/nor	somewhat	very	
1. experienced	◯	◯	◯	◯	◯	inexperienced
2. effective	◯	◯	◯	◯	◯	ineffective
3. efficient	◯	◯	◯	◯	◯	inefficient
4. customer-focused	◯	◯	◯	◯	◯	organizationally-focused
5. service-oriented	◯	◯	◯	◯	◯	technology oriented

Figure 3.3 Example of semantic differential scales.

The semantic differential scales shown in Figure 3.3 were used to help stakeholders choose between two logos being considered for a university's technology services department.

These scales were sent to department employees so external stakeholders could understand how people perceived the qualities of the two logos. A final question asked which logo they preferred, and why. Paradoxically, results showed that people preferred the logo that did not have a quality employees initially said the logo should have—that it should feel "cutting-edge."

Instead, the preferred logo was perceived as "conservative." This helped stakeholders understand that the *idea* of what the logo should convey was different than what people actually liked. Stakeholders ultimately chose the more cutting-edge, "forward-thinking" logo, but anticipated a negative response and managed it with messaging at launch affirming the initial desired qualities that were the goal of the redesign.

Research sources

These research sources are in addition to the results of traditional usability tests.

Demographic data

Statistical information about a population typically includes gender, age, household income, employment status, and location. Because demographics don't include context, analyze them as part of a broader research plan instead of relying on them on their own.

Customer feedback

Records of correspondence describing user issues with a product or service are helpful, especially when trying to prioritize design work. Some feedback includes direct issues that people have, while other feedback includes situations that must be interpreted to understand the root of the problem. Reviewing customer feedback is useful on its own, and also complements other methods.

Analytics

Analytics gathered for websites or mobile applications provide concrete statistics about what parts of an application are most frequently visited, popular user pathways, how much time people spend in specific locations, and other usage data. These analytics can typically be viewed in context of visitor demographics, such as location, browser, and OS type. As with general demographic data, reviewing analytics should take place alongside qualitative methods to provide a more complete picture of audience characteristics and behavior.

Elements of interface personality

A successful interface design establishes its personality instantly and over time to help create a positive impression. For our purposes, personality is conveyed visually through the characteristics of what people see: the way in which layout, type, color, imagery, and controls and affordances are represented. This affects how people interpret what they can do with an application and how they characterize it.

How an application is accessed or delivered affects user expectations as well. A web-based application may have different visual characteristics than a mobile application, and characteristics may further change based on the nature of the specific delivery device. The elements that affect interface personality can be represented as shown in Figure 3.4. (Feedback and responsiveness are not included, since they are not visual characteristics.)

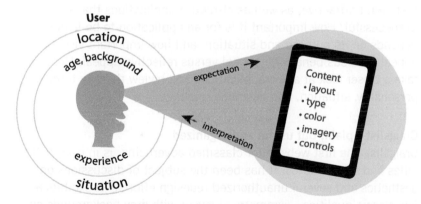

User situation and characteristics   **Content and delivery characteristics**

Figure 3.4 Elements of visual personality.

Aesthetics and interface personality

There are two ways impressions can be characterized at the visceral level: how approachable (or useful) an application appears (i.e., "Does it look like this will allow me to do what I want?"), and whether we like what we see, or find that some aspect of it resonates with us on a personal level. Researchers have tested website designs to understand how people perceive design characteristics and usability. They tested *classic* aesthetic qualities (organization, cleanliness, symmetry), which fit our notion of approachability, as well as *expressive* aesthetic qualities (harmony of design, harmony of coloring, dynamic expression)[4], which correspond to likability. We know that the more appealing users find a website, the more usable they perceive it to be.[5] The research showed that perception of classic aesthetic qualities has an edge over expressive qualities when it comes to measuring perceived usability. That tells us that personality matters to users and is relevant to usability as long as the classic qualities are evident and not overshadowed by expressive ones.

How much personality does an application need? Or, how important is it to be likable?

Whether a person (or in our case, an application) is likable—that is, appealing—is a key attribute of personality. In the realm of application design, we know that visual appeal affects users' overall impressions. However, there are plenty of successful applications that aren't attractive, as well as attractive applications that are unsuccessful. How important it is for an application to be likable depends on its purpose and situation, and how important visceral appeal is versus behavioral appeal versus reflective appeal. Here we take a closer look at a few applications and review them in terms of personality, situation, and aesthetic qualities.

Craigslist—plain, but useful and organized

Craigslist, the first website for classified advertising, is in over 700 cities and 90 countries. It has been the subject of discussions on aesthetics and several unauthorized redesign efforts.[6] It exhibits a few classic qualities—symmetrical layout with gray backgrounds on each side, simple, text-only, two-color interface, organized content.

[4] Tractinsky, N., and Lavie, T. (2004). Assessing dimensions of perceived visual aesthetics of web sites. *International Journal of Human-Computer Studies* 60, 269–298.

[5] Tractinsky, N. Aesthetic and Apparent Usability: Empirically Assessing Cultural and Methodological Issues. *CHI 97 Proceedings*, Atlanta, 1997, pp. 115–123.

[6] Honan, M. (2009, Aug. 24). Extreme Makeover: Craigslist Edition. *WIRED*. Retrieved July 9, 2012, from *http://www.wired.com/entertainment/theweb/magazine/17-09/ff_craigslist_makeover/*; LeFebvre, R. (2012, July 12). Enjoy a Better User Experience with Craigslist for iPhone and iPad. Cult of Mac. Retrieved July 24, 2012, from *http://www.cultofmac.com/178770/enjoy-a-better-user-experience-with-craigslist-for-iphone-and-ipad/*.

Its personality is exceedingly bland, and there are no expressive qualities. The fonts are plain; the colors based on default HTML markup (Figures 3.5 and 3.6).

WIRED magazine asked several top designers to redesign craigslist, and published the results.[7] Redesigns range from purely expressive (Pentagram's design by Lisa Strausfeld and Luke Hyman that does

Figure 3.5 Craigslist's local website for Boston, MA.

[7]Honan, M. (2009, Aug. 24). Extreme Makeover: Craigslist Edition. *WIRED*. Retrieved July 9, 2012, from *http://www.wired.com/entertainment/theweb/magazine/17-09/ff_craigslist_makeover/*.

Figure 3.6 Lifelike Apps' unauthorized interface design for craigslist can be purchased to change the display of craigslist content.

away with categories altogether to form words into an image of founder Craig Newmark's face), to classic (Matt Willey's from Studio8 Design and SimpleScott's submissions that introduce a bit of color and refined typography and layout), to focused on functionality (the submission from Khoi Vinh and the team from NYTimes.com that focuses on search and separates sales and purchase features).

Craigslist has kept a minimalist design for its entire existence, however, despite the availability of alternate interfaces for purchase and free ideas from designers. Few changes, such as links to mobile and tablet versions, have been made to the website since its launch. Clearly, the owners don't feel the need to add personality to the website. Their position as the oldest and best-known in their space is enough to keep the website going strong, and its owners must feel that the website's understated personality is not an impediment to profit and success. In their case, an organized website, while unattractive, is organized *enough* to be massively useful for people all over the world.

The craigslist example shows that there's more than personality at play when it comes to success. Decisions about personality in interface design are just one part of what's presented to users. Characteristics of endearment, such as familiarity and integrity, play a role. Craigslist didn't start out in 90 countries. It started in one city. It kept the basic characteristics of its look through upgrades and expansion, which makes the website familiar whether you use it daily or every few years. The constancy of the interface plays into the perceived integrity of the service.

Just as people have a frame of reference affecting their interpretations, organizations have a frame of reference affecting how and why they represent themselves. Factors such as organization type and structure, staffing and skills, competition and position, culture, and self-image all affect how organizations present themselves in their products and services.

Craigslist.com personality summary
- Some elements of classic aesthetics—simple, symmetrical, organized.
- No elements of expressive aesthetics.
- First to market.
- Started locally and grew globally (original design was fairly comprehensive, adaptable to different languages and cultures).
- Focus on one thing: classified advertising.
- Likable enough to be used by millions worldwide.

Labbler.com—cool, clean, and controlled
Labbler.com is a website and application designed to connect music artists with media and service providers in the music industry. The interface has classic qualities—the templates are clean and well organized, a result of generous use of space around the widgets and a controlled, pale background color palette with pops of bright color corresponding to sections of the application (Figure 3.7). The application displays detailed information such as music tracks, which are represented visually in the interface and tables of track listings.

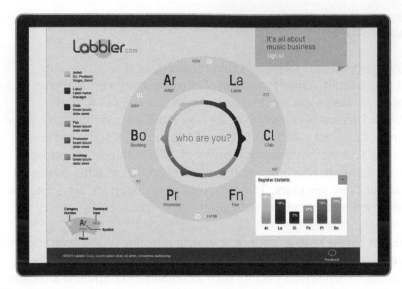

Figure 3.7 Labbler.com home page has a scientific look. The website is "all about the music business." Image courtesy Martin Oberhäuser, *http://www.oberhaeuser.info*.

Despite the need to display common data tables, the presentation does not feel generic. Expressive qualities are evident in the carefully designed typographic styles, subtle mix of flat color fields and shading, and custom, but clear, icons. Part of the expressive aesthetic is up to the user—several screens feature large profile images, and users may add custom images to tracks (Figure 3.8).

The home screen uses navigation as the interface, and personality is established there through the distinctive typeface and the round graphic that functions as the navigation. The element-like symbols, the monochrome colors in the palette, and the round graphic lend a scientific look to the home page. The real-time chart showing the breakdown of registered users sets the tone that the website is dynamic and helpful. The interface, other than displaying data and information relating to and about music, does not convey a sense of music in the design. The logo, however, shows abstract gears of a cassette tape in the round "bowls" of the letters "a" and "b." Those details are lost when the logo appears smaller on subsequent screens in the application.

Much of the success of the visual design is due to careful use of color and shading to create contrast that differentiates features from background and content, as seen in the local navigation, dropdowns, and "Add or Upload Tracks" button. Beyond the home page, much of the personality of the interface is defined by the user via images

Figure 3.8 Labbler.com successfully displays table data, complex navigation, controls for listening to and editing music, social media features, and profile information in a clean and approachable interface. Image courtesy Martin Oberhäuser, *http://www .oberhaeuser.info.*

and videos they upload. As a result, the interface itself does not need a strong personality, but the simplicity of the individual screens is a bit deceptive. Graphic style pages (Figure 3.9) show the extent of the interface design and the careful consideration it took to create this consistent and "simple" visual language, in addition to the design of about a dozen screen templates. Labbler.com is new, and we do not yet know if the attractive interface will help it succeed.

Labbler.com personality summary

- Elements of classic aesthetics—simple, some symmetry, organized; limited, controlled colors.

- User-generated expressive elements—photos and videos, bright colors coded to website sections, and a mix of flat and shaded finishes.

- Focus on industry and needs of groups of people in that industry.

- Attractive combination of expressive, classic, and useful; likable.

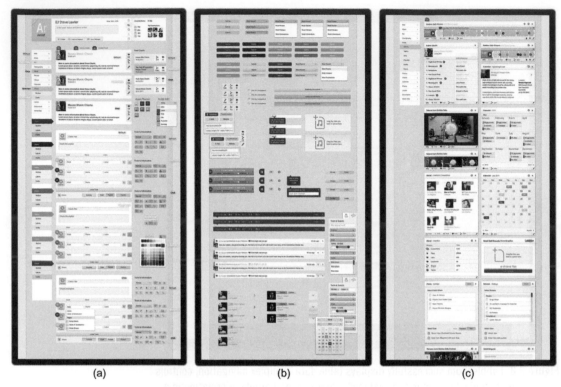

(a)   (b)   (c)

Figure 3.9 Labbler.com graphic style pages show the wide number of elements designed for this seemingly simple-looking interface. Images courtesy Martin Oberhäuser, *http://www.oberhaeuser.info*.

Epicurious—light-hearted and approachable

The Epicurious iOS application is a visual database of thirty thousand recipes from *Bon Appétit, Gourmet*, and other national magazines, with shopping list and recipe-sharing features. The application balances searching and browsing with expected and unexpected features that are friendly and clear. Recipes can be found with keywords or a visual faceted search. Browsing begins with over 25 dynamic categories, including the seasonal "Summer Desserts," along with unusual categories, like "Family Reunions" and "I Can Barely Cook." Both the search and browse features use tiny, internationally recognizable icons of foods and preparation techniques, like grilling. Rather than use the iOS picker, search categories appear in sets of horizontally scrolling rows with subcategory names and icons. The visual design of these features, including the custom picker, allows the application to express personality consistently across platforms.

The application uses the color red extensively in both the background image of red jalapeño peppers as well as in buttons (Figure 3.10). The pepper photo provides an abstract background texture that unites the application with the epicurious.com website look and feel. The

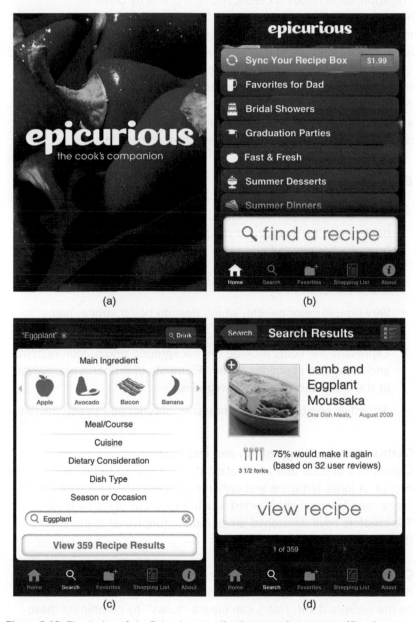

(a)   (b)

(c)   (d)

Figure 3.10 The design of the Epicurious application appeals to anyone. Visual characteristics express the brand through logo, photos, icons, and color. Use of familiar and custom controls is straightforward and clear.

distinctive, bold, semi-script logo font consistently appears in white on a colored or photographic background in the website and all application versions.

The application layout is classic, using a primarily centered arrangement on the home and search screens. Other screen templates mix centered alignment with left-aligned content for lists, while recipes are primarily left-aligned. Despite the expressive background image and use of color, the application looks approachable; for example, rather than the typical "stars" rating system, Epicurious uses forks. These details, bright color, bold background image, and extensive icon system all help give the application a friendly and engaging personality, while delivering high-quality recipes and list management features.

Epicurious personality summary
- Elements of classic aesthetics—symmetry in the centered layout screens, organized in the left-aligned layout screens. White background for results and recipes make the content stand out from the background.
- Gray icons used through the application are simple visually, yet aid in use cognitively.
- Very limited color palette, which despite being strong, helps photos of food stand out.
- Expressive elements include the background photo, icon system, and heavy use of shades of red. Elements of humor are conveyed in the icons and browsing categories.
- Attractive combination of expressive, classic, and useful; likable.

Clothia—trend-setting, useful, and inspiring
Clothia is a website and application that helps inspire fashion-minded people. It looks feminine and ephemeral due to the pale pink, white space, and trendy, light-hearted illustrations, but don't be fooled. The creators have developed an extremely functional application (Figure 3.11).

Clothia allows users to upload their own images, grab images from the web, and find images of fashionable clothing and accessories on the website itself. Users can create "looks" by combining these images any way they choose—effectively letting anyone do what fashion editors do (Figures 3.12, 3.13, and 3.14). Images on the

Figure 3.11 Clothia.com home page.

Figure 3.12 Interface to create "looks" makes it easy for anyone to try their hand at being a fashion editor.

website are linked to product details and purchase information, but the application feels more about practical fun than shopping. The main benefit is that users can plan wardrobes, outfits, and purchases visually with a drag-and-drop interface.

All drag-and-drop functionality is in the "Create" area of the website, which uses a unique template that doesn't look like a web page. It looks like an application, with most of the screen taken up by an empty area with instructional text that cues use with pale gray text: "Drag items here. Create your head-to-toe look by dragging items from All Items or My Items tabs." The tabs are clearly visible to the right.

Figure 3.13 The main screen of the Clothia iPad application differs from the web version (Figure 3.11).

(a)   (b)

Figure 3.14 Creating looks in the (a) mobile version and (b) web version. Controls in the mobile version are standard for iOS, rather than the elegant custom elements in the web version. Use of custom interface elements and behaviors would allow for consistency, and more control over the personality across platforms.

Icons of easily recognizable clothing categories help users get started. Icons are flat, yet still connote "clickability" through their position to the right of the "Create" area. Visually, elements play a game of contrast, mixing classic, minimal aesthetic characteristics like super-thin lines and simple, pale buttons that highlight on rollover with expressive and unique illustrations and fonts. The logotype is adaptable to a simple and unique application icon. The high yet controlled level of expression lends visual activity to the images of clothes and accessories without overwhelming the fashions.

An application for fashionistas, Clothia put forth a personality that said "fashion" at launch. By keeping photos focused on clothes and accessories and not models, the website can appeal to anyone interested in fashion, regardless of age, gender, or body type.

Clothia personality summary

- Elements of classic aesthetics—clean, lots of white space, some symmetry, organized, single accent color with black and white.

- User-generated and system-supplied expressive elements—photos, illustrations, and icons.

- Focus on enabling management and discovery of fashion with online capabilities.

SuperTracker—useful and usable

SuperTracker is a web application by the United States Department of Agriculture designed to help people track their food intake and activity to improve health. Nutritional information is based on the federal food composition database, a standardized resource cataloging nutritional value for over 8,000 foods.[8] Unlike competitor applications, SuperTracker will always be free and doesn't contain advertising.

Aesthetically, SuperTracker has some classic qualities and some expressive qualities. There are several application templates that are organized but don't present a strong visual hierarchy. On the most functional templates—the food and activity trackers—the appearance is cluttered, not clean, and it can be hard to tell where to click (Figure 3.15).

[8]Conaboy, C. (2012, Feb. 13). Cyber Tools Foster Fitness. *The Boston Globe.* Retrieved July 10, 2012, from *http://articles.boston.com/2012-02-13/arts/31052298_1_track-fitness-application*; NDL/FNIC Food Composition Database. (2011, Dec. 7). Retrieved July 20, 2012, from *http://ndb.nal.usda.gov/.*

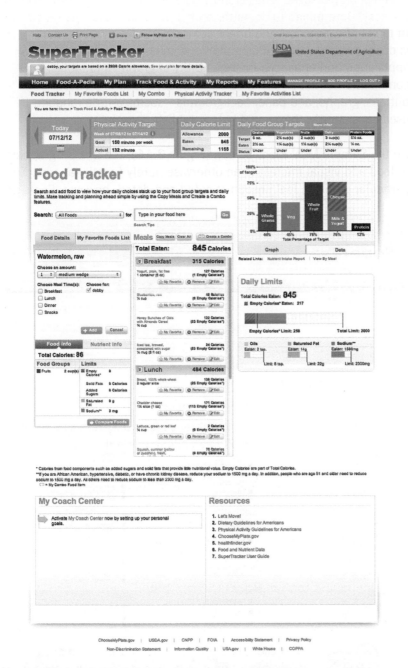

Figure 3.15 SuperTracker's Food Tracker screen.

In terms of expression, the bright color palette feels upbeat and is coded to food groups. Color-coding is consistent across the application and enhances the readability of graphs and tables. A combination of flat and shaded areas throughout the interface—in buttons, graphs, and panel backgrounds—seems a little random. If used consistently, they would help establish personality.

On the Sample Meal Plans screen (Figure 3.16), the line art graphics of food add visual interest to an otherwise purely functional area. The particular graphics feel unsophisticated and dated, however. Fonts are

Figure 3.16 SuperTracker's Sample Meal Plans screen.

appropriately plain in style, as are their sizes and weights. Similar to craigslist, SuperTracker needs to be really useful for a huge number of diverse people.

SuperTracker personality summary

- Some classic aesthetic characteristics. Personality characteristics vary depending on the template. Some symmetry, some organization.
- Could be improved by perception of approachability, and clearer organization of complex screens.
- Limited expressive color, use of shading, and use of generic line art.
- Government application.
- Nonobjectionable characteristics.

Special opportunities for conveying personality

The four examples have different personalities. We know that characteristics of personality are conveyed through layout, type, color, imagery, and controls and affordances. We have introduced a language for discussing and qualifying them in terms of classic and expressive aesthetics.

There's another opportunity to express personality that crosses these boundaries. We call this "voice of the system" messaging: system status and help messages that convey personality through tone of voice. This messaging is a type of content in response to user behavior:

- Tips
- Help
- Error messages
- Status updates

VOS messaging often combines text and an icon within an element such as a lightbox or popup, all of which receive a unique visual treatment. It ranges from afterthoughts to masterful expressions of personality and is a unique opportunity for tone of voice to delight instead of scold, be personable instead of mechanical, or be just plain helpful in a way that represents your application's personality (Figures 3.17, 3.18, and 3.19).

boston craigslist > for sale / wanted > choose category

log in to your account
(Apply for Account)

AVOID SCAMS BY DEALING LOCALLY -- IGNORE DISTANT BUYERS (SCAMMERS):

1. Most cashier's check or money orders offered to craigslist sellers are COUNTERFEIT -- cashing them can lead to financial ruin
2. Requests that you wire money abroad via Western Union or moneygram for any reason are SCAMS
3. Learn more on our scams page -- avoid scammers by dealing locally with buyers you can meet in person!

Please choose a category:

○ antiques - by dealer
○ antiques - by owner
○ appliances - by dealer
○ appliances - by owner
○ arts & crafts - by dealer
○ arts & crafts - by owner
○ auto parts - by dealer
○ auto parts - by owner
○ baby & kid stuff - by dealer
○ baby & kid stuff - by owner *(no illegal sales of banned cribs, e.g. drop-side cribs)*
○ barter
○ bicycles - by dealer
○ bicycles - by owner
○ boats - by dealer
○ boats - by owner
○ books & magazines - by dealer
○ books & magazines - by owner
○ business/commercial - by dealer
○ business/commercial - by owner
○ cars & trucks - by dealer
○ cars & trucks - by owner
○ cds / dvds / vhs - by dealer
○ cds / dvds / vhs - by owner *(no pornography please)*
○ cell phones - by dealer
○ cell phones - by owner

Figure 3.17 The design of this craigslist warning seems like an afterthought.

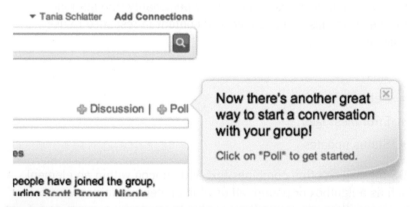

Figure 3.18 This tip from LinkedIn doesn't have a lot of personality, but the "yellow sticky" color and treatment are appropriate for the website's professional characteristics.

(a)

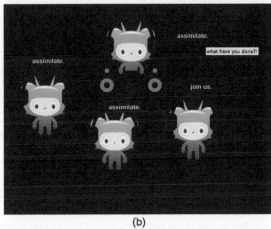

(b)

Figure 3.19 Turntable.fm, which allows people to DJ for their friends, uses appealing cartoon graphics to entice people, and on rollover, provides a standard HTML tooltip reading "please don't click this exactly 3 times." Clicking three times swaps in a new graphic of "assimilated" listeners, with a mock-horrified tooltip reading "what have you done?"

Establishing criteria for personality

Determining criteria for how an interface should look to appeal to users, meet their expectations, and help them use the application is essential to success. Just as applications have requirements for functionality, they may also have requirements for the visual interface. A designer needs to review supplied interface requirements critically and may need to seek out additional requirements to have a complete picture of what affects the interface.

Criteria for personality "live" in different places, some visible and some not (Figure 3.20). They live in the user's mind in the form of

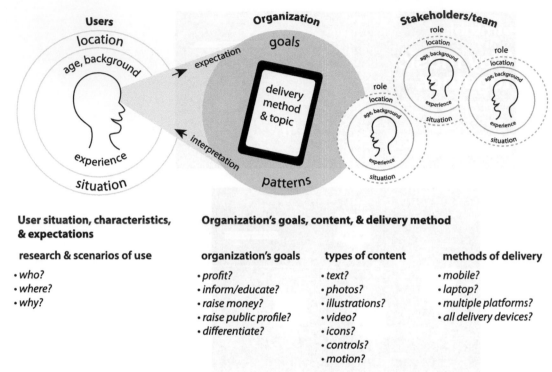

User situation, characteristics, & expectations

Organization's goals, content, & delivery method

research & scenarios of use	organization's goals	types of content	methods of delivery
• *who?*	• *profit?*	• *text?*	• *mobile?*
• *where?*	• *inform/educate?*	• *photos?*	• *laptop?*
• *why?*	• *raise money?*	• *illustrations?*	• *multiple platforms?*
	• *raise public profile?*	• *video?*	• *all delivery devices?*
	• *differentiate?*	• *icons?*	
		• *controls?*	
		• *motion?*	

Figure 3.20 This diagram adapts and expands Figure 3.4 to show where criteria that affect interface personality "live," as well as sample questions of which the answers help provide a complete picture of the expectations and biases that affect design.

experiences and expectations. They live in the organization in the form of interfaces from iterations of previous or other applications, style guides, business missions, and project goals. They live in minds of stakeholders in the form of release dates and targets to be met, preferences, and biases based on experiences; and they live in the minds of designers and developers in the form of preferences and biases. Getting a complete picture of the state of these expectations and biases involves asking questions and conducting or reviewing research that answers those questions.

Personality clues in personas

Composite models of users are commonly known as personas[9]. Personas serve interface designers by providing examples of who the application users are, where they're likely to be accessing the application, why they're using it, and what they're using it for.

[9]Cooper, A., Reimann, R and Cronin, D., (2007) About Face 3: The Essentials of Interaction Design, p. 21.

Personas don't hold explicit answers for personality, but contain clues that feed into personality design.

Personas supply the necessary who, where, and why. The *who* defines user characteristics and expectations; the *where* defines context and situations that might affect the user experience; and the *why* defines goals and expectations. From the clues, designers can imagine characteristics that will be appropriate for users. We'll review sample personas in the case study later in this chapter.

Uncovering organizational requirements

Ideally, each interface design project comes with a well-researched and sound description that clearly states rational organizational goals at the outset: who the application is for, what it should do for the organization, and what the benefits are for users. Designers need to review whatever documentation they get in detail, and question anything unclear; designs that make sense can only come from understanding project and audience goals.

Team workshops

Team workshops are good for getting goals, bias, and expectations out in the open, and are a great way to uncover organizational requirements early on in a project. We focus part of the agenda on identifying user types, typical personas of use, and "pain points" or driving issues, and part on desired personality characteristics.

Listing team member's adjectives about how they want the application to be perceived by users, discussing them as a group, and narrowing the list helps establish criteria for visual characteristics.

Stakeholder interviews

These interviews provide similar benefits to workshops, but are conducted one-on-one with each stakeholder. Stakeholder interviews help designers understand the why behind high-level expectations. A common mistake designers make is to accept stakeholder preferences and proclamations out of hand, without question. Answers to business questions need not be backed up with spreadsheets and financial reports; a few simple sentences of elaboration will do. Not understanding the why behind expectations leads designers to make assumptions about how to design something to address what they perceive as the stakeholder's issue. Assumptions are problematic when getting feedback on designs, as they are often wrong.

Assessing identity requirements

Identities, typically the logo and related visual assets that help characterize a personality, can stem from different levels: the organization that made the application, the application itself, and the system if the application is part of a suite of related programs. Since personality depends on the context, goals, and personality of their parent organizations, there's a wide range of personality characteristics that an application can portray.

In the case of Blurb, a company that provides tools for people to make their own professional-quality books, there's Blurb the company, and there's Blurb's applications (Figures 3.21 and 3.22). When it comes to personality, part of the decision-making process involves asking and answering questions like these: "When people are using our software, should they perceive one personality— the application's—or two personalities—the company's and the application's?" and "Which should be more prominent? Why?" Answering questions like these involves having a user experience strategy based on understanding where the user's mental association lies—with the company or the application—and where it should lie to achieve business goals.

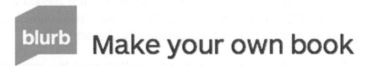

Figure 3.21 Blurb company logo and tag line.

Figure 3.22 Blurb product identity. Blurb uses the company's logo for applications as well. This approach is common for new companies, as they are working to establish a recognizable business at the same time they are establishing a product.

Dealing with bias and disagreements

Everyone has their own frame of reference that they bring to the design process; no one is completely objective, nor should they be.

This is why a sound rationale is crucial. People will always have opinions, and designers cannot and should not try to control them. As we show throughout this book, grounding design decisions in a rationale based on knowledge and understanding allows teams to make and discuss design decisions with a shared vision. When whim comes up—as it does and should as part of the expressive nature of aesthetics—it should be acknowledged as such.

Cases where members of the team, stakeholders, or users have opinions about an aesthetic characteristic but cannot explain them are not unusual. When preferences are based on whim instead of rationale, they need to be acknowledged, but set aside. All options should be evaluated based on criteria. Designers who cannot explain their preferences or rationale must either define the benefits of their whim or be willing to make changes. In either case, testing design characteristics can be done via several of the research methods discussed earlier in this chapter; the semantic differential, A/B testing, and conceptual prototype testing all help teams understand how people interpret visual characteristics.

Another common issue teams face involves disagreements about how to solve a design problem. These commonly take the form of "holy wars" fueled by dogmatic adherence to or adoption of a principle, or stalemates when there is more than one possible, good solution. These issues come up in the concept/personality direction-setting phase and can arise repeatedly throughout detailed design. If a team can't agree and is unwilling to flip a coin, getting outside feedback from users can break the deadlock. Iterating and testing several solutions that fit or are based on the principles that are at odds provide the missing criteria needed to make a decision. Online usability testing services are fast, easy, and inexpensive. If confidentiality is a concern, either have participants sign nondisclosure agreements or generalize the content to focus on the visual characteristics in question.

Content

Although this book does not address digital content in detail, an application's content both conveys personality and influences what types of personalities are appropriate. The content you have to work with affects how you use the design tools. When designing an application for MIT's HyperStudio to help scholars discover patterns in correspondence between the United States and Iran, we knew the vast majority of the interface would be black text (Figure 3.23). That fact, the characteristics of the subject matter, and the application's user base and their cultural expectations, led us to design a highly classic interface. We used simple icons and bright colors without specific national or religious connotations to contrast all the text, as well as to lend some expressive quality to the interface.

Content considerations cover imagery as well as text. In the case of iOS's Photos interface, users need to interact with photos they've

Figure 3.23 Annotating records of correspondence is the primary feature of this application for scholars of U.S.–Iranian policy. The interface is text-based. As such, classic aesthetics dominate the design.

taken, and the less interface overhead, the more the photos come to the forefront (Figure 3.24). Using slightly transparent task bars, glossy buttons, and simple iconography—all of which fade away after a few seconds, or after the user taps the screen—lend a cool, professional feel to the application.

Figure 3.24 The iOS Photos application overlays photos with tools that recede into the background, allowing users to concentrate on what's important: the photo itself.

Type of delivery—integrating technical requirements

Many interface projects begin with a method of delivery in mind. In these situations the method of delivery becomes the overarching requirement, and it affects interface decisions. Technology-led design results in dull interface personalities, with craigslist an obvious and familiar example. Applications that rely solely on default widgets also fall into this category (Figure 3.25).

It's no secret that interface designs are affected by the technology used to present them. As the number of devices continues to explode, deciding what, if any, interface patterns to adopt is a huge part of establishing personality. The number-one personality mistake we see is when teams adopt design patterns wholesale to be their interface design, closely followed by when they take a hybrid approach and avoid integration, such as designing an appealing header and adding it to an otherwise generic, technology-driven interface (Figure 3.26).

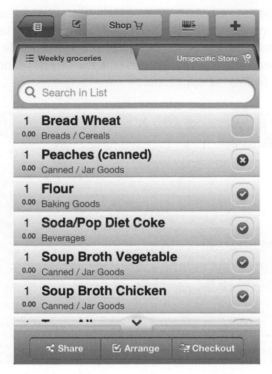

Figure 3.25 Because Grocery Gadget's shopping list interface relies on limited customization of default iOS UI widgets, it's useful and easy to understand, but the few completely custom elements onscreen are so overshadowed by the main UI that the application has no personality of its own.

Interface design patterns and default widgets exist to speed design and development and promote consistency across applications, but because they must literally be all things to all applications, they must also by definition be personality-free. At best, they convey limited characteristics of the chosen platform, such as Aqua's rounded-corner form buttons on the OS X version of Safari, or the crisp, high-contrast form elements on Android that reflect the platform's developer-friendly aesthetic. But pure reliance on default elements without additional personality styling results only in generic-looking applications that are functional, but emotionally unsatisfying.

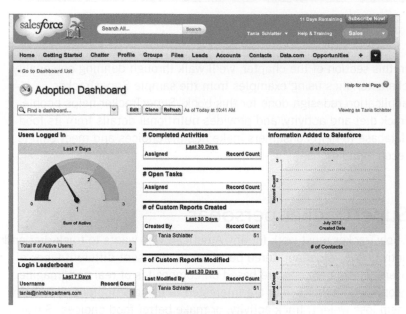

Figure 3.26 The pleasing effect of the header with the cute cloud logo and palm trees fades quickly when the eye falls below to the generic dashboard UI.

Figure 3.27 The iOS picker is very strong visually and can dominate small phone screens. The iOS application StatsWidget integrates a similar control, but applies subtle treatments to it that harmonize with the application's design, yet still clearly indicate what type of control it is and how it should work. This is a great example of visual usability—combining affordances people expect with custom characteristics that work aesthetically and convey personality.

In this section of the chapter, we'll walk through defining personality characteristics using examples from the sample SuperTracker application redesign done for this book. SuperTracker helps people track diet and activity, and provides nutritional details from its food database to help consumers make healthy choices and meet calorie recommendations.

SuperTracker personas

SuperTracker must work for any American who wants to track diet and activity. We've defined three personas to represent different types of users. These personas are based on composites of real and imagined people who either use or are interested in using a digital tool to help them lose weight, track activity, or make better food choices. Since we're designing for the book and not for an actual client, these lightweight, or ad-hoc, personas[10] are sufficient to help us make empathetic decisions. Ideas for appealing personalities come from clues in the personas.

Diet and activity persona 1: Betty

Betty is 70 years old, and a widow. She has enough money for what she needs and a little travel if she budgets carefully. She is healthy—takes only a multivitamin and calcium, no medicine—and is active, walking half a mile to a mile most days or going to the gym. She drives elders in her community on errands, and takes trips to see family a few times a year. She uses her laptop regularly to research airfare and travel deals, monitor her recent Match.com account, and keep up with email from family.

Betty gained 15 pounds in the two years after her husband died. She is mindful of food portions and nutrition. She tried a diet system that includes prepackaged food, didn't lose weight, and was disgusted with the cost. Determined to do better on her own, she eats small meals that she prepares herself. She loses a few pounds, and then her weight loss stalls again. Betty is frustrated and mystified.

[10] Norman, D. (2004, November 16). Ad-Hoc Personas & Empathetic Focus. Don Norman's jnd.org website / human-centered design. Retrieved February 18, 2013, from http://www.jnd.org/dn.mss/adhoc_personas_em.html

Betty brings up characteristics that need to be taken into consideration in the interface design. She's older, and that will affect type size and control area. She also sees herself as active and "doing the right things." Emotionally, she may be more defensive than open to critique about her diet and weight.

If we consider characteristics for what Betty's dream application would be like, a friend comes to mind. Reading into Betty, we imagine that she wants sympathetic, knowledgeable advice from someone who understands her. She's not interested in taking orders from a coach. A friend would be sympathetic, but not endlessly, and would provide gentle but persistent reminders and advice, especially when they find out how much cheese Betty eats on a daily basis.

Diet and activity persona 2: Danny

Danny is 36 years old. He's always been able to eat whatever he wanted and have the energy needed to play pickup or team basketball once or twice a week. Because Danny's dad was diabetic, Danny had his blood sugar levels checked a few years ago. Results were normal, and Danny wasn't concerned—but since he became a dad last year, it's on his mind, as is the paunch in his middle now that he plays ball only occasionally. After a more recent blood test, Danny discovers his results are in the high range of normal, and Danny's doctor suggests he make some changes to his diet and activity.

Danny carries his mobile phone at all times. He's a manager for an internal IT team at a medium-sized software company, and is often on call. He goes out to buy lunch during the weekday with members of his team. He's looking for an application he can access on his phone that will help him track what he eats, motivate him to eat better, and get more regular exercise into his life.

For an application to work for Danny, it needs to be mobile. From the personality standpoint, if we imagine what the perfect application for Danny would be like, someone who would motivate him to make healthier food choices and inspire him to be more active on a daily and long-term basis comes to mind. A coach like the one he had for high school basketball, who occasionally shamed him into action, could motivate him. Someone who just plain has the facts about what Danny eats, calls him on poor choices with information rather than dominance, and makes the outcomes of his choices hard to ignore could motivate him as well.

Diet and activity persona 3: Sonia

Sonia is a single mom with 11-year-old twins. She works at a large insurance agency, and is at her computer all day. Sonia has little control over what the twins eat during the week. They get lunch at school and snack at the recreation center in the afternoons. On the weekends, Sonia loves to cook. On a typical Saturday morning, she does the grocery shopping early, and takes the kids to athletics. Later, the family watches a few movies and enjoys her cooking. Sonia knows both kids are big for their age, and not just tall. She has a hard time saying "no" to the processed salty and sweet snacks they like. She knows she should limit snacks from the vending machine after practices and cook healthier meals from the cooking magazines she browses in the checkout aisle, but she doesn't know how to start making changes.

Sonia has a laptop at home. She'd love a tablet or an e-reader for her commute, and is thinking of splurging on herself for Christmas. In terms of an interface, Sonia's used to complex enterprise applications from her work. If we imagine what type of personality would appeal to her, she would appreciate guidance from a teacher or other professional authority.

Interpreting personas

Potential personalities for the interface come from imagining possibilities based on the personas. We imagine and brainstorm when we're engaged with the personas, because we feel connected to and empathy for the people they represent. How we interpret the personas is influenced by our individual subjectivity. Our interpretations are not based on whim, but what we've experienced directly in life—people we know who made up Betty and the other personas. This is a good thing, as empathy and connection drive more meaningful designs. As long as we acknowledge our biases, adding them to the interpretation of Betty lets us imagine richer possibilities than if we constrained ourselves to the "facts" of the persona.

Criteria and requirements for the visual interface

Some requirements for visual interfaces are "hard," and based on fact, like needing to adhere to accessibility standards for publicly funded work. We consider meeting the needs of users described in personas and addressing stakeholder preferences as requirements as well, even though they may be "soft." All requirements come under scrutiny during the design process, and priorities change. Starting out, defining requirements for the visual interface means pulling together everything we know that will affect the interface— all relevant hard and soft criteria we've collected—for review before beginning visual interface design.

In a formal design process, we document criteria in a *design brief*, and share it with stakeholders to get agreement or generate discussion before visual design begins.

An interface design brief may contain:

- A statement of general and specific business goals for the interface in bullet-point form.
- Copies of or links to the existing website or application, related websites or applications, and any brand or identity standards that apply.
- Technical information, such as platform style guides and links to demo code.
- A simple, brief competitive survey and analysis of interface characteristics for one to three competitor websites or applications.

- Notes about what types of content the application will display, as well as very high-level notes about where it will come from.

- Notes about what types of images will be shown (if known at this stage) and where they will come from.

- User requirements—explicit information about user characteristics that affect design, such as age, familiarity with the device, and accessibility requirements.

- High-level insights from user research.

- Initial user personas.

- A list of adjectives describing the ideal redesigned or new application, which will inform the personality.

- A proposed approach, or starting point for the visual design. This could be a description of a high-level rationale based on requirements, sketches, or image collages[11] that represent one or more proposed "look-and-feel" directions.

Despite the long list of contents, the design brief should be as short and straightforward as possible. It serves to help ground discussions about prioritization of requirements and provide a blueprint for visual interface design. Ideally, requirements are approved and prioritized before visual design begins, but in reality this is seldom the case, and design needs to progress based on what's known and agreed to at the time, even if it's incomplete or changes.

[11] Image collages that show the feeling that a design could convey are called "feely boards" or "mood boards." They are most commonly used to define visual characteristics for highly expressive brands, nondigital products, clothing lines, and interior decor, and apply to any type of design.

SuperTracker requirements

For the SuperTracker redesign, we adopted the best practice of "designing for mobile first"[12] to home in on the most important features and figure out how to present them on the small screen. We also constrained our redesign to food-tracking screens, as tracking diet was most important to our personas. Once we'd set these two primary requirements, we focused on additional criteria.

Business requirements, project goals, and content

Our primary goal was a visual redesign and adaptation of SuperTracker's food-tracking features to mobile platforms, not an overhaul of the application's complete user experience. We planned to maintain the application's current content and functionality, in keeping with the project's stated goals:

> Provide consumers with the practical application and "how-tos" to empower them to make healthy food and activity choices....

- **SuperTracker** empowers consumers to build a healthier diet based on personal preferences that also meet nutrient needs and stay within their Calorie allowance.

- Americans [*sic*] eating styles vary greatly based on many factors including culture, lifestyle preferences, and health status. Features within **SuperTracker** allow flexibility to link and create unique combinations to accommodate personal preferences.

- The expansive food database allows consumers to develop an infinite number of eating patterns that meet nutrient needs within an appropriate Calorie allowance that they enjoy and can maintain over time.[13]

---

[12] Luke Wroblewski's book *Mobile First* goes into more detail about the advantages of this strategy. Wroblewski, L. (2011). *Mobile first*. New York: A Book Apart.

[13] SuperTracker Backgrounder (2011, Dec.). ChooseMyPlate.gov. Retrieved July 23, 2012, from *http://www.choosemyplate.gov/newsroom/ST/SuperTrackerBackgrounder.pdf*.

Reference materials

We had many reference sources from which to draw during the course of the project:

- The existing application.
- The related ChooseMyPlate.gov site.
- Graphic standards for the MyPlate logo, type, and colors.
- The World Wide Web Consortium's Web Accessibility Initiative guidelines (*http://www.w3.org/WAI/*), which are required for government applications, but the right thing to do regardless.

Technical requirements

Since we weren't actually coding mobile or web applications, we had few technical requirements. Nevertheless, even visual sketches for these platforms required understanding the different guidelines and conventions to follow for each one.

- Design for mobile, in both small form factors (phone) and larger ones (tablet).
- Design for web browser.

Competitive survey and analysis

We used SuperTracker and competitor applications and evaluated them based on usability heuristics[14] to help us understand SuperTracker's strength and weaknesses. We considered the overall user experience, not just the interface.

SuperTracker's strengths included:

- A food database that covered common prepackaged snacks and meals, and was based on independent scientific analysis of food composition, not manufacturers' claims.

---

[14] Many sets of usability heuristics exist. Jakob Nielsen's list is one of the most well-known, and is available at *http://www.useit.com/papers/heuristic/heuristic_list.html*.

- The ability to track quantities more accurately than other applications we tried.

- A connection to educational initiatives and content from ChooseMyPlate.gov.

- If used as designed, a very clear status of nutrition and calorie consumption.

SuperTracker's weaknesses

The application also had several weaknesses:

- An awkward, overly complex food entry interface.

- No mobile application.

- Feedback when daily limits were exceeded looked like errors, which was discouraging.

User requirements

We assumed the following user requirements:

- Must work on mobile platforms to fit into daily life and help make healthy choices away from home.

- Must work for older adult's vision—a feature partially addressed by accessibility requirements.

- Food entry flow needed to feel simple, smooth, and intuitive.

- Application must provide guidance that's firm and informative without being overly critical.

User research findings

We used SuperTracker daily to give us direct knowledge of how it met our needs. This also helped us imagine how it could help the users in our personas. We discovered:

- SuperTracker was most useful when it provided status about where we were in our daily calorie limits and nutritional goals.

- When we exceeded calorie, fat, or salt limits, the application's feedback felt like scolding, not guidance.

- It would be nice if feedback recognized successful and detrimental behavior patterns.
- Food tracking felt slow and onerous. Tracking food intake is rarely going to be fun, but it should at least not feel like an unpleasant chore.
- The design of the food-tracking area made it hard to tell at a glance what we'd eaten and how many calories each item contained.

Desired personality

Even though a coach personality might work for Danny, it wouldn't for Betty. We needed to define characteristics that would work for all three personas. We wanted a personality that would motivate with information and feedback. Information in the personas suggested the application needed to be:

- Helpful
- Knowledgeable, very smart
- Devoted—always there when needed
- Caring, nonjudgmental

We imagined and brainstormed characters with these attributes to visualize what form these qualities could take. We thought about what made SuperTracker different from competitor applications. It didn't have the slickness of commercial applications, but there was no barrier to entry—it was free for anyone to use, and tied into federal education initiatives Americans might already be familiar with. Its database, while smaller than those offered by its competition, relied on independent analysis of nutritional information, not what manufacturers claimed their products contained. And while logging foods was more cumbersome in SuperTracker than similar applications, ease of entry could be addressed in interface design.

SuperTracker was smart and helpful, and its personality should take advantage of that. We came up with the concept of Pepper, a knowledgeable, technology-savvy assistant who's professional, sophisticated, devoted, and always there with the facts. We'll show how Pepper took shape though layout, color, type, imagery, and controls and affordances.

Approach

With Pepper in mind, we could determine our starting point for the design.

- Design for mobile first. Any issues we had with hierarchy and layout would be addressed for mobile platforms before redesigning the web version.
- Start exploring the expression of personality characteristics in a new logo design.

Exploring a personality's possibilities

Kevin Mullet and Darrell Sano define the principles of style as distinctiveness, integrity, comprehensiveness, and appropriateness. In their words,

> Effective styles must be **distinctive** enough to be readily identifiable. They must possess an **integrity** that reflects the central ideas of the worldview they represent, and be **comprehensive** enough to generalize across a range of design problems. Finally, and most importantly, they must be **appropriate** for the problem, the designer and targeted consumers.[15]

These principles help qualify the personality of our designs. Our sample designs were done for this book. Other than getting user feedback on designs, we were able to go with our assumptions, but when we design for clients, we need to be prepared to explain and defend assumptions we make in the design process. If we were working with a team, some folks on the team might feel we nailed appropriate characteristics and wish us good luck with the design, while others would be uncomfortable with the leaps we've made.

Defining characteristics for personality involves educated guesses. It takes what's known (the more the better) and uses intuition and experience to go from there. Allowing this level of creativity into the thought process enables us to explore possibilities and evaluate more than one right answer. This is true of defining potential application-level characteristics of personality, as well as defining layouts, fonts, colors, etc., at the detailed interface element level.

Successful personalities are imaginative. Think of the MailChimp email campaign application (Figure 3.28). MailChimp wasn't designed based purely on fact; it was summoned from an understanding that people creating email campaigns are probably in a cubicle, may create email campaigns frequently, and would probably like a little levity in an otherwise tedious task. The interface's design isn't too different from others that enable management and reporting. However, the addition of the chimp, the playful logo, and messaging

---

[15] Mullet, K., and Sano, D. *Designing Visual Interfaces*, p. 215.

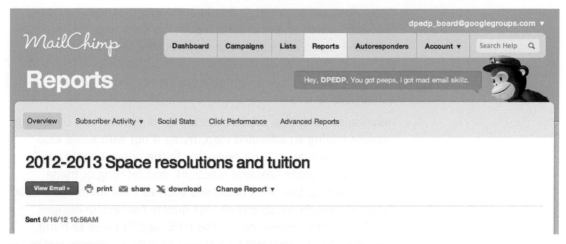

Figure 3.28 MailChimp's mascot and playful messaging help give it a distinctive personality.

"transform[s] an otherwise mundane task into an experience that people look forward to, and sometimes even miss."[16]

These characteristics have a big impact on the interface. The solution isn't to add a mascot to your application; it's to allow imagination into the design, and look for ways to let that imagination show through.

As a creative process, imagining needs to be free from criticism until it can be explored enough to be evaluated. This doesn't mean that it takes months to define successful personalities; the design team shouldn't be free from time constraints while everyone else codes late into the night. It does mean:

- Anyone can come up with possible characteristics of personality, as long as they're aware of project goals and criteria.
- Some ideas will be more appropriate than others, but ideas informed by the criteria are worth exploring.
- Defining attributes for personality will be more successful if done openly, such as in a working session.
- Defining attributes for personality can and should be done as part of a schedule that applies to the overall project.

[16]Walter, A. (2010, Apr. 23). Emotional Interface Design: The Gateway to Passionate Users. *Think Vitamin.* Retrieved July 23, 2012, from *http://thinkvitamin.com/design/emotional-interface-design-the-gateway-to-passionate-users/.*

- Once ideas are recorded, formally or informally, they should be evaluated based on the criteria/requirements, and defended if needed based on rationale or the reasoned decision-making that led to them. While imagination and subjectivity are part of defining personality, a personality still needs the underpinning of a plausible rationale.

- Iterating is designing; explore more than one direction. Designing involves having an informed idea, trying it out with some kind of sketch, evaluating it for relevance to the criteria and overall emotional response (visceral reaction), and refining or trying again. Famous, seasoned designers such as Paul Rand and Paula Scher are known for admitting that hugely successful designs (the Traveler's/Citibank logo,[17] the UPS logo[18]) came to mind instantly after understanding the project criteria. Unless you're that famous, and your interface that simple, you need to explore, sketch, and evaluate several ideas. *Sketchboarding* is a method of idea generation through structured sketching. Intended for user experience design, it's a great way to involve the team in the design process for interface design as well.[19]

- You *can* qualify aesthetic characteristics, appropriateness, and "likability." Results will be more accurate if you test designs with participants who are truly representative of your user base. (See our discussion of test methods earlier in this chapter.)

- Client and stakeholders' personal opinions matter, and need to be acknowledged and understood. Always show a design that includes client and/or stakeholders' personal opinions, if they expressed them clearly and voluntarily. Only when you've explored their ideas can you gently explain (relying on your sound rationale) why they aren't appropriate, while showing what you believe is a better solution.

- Even a good rationale isn't bulletproof. It's a shield that deflects and protects with rationality and sensitivity.

[17] Curtis, H. Artist Series: Paula Scher. Retrieved from *http://hillmancurtis.com/ artist-series/paula-scher/*.

[18] From Tania Schlatter's discussions as a student with Paul Rand in Brissago, Switzerland, 1991.

[19] Schauer, B. (2007, Dec. 14). Sketchboards: Discover Better + Faster UX Solutions. Adaptive Path website. Retrieved July 27, 2012, from *http://www.adaptivepath.com/ideas/sketchboards-discover-better-faster-ux-solutions.*

Avoid common mistakes

A little personality applied consistently is better than designing some sections or aspects of an application and not others. Designing an appealing application and treating a "help" section or messaging with little or no attention to design undermines personality.

Consider these questions while evaluating your designs:

- Does your intended audience consider the interface approachable? Does the interface look organized? Is it represented in a way that it feels familiar to the audience?

- Does visual design distract or get in the way of the application fulfilling its role?

- Do people know what application they are using? Can they differentiate the interface from competitor products?

- Does the interface design help users know where to start? Do they have an accurate understanding of what they can do on the screens?

- Have you applied design characteristics consistently to all areas of the application?

Make informed decisions

- Do the visual characteristics appeal to your audience?

- Does the interface represent only what's necessary for the application to perform its role successfully for users, with the addition of small elements that convey delight and/or meaning, without distractions?

- Do the visual characteristics still work if content, navigation, or features are added?

- Do the visual characteristics relate to other applications or communications that represent the organization in some way?

- Can the visual characteristics be adopted by new templates?

- If necessary, can your personality accommodate third-party customizations such as additional logos, colors, or type changes?

- Do the attributes that convey personality work across platforms and devices?

- Can the attributes that convey personality be easily changed if necessary, such as adding another color for a new section of the application? Are personality attributes maintainable? (For example, cropping round photos requires photo editing software the maintenance team may not know or have time to learn; changing out square or rectangular photos requires little to no special expertise.)

- Are the attributes that convey personality extendable to a sibling application?

Elevate the ordinary

- Does the personality add to the meaning of the application in a clever, surprising, or playful way, such as in Figure 3.29?
- Do users feel personally connected to the personality?
- Do interactions with the application feel like a dialog?
- Does the personality delight its users?

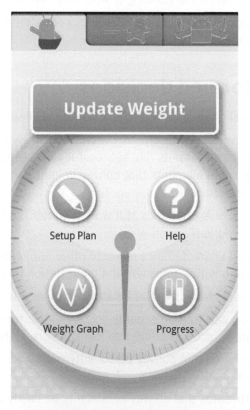

Figure 3.29 Icons used in a version of the Noom Weight Loss application, which was only available for Android, playfully used the Android character.

Part II
The Visual Usability Tools

Layout

Our exploration of the visual usability tools begins with layout: positioning elements in a structure that people understand, and making decisions about and defining templates for what should appear onscreen. Creating layouts based on a rationale that accounts for use, behavior, and aesthetics sets the stage for screens to communicate in a helpful, appealing way, and is covered in detail in the case study later in this chapter.

The meta-principles of consistency, hierarchy, and personality affect layout, and layout in turn informs them. Successful layouts support and reinforce the meta-principles through consistent visual hierarchies that help people know where to look and when, and arrangements that communicate the application's personality no matter what device someone is using. Unsuccessful layouts undermine the meta-principles with guessing games about where to locate information, what information is important, and what's related in a way that runs counter to the purpose and chosen personality, ultimately sending confusing messages.

The language of layout

Basic terminology for layout—words such as *alignment, proximity, grid, scale*, and *white space*—are used in aesthetic criticism and design discourse across mediums. To these we add terms specifically for designing for screens: *screen size* and *templates*, and subterms like *responsive.*

Screen size

Knowing the screen sizes and behavior you are designing for (e.g., if screens rotate and need to support more than one format) is the first step in layout. The screen provides a frame in which to present content and interface elements, but relationships between elements and the frame, and elements to each other, need to be considered in all screen sizes individually (Figure 4.1). Application interface design almost always involves modules, not discrete pages. Instead of considering a layout as something completely static, consider it as a thoughtful, changeable placement of modules that matches how users expect to interact with an application and delivery platform.

Core layout principles apply no matter the screen size. The important thing is to integrate these principles with an understanding of how screen elements relate to one another, so that your layouts flex intelligently if they need to do so.

Figure 4.1 Screen sizes vary dramatically. Aspect ratios affect layout and positioning.

Position

Consider Figure 4.2 from the USDA's SuperTracker food- and exercise-tracking tool. The dots introduced in Chapter 2 illustrate the principles of positioning elements, showing how whenever there are one or more elements in a space, visual relationships between elements are created. Layout involves positioning elements to form perceptible, useful relationships. A key part is analyzing the content elements you have to work with, and thinking about how they help each other make sense.

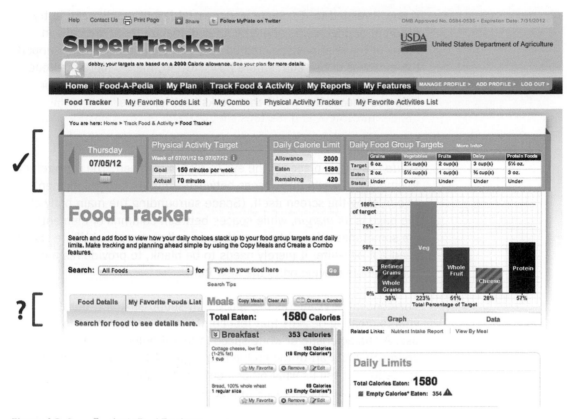

Figure 4.2 SuperTracker's Food Tracker screen.

Four SuperTracker features at the top of the screen—Day, Physical Activity Target, Daily Calorie Limit, and Daily Food Group Targets—provide a snapshot of status at a glance. They're all positioned in a row and treated with a blue background, so we interpret their placement and treatment to indicate they're related. Lower on the screen, position and grouping are less clear. There's so little space between the Food Details tab, the My Favorite Foods List, and the Meals head text that it's hard to know which of these items (if any) the Meals head relates to. In this crowded part of the screen, alignment and proximity aren't enough to tell us what goes with what.

Balancing the relationships created by positioning elements on a screen is a puzzle. When one element is moved to solve a problem, it can create another. For example, if the Meals head were moved up to separate it from the Food Details and My Favorite Foods List tabs, it might appear to be floating, and it wouldn't be clear what elements, if any, it related to. To create a successful layout, you'll need to try different arrangements of elements and analyze them critically in terms of the relationships created between elements. Do they support the personas of use and feature flows? Often, there's more than one possible arrangement. Testing layouts that meet requirements can help you choose the layout that works best for users.

White space

White space is a place for the eye to rest in a screen. The term refers to empty areas, whether spaces between columns, around elements, or bordering the screen itself. (Space surrounding the main body of the page is its *margin*, while spaces between columns or elements are sometimes referred to as *gutters* as well as margins.) White space need not be white; it merely needs to be blank, to provide resting space before moving on to the next item.

The concept of visual resting space may sound abstract, but it's vital to creating designs that feel comfortable and pleasant to use. A characteristic of white space is that it helps screens look approachable. Part of the problem in Figure 4.2 is a lack of white space to help tell us what other elements the Meals head belongs with. Let's take another look in Figure 4.3.

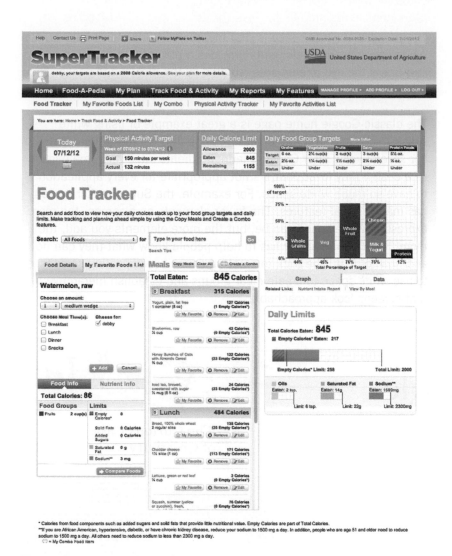

Figure 4.3 SuperTracker's Food Tracker screen.

Although there are a few empty areas, most of the screen is taken up with small, densely packed type; form widgets and editing tools; and progress charts. With so much going on, and inconsistent visual hierarchy to help distinguish what's most crucial, the layout makes what can already be an anxiety-provoking task—tracking one's food intake in the hope of losing weight—more fraught, because there's too much information presented to parse at once. Careful use of white space, which we'll add as part of our sample redesign of this application, will make this screen more inviting.

The paradox of white space is that blank areas emphasize busy areas. White space between elements provides a place for the eye to rest, and draws the eye to elements *isolated* by the most white space. The more white space, the more attention is drawn.

The classic Google home page is a great example of using white space to draw the eye and create an appealing screen (Figure 4.4). For several years after Google's launch, clients cited its home page as a design they loved, but it's not appropriate for every application to have so much white space. For example, the SuperTracker screen has many central features. The fewer elements on a screen, the more expressive white space can be, but the more elements you add, the more "work" white space has to help people know what they can do and how to do it. The trick to creating dense but appealing screens is to use white space to create clear groups and establish hierarchy so that screens look approachable.

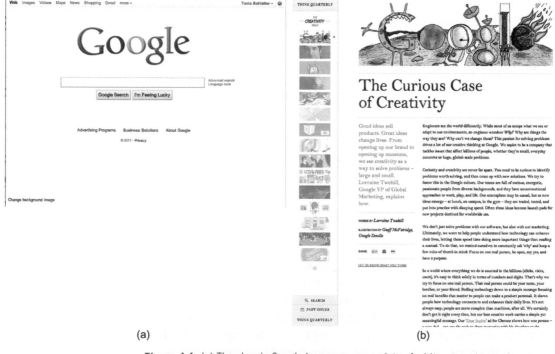

(a)   (b)

Figure 4.4 (a) The classic Google home page uses lots of white space to create an approachable design and draw the eye to a specific element. (b) Google's publication Think Quarterly also has few elements, and uses white space and grouping for an inviting look.

Margins

Margins are a type of white space between the edges of a container and the elements within that container. They can make the difference between a comfortable layout and a crowded one (Figure 4.5). Margins aren't just the space around the edge of a screen; anytime an element contains smaller elements, there need to be margins separating the child elements from their parent, as well as from each other.

Determining how much space should be used for margins is part of the layout process, usually done as a refinement after determining general placement of elements. When multiple elements serve as containers on a screen, the margins for each container should be consistent.

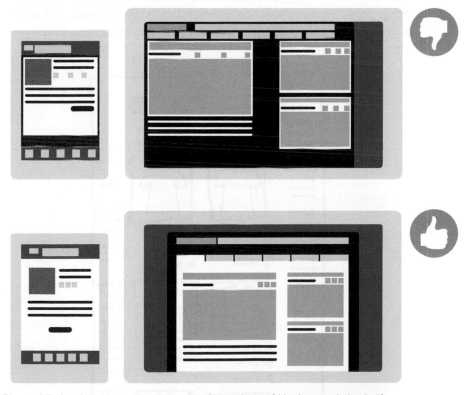

Figure 4.5 Comfortable, deliberate positioning and use of blank space help clarify relationships and make screens approachable. Margins are too tight to the frame edges (top left), making the screen feel cramped. Margins are too tight and the gap between widget columns is too wide (top right), which feels unbalanced. Margins are comfortable and positions create clear groups in the bottom illustrations.

Proximity, scale, and alignment

Proximity, scale, and alignment are the principles that cause the eye to interpret SuperTracker's closely positioned mini-dashboard elements as related. They're also the principles that cause confusion about what text the Meals head refers to. If shape, color, and size are the same, visual relationships are affected by proximity—how close elements are to one another.

Proximity

Imagine you have multiple product images presented in a grid on a screen. Each product has a photo, title, brief description, and a small "Buy" button or link to more information (Figure 4.6). It's crucial to position the button clearly as part of the group of elements that it belongs with. In this type of situation, it's easy to make the mistake of not providing enough space between groups of elements, but when a group isn't defined clearly enough, it's hard to determine which product the button goes with.

Figure 4.6 This simple illustration represents a product display screen and shows a common problem—an unclear grouping of elements. If items in a group aren't close enough to each other, and are too close to elements outside the group, it's hard to know what goes with what.

Scale

Scale—or the relative size of elements—is directly related to visual weight and the interpretation of importance. When elements are the same size, they can look related. When using scale to indicate importance and define hierarchy, size differences need to be clear, but not so different as to overpower.

Alignment

Alignment is another way to make a layout appear organized. In the SuperTracker example (Figure 4.3), the four mini-dashboard features are aligned with one another near the top of the screen. Each feature consists of several elements, all of which are also aligned to arrange information and expose its relationships. (This alignment isn't always successful; for example, the day of the week feature title, "Thursday," should be positioned the same way as other text heads to more clearly show it is part of the group.)

In typographers' practice, type is typically aligned by its baseline—the invisible base the letters rest on (see Chapter 5 for details). Nontype elements may be aligned based on their center, top, or bottom. All elements may also be aligned *flush left*, or left-aligned; centered; or *flush right*, or right-aligned (Figure 4.7). The key to using alignment

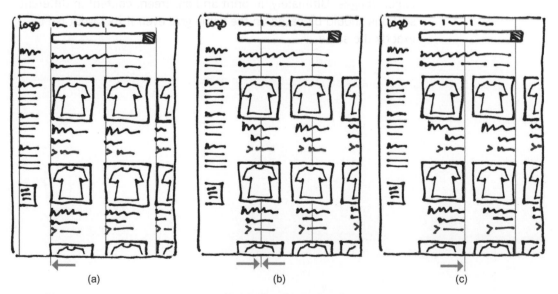

(a)   (b)   (c)

Figure 4.7 (a) Flush-left alignment of elements under shirts. (b) Centered elements under shirts. (c) Flush-right alignment of elements under shirts. The flush-left alignment creates the least awkward, unintentional white space between columns.

successfully is to pick an alignment that supports grouping and reduces visual activity and stick with it. When in doubt, align elements flush left for use in the Western world.

Grid

A *grid* is a set of invisible vertical and horizontal lines fixed at consistent intervals that provide a structure for layout. Grid lines supply a modular framework for placement, alignment, and the relative size of elements (Figure 4.8).

Grids are a powerful layout tool because they take some guesswork out of the design process. A grid defines rules for the width of margins, width of columns, the space between items, the size of image areas, and how everything aligns to guide the eye along specific paths on the page, as well as give the eye places to pause and rest.

The most common example of a grid in action is a newspaper, which is broken out into clear, vertical columns. Just as in newspapers, the way a grid is used in applications may vary from section to section. A paper's local news section, meant to be businesslike and informative, may use narrower columns and pack in more content than its arts section, which may have fewer, wider columns and larger images. Ultimately, in print and onscreen, content in different sections should be based on the same grid even if its layout isn't exactly the same.

Figure 4.8 Overlaying two different days' front pages of *The New York Times'* online edition reveals evidence of the grid underpinning both layouts. The grid provides a structure that informs the placement and size of elements. Depending on the content and desired impact, image widths can run one, two, three, or more columns.

Grids and alignment in practice

Designing a grid to support a particular layout is a project in itself.[1] That effort is complicated by designing for a variety of screen sizes (Figures 4.9, 4.10, and 4.11). There are several CSS-based grid systems, such as Blueprint (*http://blueprintcss.org*) and 960.gs (*http://960.gs*), that provide designers and developers with starting points for layout. These systems often work with a large number of grid columns—from as few as 12 to as many as 24—to offer the most variety in size, placement, and alignment options. However, the risk of so many columns is that if not used judiciously along with a strong information hierarchy, you may end up with a densely packed layout that feels heavy and overwhelming despite its underlying structure.

There are a variety of valid ways to approach layout. Simple applications, or those for small screens, may rely on margins rather

[1] For more on designing and working with grid systems, see Khoi Vinh's *Ordering Disorder: Grid Principles for Web Design*.

than a grid to help define structure, as there aren't enough positioning options for a grid to be useful. For large screens with many elements, designers create or select a grid based on known content. If starting from scratch, a designer may place elements without a grid, making decisions based on flow and what users expect, and refine alignment before design is finalized. A refined alignment places elements along the *fewest number* of horizontal and vertical lines, whether or not those lines are part of a formal grid.

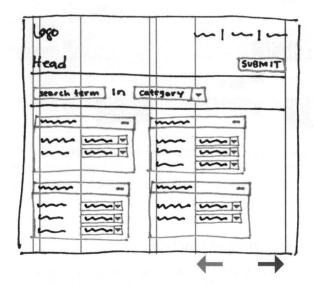

Figure 4.9 A simplified example of aligned placement on a large screen. Elements are aligned both flush left and right along the fewest possible lines. Mixing alignments works here because most elements are left-aligned, while the right-aligned items are in a different group that follows conventions for that type of content. Elements within containers should be aligned consistently, which makes the overall screen feel organized.

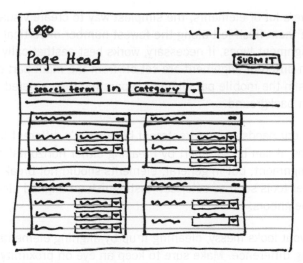

Figure 4.10 Yellow lines show baselines for consistent alignment. Text, buttons, and dialog boxes are all aligned to the base of the text. Red lines are "hang lines" for hanging elements down from a consistent point.

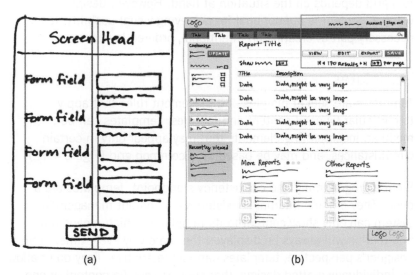

(a)   (b)

Figure 4.11 (a) A small screen with few elements may successfully use more than one type of alignment if hierarchy, groups, and structure are clear. Form elements are flush left to blue lines, and header and button elements are centered to the red line. (b) A larger screen with more elements requires more structure and consistency to look organized. Elements are flush left, with the exception of the few elements in blue boxes, which are of a different type and are flush right.

If you have a lot of elements, the simplest way to create visual order is to align them flush left along the fewest number of vertical lines. Mixing alignment types, if necessary, works best aesthetically when areas with different alignment are set off from the main part of the screen, as in the mobile paradigm of separating the centered top text on its own background.

If an element needs unique treatment because it's different from other items, it can be set apart by breaking either horizontal or vertical alignment, but in general, elements should not break from both. Other tools such as color can distinguish an aligned element from its neighbors.

If your layout looks messy, cleaning it up by aligning elements will make a big difference. Make sure to keep an eye on proximity and grouping so that hierarchy is still clear when refining alignment and using a grid.

Finally, designing with a grid is optional; how strictly you adhere to a grid depends on the situation at hand. However, designing using alignment is *not* optional for achieving visual usability. It's a necessary part of creating an intentional, ordered layout.

Templates

Templates are sets of margins and placement rules that apply to particular types of content and features. Templates can be modular, incorporating elements that may appear only in certain circumstances, and may be based on a common grid (Figure 4.12).

From a programming and consistency standpoint, templates are a boon. They enforce internal consistency—a content management system can only show content in its templates, which means that information will always be displayed the same way every time. From a designer's perspective, templates can feel restrictive. They don't allow for individually crafted designs that support specific content or one-off situations, and designers accustomed to fine-tuning every aspect of a handcrafted website may find themselves frustrated by template-driven systems. Nevertheless, there's room for creativity in template design, as shown in Figure 4.18(b) later in the chapter.

Templates are defined by the similarities and differences between content elements that appear together. E-commerce offers a simple example: a retailer who sells everything from T-shirts to furniture to diamond jewelry may want to display each type of merchandise differently. If they can design one template flexible enough to show or hide content, their job will be easier.

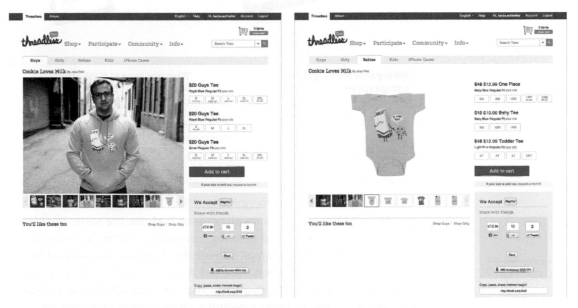

Figure 4.12 This Threadless.com product template can display different product images and sets of sizes.

Layout and the meta-principles

Layout and consistency

When considering how to lay out an application, you must address internal consistency—how the layout applies to all screens and widgets—as well as external consistency—how the layout of related or similar applications sets expectations for this one (Figure 4.13).

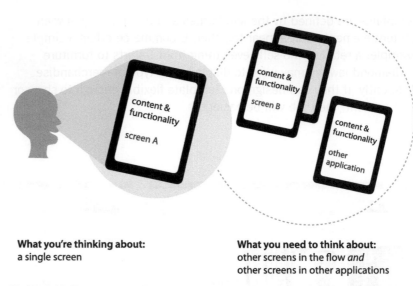

What you're thinking about:
a single screen

What you need to think about:
other screens in the flow *and*
other screens in other applications

Figure 4.13 No screen stands alone. It must always be considered in context of the whole application, as well as related applications, to make informed decisions about what users expect.

Using templates ensures margins, headers, and navigation elements will be placed consistently on all screens that use the same template. When designing layout and defining templates, review the content and features that will be on all screens (or as many as possible) to find commonalities between different types of tabular data, content structure, and basic data elements, such as products for sale; these parallels allow you to begin creating a shared visual language for similar elements grounded in grids, margins, and use of white space. (See "Merging templates" later in this chapter for more about this.) Review other applications with similar features to see pluses and minuses of existing approaches, and review platform and application conventions as well. These exist to help people quickly grasp new and unfamiliar systems; don't break from convention or expectation without a good reason.

Layout and hierarchy

Layout literally reinforces information hierarchy by creating an intentional order for reading information. Although this order changes slightly depending on the nature of the language (e.g., right-to-left versus left-to-right), the fundamental assumption that the most important content and features should stand out visually remains the same, and applies regardless of whether a layout changes across devices. The structure and rhythm of the screen influence hierarchy. Recall Figure 2.1, shown again here as Figure 4.14.

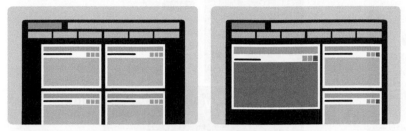

Figure 4.14 Because all four items on the left are of equal size and visual weight, the only cue to their relative importance is their perceived top-to-bottom, left-to-right order. On the right, the single large item to the left of the two smaller ones clearly indicates its priority. The contrast in size, combined with the larger element's positioning, confirms its place in the hierarchy.

Layout and personality

Layout reinforces an application's personality, and an application's personality should harmonize with its purpose. White space supports websites and applications that want to be perceived as open and friendly. Layouts with many small, carefully arranged product images can promote the idea that an e-commerce website offers more merchandise than anyone else. A staid, simple design that adheres tightly to a grid can reinforce the sense that an application is the place for people to get work done, not to play.

Layout also helps personalities retain their core qualities across platforms. Compare the JetBlue application we reviewed in Chapter 1 to the JetBlue website shown in Figure 4.15. Both rely on a boxy design that literally exposes the underlying grid to chunk navigation and key functional elements, but the extensive use of white space, even between icons and their labels, makes both screens feel open and inviting. The primary difference between the two is navigation placement—in iOS, it's near the bottom for quick access with a thumb, while on the website, it's in a traditionally prominent location at the top.

Figure 4.15 (a) JetBlue application and (b) JetBlue website.

Highly similar positioning reinforces JetBlue's personality on the "book a flight" tools on both iOS and jetblue.com (Figure 4.16). With minor exceptions, such as the different main header treatments, these could be the same screens. Widget placement is virtually the same across platforms, and the most obvious change—the form field icon shifts from left on the web to right on iOS—could exist to improve ease of use on mobile devices regardless of whether users are right- or left-handed. There's less white space in the iOS application due to the need to maximize limited screen space, but generously sized form fields are friendly and welcoming.

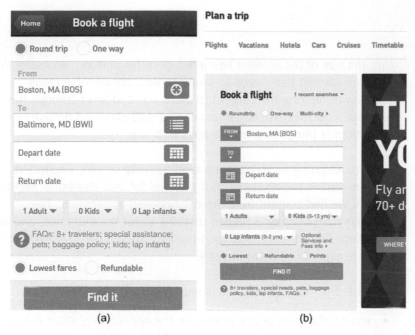

Figure 4.16   (a) The JetBlue iOS application's flight booking tool. (b) The same tool on jetblue.com.

With the size of the screens being designed for in mind, and sample or actual content that needs to be presented, layout for screens begins with filtering the content, feature set, and flows through the audience's perspective, situations of use, and expected behaviors, and grouping things so that like goes with like.

When redesigning SuperTracker's food-tracking screen, we started with the mobile phone layout, but planned for web and tablet versions as well. We had content from the existing web application. The personas from Chapter 3 helped us think about the audience, and we used SuperTracker and other food-tracking applications for several weeks to experience them directly.

We started defining the mobile layout by asking ourselves:

- *What's the number-one feature in the application? What feature do people use more than any other?* Knowing the primary reasons why people use the application allows you to make rational assumptions about necessary template types.

- *What screens or widgets support the primary action(s), such as the ability to view and edit details?* Because a mobile phone screen is so small, we knew we'd have to break apart features that were on a single screen in the web application, decide where to put them, and figure out how many screens we needed to support those key features.

- *What's the primary sequence of use? Secondary?* Priority and sequence help dictate hierarchy, which informs the order and placement of objects on the screen.

- *How does the technology affect the interface? What are the screen sizes? Are there any parts of the screen that need to be used in a particular way? Are there any widgets device manufacturers require us to use? What are the pros and cons of custom widgets versus platform-defined ones?* Every device has its own interface control conventions, and those conventions—or uniquely designed ones—affect an application's personality. Refer to each device OS developer's guidelines for layout, navigation, and control conventions.

- *How do other applications in this space approach the layout?* Where was there room for improvement? We surveyed and used similar applications to get a sense of conventions for logging food and tracking exercise, and found that they were more concerned with collecting the gist of users' food consumption and activity. Because these applications' features were less detailed, they had simpler interfaces, meaning one challenge for SuperTracker's redesign was to make food logging as easy as its competitors did.

- *How can the layout of the original application inform design of a mobile version?* Our analysis of SuperTracker's layout, as well as our use of the application itself, helped us see relationships between elements that we wanted to keep, and opportunities for improvement.

- *Are there any layout implications from related communications?* We considered how SuperTracker is related to other MyPlate initiatives. The MyPlate icon has graphic standards, including a color palette and usage rules, but there are no other applications that are part of the MyPlate program. Had there been, we might have needed to use their navigation structure and the same basic template, or at least the same header, footer, and navigation location.

Feature and data considerations

SuperTracker's most useful features relate to food and activity tracking. They're also the most complex in terms of number of elements, functionality, and interaction. When beginning a new layout, we like to start with the most complicated set of features. Starting from the hardest point not only gives us a sense of how dense the application's information hierarchy might be, it allows us to create conventions for managing as much of that hierarchy as possible, from different header levels to alert messages. Layout conventions established on the most complicated screen are likely to work on simpler screens as well.

Whenever possible, we work with sample data for the application, which helps determine overall content density and establish line lengths. We sometimes fill a table with *lorem ipsum* text, but don't finalize the design unless we have sample text. If the real data comes in and is much, much longer, table columns may no longer be wide enough to accommodate reality.

Conversely, any application that displays results is going to have situations in which much less data is shown, or none at all. When working through initial worst-case scenario layouts, we try them with half the data to make sure layout conventions still hold, and then with no data. The layout must work in all circumstances; if not, it's literally time to go back to the drawing board.

Mapping features to screens and layout

Figure 4.17 (a) After placing elements based on conventions, personas, and what our use had shown was important, we looked for elements that were redundant, unnecessary, or had too much or too little visual prominence, as well as opportunities to emphasize or express personality. (b) We then refined the layout.

Our initial black-and-white layout for the mobile application's food-tracking screen focused on the most common task of entering foods and editing and deleting entries (Figure 4.17). We knew we couldn't show all the charts or the food and nutrition details on the same screen as the list of foods eaten; the screen was too small. So how would users get to those features?

- We mapped the web application's navigation to a few functional areas, and used standard mobile navigation controls for access to those sections of the application on the bottom of the screen.

- We made search prominent, but placed it so it would not obscure daily status; this way, users could quickly see their status while making a decision about what to eat.

- A standard toggle control provided access to daily status charts that didn't fit on the screen. Placing the toggle directly under the primary chart reinforced their relationship.

- Rather than replicate the four mini-dashboard features—Day, Physical Activity Target, Daily Calorie Limit, and Daily Food Group Limits—we decided that daily activity status could go in the activity section of the application, and that this screen could focus just on food.

- Since selecting a food from a list of favorites is related to finding a food, we provided favorites list access with the search feature.

After placing elements for the flow of adding a food, we took a critical look to determine whether all elements were necessary, whether their visual weight generally reflected their importance, and whether there were any opportunities to add personality. Based on our analysis, we made the following changes:

- Deleted the screen header, which felt redundant with the screen content.

- Reduced the prominence of the "combine foods" and "choose from favorites" features.

- Added icons to the meal categories to begin introducing personality.

- Removed text prompts reading "What you ate today" and "What did you eat today?"

See Figures 4.17b, 4.18, and 4.19 as examples of changes made.

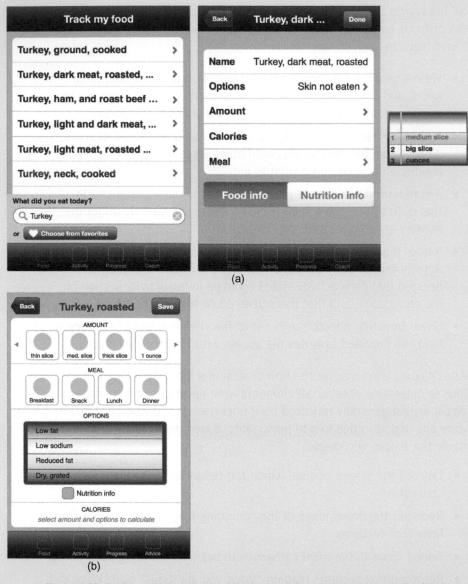

Figure 4.18 Finding a food requires a different layout from food tracking. (a) Our first layout focused on mapping the food-selection interface to mobile platform conventions. Even though mobile users are accustomed to sequences involving several screens, we wanted to see if we could elevate the ordinary by streamlining data entry and making it more appealing. (b) Our second layout presents controls for entering food details and quantity on a single screen. The controls use icons, represented by circles, for selecting some details.

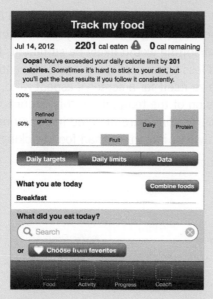

Figure 4.19 Designing feedback as part of the flow helps it integrate with design, instead of being treated as an afterthought.

From screens to templates

To define the food-tracking screen as a template—a structure that could work for similar features, such as tracking activity—we assessed user goals and decided which data was most important to communicate at any given time. Having a live application helped, as it showed where overlaps existed within data types. (Without an application to work from, we would have sketched a few screens with similar content types.) We also considered business, design, and technical requirements, and factored those into our template exploration.

Even though we'd focused on redesigning just one screen of the web application—the food-tracking screen—we still had to consider how its features and flows played out across platforms. We started with a handheld mobile device in portrait mode, the smallest, narrowest screen available, and determined we'd need at least three templates: one for status and food consumed, one to enter foods, and one for nutritional details. Mobile conventions supported the idea of multiple screens to perform a single task, providing the screens flowed logically. In landscape mode, our screen could just get a little wider.

On tablets (Figure 4.20) and on the web (Figure 4.21) in landscape mode, we had far more real estate for our layout. A single template for food detail input and editing would likely be sufficient. But a tablet in portrait mode has less horizontal space available, and a responsive design should optimize itself for a screen's aspect ratio, implying we'd need a modified version of the template in this circumstance. Again, device usage and conventions were factored into feature priority: with viewing charts slightly less important than food tracking, charts could be shown on demand.

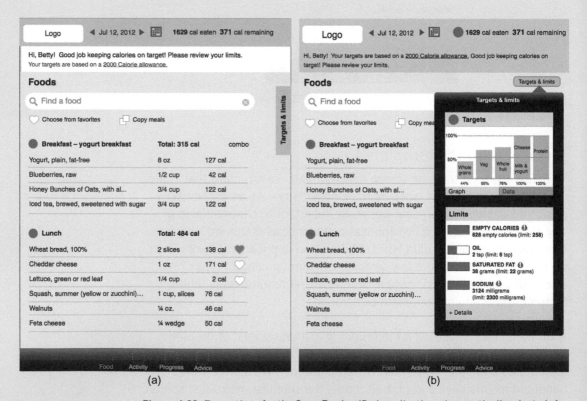

Figure 4.20 Two options for the SuperTracker iPad application when vertically oriented. A sliding tab or popover could display charts on demand. The "Find a food" search bar could have remained on the bottom of the screen as in the mobile phone layout, but we decided to move it up so that the tablet layout would be more consistent with the web version.

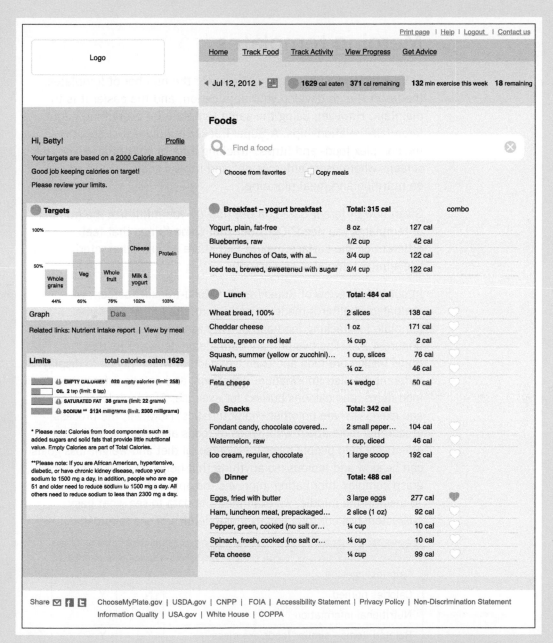

Print page | Help | Logout | Contact us

Home   Track Food   Track Activity   View Progress   Get Advice

◄ Jul 12, 2012 ►   1629 cal eaten   371 cal remaining   132 min exercise this week   18 remaining

Foods

🔍 Find a food   ⊗

♡ Choose from favorites   ⎘ Copy meals

Logo

Hi, Betty!   Profile

Your targets are based on a 2000 Calorie allowance

Good job keeping calories on target!

Please review your limits.

● **Targets**

			Cheese	Protein
Whole grains	Veg	Whole fruit	Milk & yogurt	
44%	65%	76%	102%	103%

Graph   Data

Related links: Nutrient intake report | View by meal

● **Limits**   total calories eaten **1629**

⚠ **EMPTY CALORIES¹** 820 empty calories (limit: 258)
  OIL 2 tsp (limit: 6 tsp)
⚠ **SATURATED FAT** 38 grams (limit: 22 grams)
⚠ **SODIUM **** 3124 milligrams (limit: 2300 milligrams)

* Please note: Calories from food components such as added sugars and solid fats that provide little nutritional value. Empty Calories are part of Total Calories.

**Please note: If you are African American, hypertensive, diabetic, or have chronic kidney disease, reduce your sodium to 1500 mg a day. In addition, people who are age 51 and older need to reduce sodium to 1500 mg a day. All others need to reduce sodium to less than 2300 mg a day.

● **Breakfast – yogurt breakfast**	**Total: 315 cal**		combo
Yogurt, plain, fat-free	8 oz	127 cal	
Blueberries, raw	1/2 cup	42 cal	
Honey Bunches of Oats, with al...	3/4 cup	122 cal	
Iced tea, brewed, sweetened with sugar	3/4 cup	122 cal	
● **Lunch**	**Total: 484 cal**		
Wheat bread, 100%	2 slices	138 cal	♡
Cheddar cheese	1 oz	171 cal	♡
Lettuce, green or red leaf	¼ cup	2 cal	♡
Squash, summer (yellow or zucchini)...	1 cup, slices	76 cal	♡
Walnuts	¼ oz.	46 cal	♡
Feta cheese	¼ wedge	50 cal	♡
● **Snacks**	**Total: 342 cal**		
Fondant candy, chocolate covered...	2 small peper...	104 cal	♡
Watermelon, raw	1 cup, diced	46 cal	♡
Ice cream, regular, chocolate	1 large scoop	192 cal	♡
● **Dinner**	**Total: 488 cal**		
Eggs, fried with butter	3 large eggs	277 cal	♥
Ham, luncheon meat, prepackaged...	2 slice (1 oz)	92 cal	♡
Pepper, green, cooked (no salt or...	¼ cup	10 cal	♡
Spinach, fresh, cooked (no salt or...	¼ cup	10 cal	♡
Feta cheese	¼ cup	99 cal	♡

Share ✉ f t   ChooseMyPlate.gov | USDA.gov | CNPP | FOIA | Accessibility Statement | Privacy Policy | Non-Discrimination Statement
Information Quality | USA.gov | White House | COPPA

Figure 4.21 With so much real estate, the web version needed structure to organize the space. Background shading defined groups of elements. The food log and search tool got the most space, giving them primary emphasis. Daily targets and limits were placed on the left rather than the right to give them more priority.

Merging templates

From a technical perspective, the fewer the number of templates, the faster it is to develop your application, and the easier it is to maintain. However, using the same template for everything might force false relationships. A SuperTracker template that supports the complex food- and fitness-tracking data might not also work for screens where users enter weight and fitness goals or read advice on nutrition and meal planning.

Given how different data can be, how do you minimize the number of templates you need? Consider that some things that feel different on the surface may in fact share enough characteristics to use similar templates or elements.

In our initial review of SuperTracker's food-tracking screen, we evaluated whether it made sense to continue to use the same template for tracking food and activity as the web version does (Figure 4.22). The two primary data elements in our revised SuperTracker are food and exercise, each of which needs to display different detailed information: nutritional and calorie information for food items, and calories burned for exercise. At a high level, food and exercise share no other characteristics. However, the process of learning more about what types of foods and exercise will most effectively help people meet their personal diet and weight-loss goals can be slow and tedious, so anything that helps an audience quickly grasp complex information improves the application experience. To meet in the middle, we examined the data to see what basic characteristics our food and exercise detail screens might share:

	Food	Exercise
Calories ingested	Y	N
Calories burned	N	Y
Nutritional information	Y	N
Related items—similar foods/exercises	Y	Y
Imagery (photo, illustration, icon, etc.)	Y	Y
User interacts with screen at least once per day	Y	Y

Looking at the content and thinking about the context of use, we decided that a modular template design that planned for the most complex data scenario—that is, food—could serve for exercise as well, using similar layout styles and screen widgets to display only the relevant information. Food or exercise name, calories ingested or burned, and any incidental content, such as nutritional information or other exercises, could be displayed in exactly the same way, despite not being the exact same content; the food screen would merely show a little more information than the exercise one. Picking the worst-case scenario to start with allows you to gracefully trim content and elements unnecessary in less complex personas. Working the other way around ultimately leads to shoehorning content and features into a layout that doesn't necessarily support it.

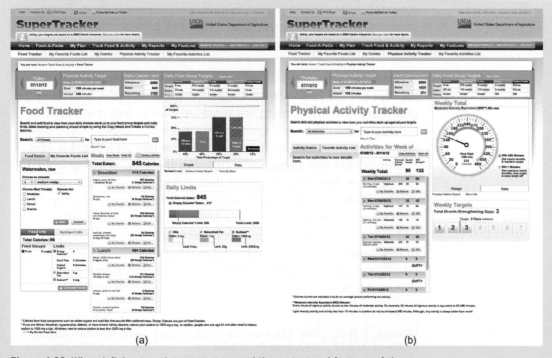

(a)   (b)

Figure 4.22 When defining templates, we compared the content and features of the food-tracking screen (a) with the activity-tracking screen (b), and determined they were similar enough to share a template.

One big bite, or a few little ones?

Different application flows require different numbers of screens depending on audience expectations and system conventions. An application geared toward at-a-glance overviews of system status, such as website analytics, needs a dashboard where the audience can see a high-level overview of a lot of data in a single location, only drilling down when they need fine details. This audience may not care how much they have to scroll to view content, as long as that single screen displays the information they consider most relevant. By contrast, shoppers on an e-commerce application may browse multiple pathways before they find what they want to purchase, and moving them from high-level category screens to low-level detail ones allows them to continually refine their choices until they've narrowed in on the perfect pair of shoes.

The maturity of the Internet, as well as the trend toward "mobile-first" design, has chipped away at older conventions about never making users scroll. After more than 20 years of web use, people are accustomed to scrolling,[2] and mobile users expect to do it, if only because their smaller screen size relative to desktop and laptop monitors means scrolling is practically inevitable.

With scrolling now considered routine, the old, newspaper-based concept of "the fold"—the point at which the viewport ends, and the user must begin to scroll to see more—becomes less important. Although Jakob Nielsen's eye-tracking research[3] shows most people spend more time looking at items above the fold on a 1024×768 screen, people still viewed content below the fold, skipping around to find other items that attracted them. This indicates that while it's still necessary to put the most important information at the top of a screen—as one would expect in a solid hierarchy—users will scroll to find out more. Incorporating design elements to suggest there's more to view lower down (or horizontally), such as images designed to cut off midway at likely screen breakpoints, helps encourage exploration (Figure 4.23).

[2] Nielsen, J. (2010, Mar. 22). Scrolling and Attention. Jakob Nielsen's Alertbox. Retrieved July 17, 2012, from *http://www.useit.com/alertbox/scrolling-attention .html.*
[3] Nielsen, J. (2010, Mar. 22). Scrolling and Attention. Jakob Nielsen's Alertbox. Retrieved July 17, 2012, from *http://www.useit.com/alertbox/scrolling-attention .html.*

Figure 4.23 The Netflix application shows partial images at the right and bottom of the screen to encourage horizontal and vertical scrolling.

If everyone knows how to scroll, why bother chunking out functionality onto multiple screens? The answer is that application flows should match audience expectations and patterns of use, and there's literally no one-size-fits-all solution. Creating lightweight digital or paper prototypes and testing with representative users can provide invaluable information about how people expect to interact with what you're designing.

Platform and technical considerations also come into play. For example, Apple recommends minimizing iPad screen transitions because they reduce "visual stability." Desktop and laptop users would never expect their entire screen to flip over or move on a regular basis; such motion would be distracting, and the same principle applies to an iPad screen. To help designers and developers work within the constraints of this principle, Apple provides UI elements, such as split-pane views and popovers, to minimize the need for screen refreshes.

From a purely technical perspective, applications searching large databases of information may have resource and performance limitations based on how quickly data can be accessed and delivered, which can influence whether search results appear onscreen after a refresh or on a separate screen, as well as how pagination works.

Balancing your audience's needs against what's possible and desired on the delivery platforms can be tricky, but is a necessary part of the design process.

Even after you've determined how many screens you need, you may still find you have to fit a lot of information on a single screen, not all of which may be immediately relevant to your users. This is where the user interface principle of *progressive disclosure* comes into play—displaying information on demand, as people need or want to view it, as opposed to simply displaying it all the time (Figures 4.24 and 4.25). Tabs, accordions, panels, and other user interface widgets that allow content to be shown as necessary support information hierarchy; hidden content is automatically a lower priority than content shown by default.

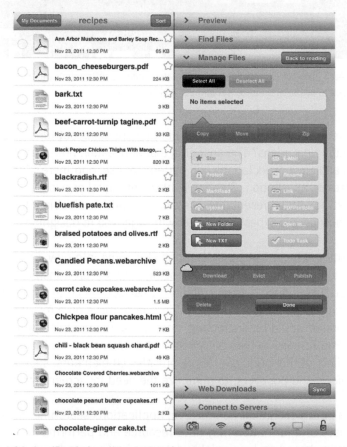

Figure 4.24 GoodReader's split-pane interface includes accordions on the right to host different types of file- and folder-management functionality. Displaying all this functionality on a single screen would be overwhelming and confusing.

Figure 4.25 Twitterrific's sidebar, normally visible in landscape mode, does not appear by default in portrait mode. Instead, a swipe in from the left reveals it when it's needed.

Avoid common mistakes
Too much information on a single screen

This mistake is closely related to lack of hierarchy, because it happens when people fail to prioritize content and features. To avoid it, ask yourself these questions:

- What are the primary tasks users must perform on this screen?
- Have you displayed only the information users need to perform those tasks?
- Have you provided cues that support next steps without distracting from the task at hand?

Arbitrary alignment

While you don't have to use a grid to design your application, providing consistent margins, placement, and alignment across screens creates a sense of order and balance.

- Have you created conventions for how items are placed and aligned on the screen relative to each other?
- Are you using similar positioning and proportions for similar elements?
- If breaking horizontal or vertical alignment conventions, are you breaking only one at a time, and only for elements that need differentiation?

Arbitrary grouping

Just as putting too much content on the page confuses your audience, so does scattering related items far from one another.

- Have you grouped related items to help people know where to look?
- Have you nested groups of related items, or positioned and aligned them near one another to reinforce their relationship?

Make informed decisions

Clear hierarchy

"Everything is important" is not a design rationale. An information hierarchy provides needed guidance to help people know where to look, what to do, and when to do it.

- Have you prioritized your user personas or stories so you know when to provide different types of information?
- Are the most important elements on the page placed near the top of the screen (or locked to the bottom, if on a handheld mobile device)? Are there other ways you could use positioning and contrast to draw attention to what's important?
- Can you minimize the prominence of less important information through progressive disclosure, displaying content and features only when needed?

Design for flexibility

A flexible template structure allows you to add more features more quickly in the future or adapt existing templates to accommodate features and information you didn't expect. If you've accounted for the most complicated situations, your design is more likely to be able to accommodate anything new that's thrown at it.

- Have you designed for the worst-case personas?
- Are your templates modular, with elements that can be added or removed as necessary?
- For screens that return data to the users, how does the layout look when there's a lot of information returned? Only some information? None at all?
- How does your application look and behave when viewed on different screen sizes, resolutions, and devices, or at different orientations?
- Does your application need to follow different conventions across platforms or shift layout with viewport size?

Elevate the ordinary

Grids can go beyond mere organization to convey personality. If appropriate, consider how exposing parts of your layout's underlying structure could enhance an application's personality and an audience's engagement (Figure 4.26).

(a)   (b)

Figure 4.26 Zappos' TweetWall provides a real-time glimpse of products people are tweeting about, randomly choosing some products to feature in larger spaces in the grid. The overall effect promotes the "thrill of the hunt"—of serendipitously finding the perfect pair of boots or frog raincoat—while simultaneously exposing what products Zappos' customers find trendy and appealing.

Also, look for opportunities to go beyond the standard patterns and conventions that apply to controls and information display. The SuperTracker wireframes in Figures 4.18(a) and (b) demonstrate one way to push past device conventions into something equally usable that expresses a little personality.

Type

5

In 1996, we designed the first website for a Boston-area university using one of the only typefaces fledgling web designers had available at the time: Times New Roman. We typeset our headers as graphics in Stone Sans to add some visual personality to the page, and adjusted our HTML type as best we could to get the level of control we wanted.

In the years since then, online typography has evolved at such a rapid pace, it's hard to believe there was ever a time before CSS and the plethora of web and embeddable typefaces now available. On the web and in web applications, there's a little ways to go in providing a precise level of control on par with page layout programs, but the landscape has changed so dramatically that there's no longer any reason to rely on typeset graphics, and native mobile applications can support typography as sophisticated as anything seen in print. Digital typography is finally a tool that can be employed to the fullest extent, but how do you take advantage of digital typefaces and put them to work in your applications?

The language of type

Typography, like the other tools we discuss, has its own language and conventions, much of which date to the earliest days of Western typography, when type was drawn by hand. The language continued to evolve with the development of the printing press, and the advent of individual metal letterforms set line-by-line.[1] Understanding how to typeset text appropriately and effectively begins with an introduction to typographic vernacular.

Although the word *font* is sometimes used to refer to any set of visually related letterforms, a font is actually a subset of a *typeface*, a

[1] Bringhurst, R. Historical Interlude. In *The Elements of Typographic Style*, pp. 119–142.

family of related letters, numbers, and sometimes icons and symbols created in different weights and styles. For example, the typeface Verdana includes four fonts: Verdana Regular, Verdana Italic, Verdana Bold, and Verdana Bold Italic. Other typefaces may include far more options, such as Gill Sans, which contains more than 35 different fonts that vary along different axes of weight, stroke thickness, and style, including versions with built-in shadows and additional fonts that support Greek and Cyrillic alphabets.

Letterform basics

Wonderful, in-depth studies of typography[2] go into detail about everything there is to know about type. These books, focused on printed type, apply to screen-based type as well. This chapter provides a few basics to help you compare typefaces to one another and make the best choices for your applications.

Serif, slab serif, and sans serif

Figure 5.1(a) shows the word "boxy" typeset in Helvetica Regular; Figure 5.1(b) is the same word in Times New Roman Regular. Note how the edges of the Helvetica b, x, and y are squared-off and straight, while the same letters in Times New Roman have pointed edges that extend to the left and right of the letterform strokes. Typefaces with pointed edges are called *serif*; typefaces without them are *sans serif.*

(a)   (b)

Figure 5.1 (a) The word "boxy" in Helvetica Regular, and (b) in Times New Roman Regular.

Serif typefaces, which date from the earliest days of typography, are generally considered more formal than sans serif ones.[3] Variations on the standard pointed serif look also exist: *slab serif* or *Egyptian*

---

[2] See the Resources chapter at the end of this book.

[3] Shaikh, A., Chaparro, B., and Fox, D. (2006, Feb.). Perception of Fonts: Perceived Personality Traits and Uses. Usability News. Retrieved June 29, 2012, from *http://www.surl.org/usabilitynews/81/personalityoffonts.asp.*

design

Figure 5.2 Museo is a slab serif typeface.

design design
(a)   (b)

Figure 5.3 (a) Rotis Semi-Sans is primarily a sans serif font, but retains a slight pointiness at letterform ends. (b) Rotis Semi-Serif is more obviously serifed, but blunts its serif ends in some locations, such as the ends of the s and the terminal (downward) stroke of the d.

typefaces (Figure 5.2), in which the serifs are rectangular rather than pointed, as well as *semi-serif* and *semi-sans* typefaces (Figure 5.3), which blunt the serifs to yield edges midway between serif and sans serif.

Designers and typographers have argued for years about whether serif or sans serif typefaces are more legible in print or onscreen, but research is so inconclusive[4] that we recommend simply using whichever typeface feels most appropriate for the application you're designing. (We'll cover how to choose typefaces later in this chapter.) Assuming you've typeset your text at a readable[5] size, in readable colors, and so on, it won't matter whether it has serifs or not.

Letterform alignment

In the version of Figure 5.1(a) shown in Figure 5.4, the line below the b, o, and x represents the *baseline* of the letterforms, the point upon which the main body of each letter will always rest.

The line above these letters represents the *midline*, the point that typically identifies where the main body of each letter begins. Letter

[4] Poole, A. (2008, Feb. 17). Which Are More Legible: Serif or Sans Serif Typefaces? Alexpoole.info. Retrieved June 26, 2012, from *http://alexpoole.info/which-are-more-legible-serif-or-sans_serif-typefaces/*.

[5] *Legibility* refers to how easy it is to distinguish letterforms from one another. *Readability* refers to how easy it is to read text typeset in a given font.

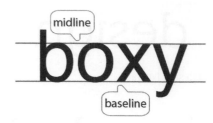

Figure 5.4 The baseline and midline of the word "boxy."

elements that extend above the midline, such as the top part of the b, are called *ascenders*, while elements that extend below it, such as the tail of the y, are *descenders*. Ascender and descender style varies between typefaces, and depending on shape, angle, and other characteristics, contributes to a typeface's personality. Letterforms in a layout are aligned at the baseline.

X-height

The distance between the baseline and midline is the *x-height*, or base size for a typeface. X-height is not standard across typefaces—for example, Helvetica's x-height is larger than Times New Roman's.

X-height affects the amount of space a font takes up on a page, since obviously a paragraph typeset in a font with a large x-height will end up bigger than the same paragraph in a font with a smaller x-height. It also influences a typeface's personality: a typeface with a large x-height may be perceived as more open and friendly than a typeface with a smaller one, but the smaller x-height font may be perceived as more workmanlike and appropriate for business use.

When looking for typefaces to pair together, compare x-heights; similar x-height is one criterion for a successful pairing. Testing multiple typefaces with CSS or an application like typetester.org can help you compare different fonts and their relative sizing to give you a sense of what's right for your design (Figure 5.5).

Font weights and styles

Fonts come in different *weights*—levels of thickness and heaviness—as well as *styles*—changes in letterform angle and shape. It used to be that the best web designers could hope for was boldfacing and

Figure 5.5 The left column is set in Verdana (largest x-height), while the paragraphs in the middle and right columns, in Calibri and Times New Roman, respectively, show that these two fonts have similar, smaller x-heights.

italicizing a small set of basic typefaces. Now, with web and mobile fonts readily available and easy to apply, designers have a much wider range of typeface, weight, and style to choose from.

Most typefaces designed for body content have fonts for a "regular" (*roman* or *book*) weight, along with bold, italic, and bold italic options. Other typefaces move well beyond that, including fonts that vary along multiple axes of light versus bold, narrow versus wide, and even italic versus oblique. (*Obliqued* type is angled, but retains the same basic letterform shapes used throughout the type family; *italicized* type uses specially designed letterforms.)

Figure 5.6 shows several examples from Helvetica Neue, a typeface that contains over 50 different fonts.

Roman

Italic

Medium (semibold) condensed

Bold

Heavy (extrabold)

Black

Thin

Condensed

Extended

Ultralight Condensed

Black extended oblique

Figure 5.6 Samples of font weight and style.

Some font families include both serif and sans serif fonts, although fonts within the same family have similar x-heights and spacing. Using fonts from a family with a wide range of styles and weights is an easy way to add contrast and visual interest.

Types of type

The breadth of fonts and granularity of typeface classification can quickly become overwhelming for nondesigners (and even for designers). Typefaces created for setting body text have far more subclassifications—old style, modern, transitional, and many more—than novice application designers need to know. While these classifications are interesting from a historical perspective, or for those who take an advanced interest in typography, for the purposes of application design, it's more helpful to classify type at a very high level: body typefaces, display typefaces, monospaced typefaces, and ornament/icon typefaces.

Body typefaces

Body typefaces are specifically designed for typesetting body content, whether in a book, on a web page, or in content displayed in a mobile application. These typefaces promote readability—literally, ease of reading—at a wide range of sizes, and while each typeface has its own personality, they don't generally "shout" at you the way a display typeface's personality will.

Most standard web and mobile font families, such as Arial, Verdana, and Georgia, are body text typefaces. Your body text typeface is part of your application's personality, and the typeface you choose reinforces that personality. Keep in mind that body text should never be bold unless you're emphasizing a few words.

Display typefaces

Display typefaces, also known as *decorative typefaces*, are designed to call attention through unique design (Figure 5.7). They're expressive, meaning they have stronger visual personalities than body typefaces. Used judiciously as an accent to contrast the body font, they're great for limited, strong statements about an application's personality.[6] The more unique and expressive the display font, the less of it should be used (Figure 5.8).

Figure 5.7 Google Web Fonts provides filters for browsing serif, sans serif, display (pictured), and handwriting fonts.

[6] A study sought to determine if fonts have personalities, and found that people do attribute personality traits to fonts. Shaikh, A. D., Chaparro, B. S., and Fox, D. (2006). Personality of ClearType Fonts. Retrieved from January 10, 2013 *http:// www.surl.org/usabilitynews/81/PersonalityofFonts.asp.*

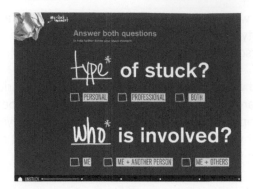

Figure 5.8 Self-help application Unstuck uses a handwriting font as an accent to create a sense of informality and approachability.

Display typefaces are for headers and headlines, not for body text. They may be designed to only show off certain details at minimum sizes, and when used below that size, can look cramped and muddy. Not every application needs a display typeface; refer to Chapter 3 for help evaluating whether display type is appropriate to help express your application's personality.

Monospaced typefaces

Monospaced typefaces, unlike body typefaces, use the same amount of spacing between all letterforms (Figure 5.9). (Body typefaces manipulate the amount of space between some letter pairs to improve aesthetics and readability; see the discussion on letterspacing later in this chapter.) Standardized spacing makes monospaced typefaces ideal for displaying computer code, which often contains indents for readability, and needs constant alignment with spaces or tabs to preserve those indents (Figure 5.10).

Monospaced typefaces can be used for display text, accent text (e.g., button labels), and even body copy, but are not ideal for long stretches of content unless part of your application's aesthetic involves evoking 1980's dot-matrix printers. Monospaced fonts can help an application be perceived as hip, clever, and geek-friendly,

Figure 5.9 Form button typeset in Courier, a monospaced font.

```
<html>
      <head>
            <title>This is a title</title>
      </head>
      <body>
            <div>Hello, world!</div>
      </body>
</html>
```

Figure 5.10 HTML code typeset in Courier.

if used successfully in an application where that personality is appropriate.

Ornament and icon fonts

Ornament (Figure 5.11) and *icon* (Figure 5.12) fonts contain illustrations instead of letterforms, and like body and display fonts, they have their own unique personalities. Because icon font glyphs must be mapped to letter keys, applying fonts like this with CSS can pose accessibility challenges; screen readers will read anything coded as text, regardless of whether what's displayed is actually a letter. However, creative, accessibility-friendly solutions for delivering icons and ornaments via CSS now exist, and are supported across many modern browsers.[7]

Figure 5.11 Bodoni Ornaments is provided for use in iOS.

Figure 5.12 (a) Dotcom and (b) Heydings are two free icon fonts.

Of course, icons and ornaments can always be applied as graphics rather than text, providing ALT attributes are added where required to meet accessibility needs. But treating ornaments and icons as

[7]Coyier, C. (2012, May 24). HTML for Icon Font Usage. *CSS-Tricks*. Retrieved June 27, 2012, from *http://css-tricks.com/html-for-icon-font-usage/*.

the fonts they are allows for on-the-fly control of color, size, and other CSS attributes, suggesting that improved browser and screen reader support could make use of icon and ornament fonts more commonplace online.

Font licensing

It's now easy to use fonts in digital applications, but it isn't always free. Although Google Web Fonts provides well over 500 different type families for free, some of the best typefaces are only available through paid licensing programs.

If you're developing a website or mobile web application, licensing fonts through Typekit (*http://typekit.com*), Webtype (http://webtype.com), or other online services can be relatively inexpensive, depending on the number of fonts you need and the traffic to your application. For native applications, read font licenses carefully to make sure they allow embedding. You may also need to contact the font foundry—the company that designed the font—to discuss pricing, which can add up quickly the more fonts you use, even if they're from the same family.

Bottom line: unless you're already certain you have the right to use a font with a specific delivery method, always check its licensing terms first.

Typesetting considerations

Type size

Type is traditionally measured in points, which are generally sized at 72 per inch. CSS supports the points unit, but due to poor type resize support from some older browsers, such as IE6 and 7, best practices moved toward relative units like *ems* that all browsers could resize.

An em is defined based on the standard body text size used in the application. For example, if your CSS declares the standard body size as 12 pixels (px), an em will be equivalent to that, and other type sizes can be defined relative to that initial size. A header that might normally be 15 px would instead be defined as 1.25 em, while a 9 px caption would be 0.75 em.

The drawback of initially defining type in ems is that there can still be unpredictable display results in older browsers. However, with use of such browsers continuing to decline, and screen resize technology now standard on web and mobile browsers, it's okay to use the more precise pixel or point measurements for web-based applications.

Weight

Type weight correlates directly with its level of visual impact. Book and roman weights of body text typefaces are most appropriate for reading long blocks of content, while bolder weights should be reserved for headers and other text that requires special emphasis, such as a selected link. Limit use of boldface to only where absolutely necessary: it can "shout at readers, putting them on edge and driving them away."[8]

Light and ultra-light typefaces can work for body text if it's typeset at larger-than-usual sizes. However, because the thinner strokes can make type harder to read, they're not really suitable for long blocks of content at standard reading sizes.

Leading

Leading, pronounced to rhyme with "heading," is the amount of space between lines of text, and is defined using the same units as text. (In CSS nomenclature, it's *line-height*.) Although intuitively, single-spacing implies that text set at 12 px would require leading of 12 px, in practice, setting leading at two or three pixels higher than text size prevents ascenders and descenders from crashing into each other, and provides enough breathing room to improve readability.

Designers may sometimes specify type as number/number, for example, Arial 12 px/15 px. This notation indicates text size with the first number, and leading with the second. Comfortable leading is essential to making an interface with a lot of type feel approachable.

Column width and justification

In general, body text should be set at narrow column widths for optimum readability. At a standard body text size of 12 points or

[8] Bringhurst, R. *The Elements of Typographic Style*, p. 56.

pixels, the ideal column width might range between roughly 40–90 characters per line.

Why the wide variation? To some extent, a "good" column width is determined by what looks best typographically, which can be a subjective judgment. Bringhurst suggests using a line length 30 times the point size, but acknowledges that lines of between 20 and 40 times that point size can work as well.[9] The World Wide Web Consortium's accessibility guidelines suggest not more than 80 characters per line in English text.[10] And a Wichita State University study found that anything between their tested values of 35–95 characters per line was readable, but that some people strongly preferred the shortest length, because it required less eye movement to read, while others preferred the longest length, because it placed more information on the page.[11]

Narrower column widths also mean less reflow when text is viewed on devices with smaller viewports than desktop machines, and less text reflow allows you to maintain similar layouts across devices.

When setting body text, we recommend aligning it *ragged left* by default—that is, with varied line ending points within a given column width. Typically, this is a browser's default view anyway, the reason being that it allows consistent space between words, which makes text easier to read. *Justified* text, which spaces out text to force straight column margins at right and left, creates neater margins (and thus is popular on layouts with highly visible grids, such as newspapers), but the varied amount of word spacing resulting from forcing text into these margins can make it harder to read. *Ragged-right* text, or text with varied line beginnings instead of endings, is rarely used for body text in functional applications, although its consistent right margin makes it a good choice for typesetting form field labels.

[9] Bringhurst, R. *The Elements of Typographic Style*, p. 27.

[10] Visual Presentation: Understanding SC 1.4.8. (2012). Understanding WCAG 2.0: A Guide to Understanding and Implementing WCAG 2.0. Retrieved July 3, 2012, from *http://www.w3.org/TR/UNDERSTANDING-WCAG20/visual-audio-contrast-visual-presentation.html*.

[11] Shaikh, A. (2005, July). The Effects of Line Length on Reading Online News. *Usability News*. Retrieved July 3, 2012, from *http://psychology.wichita.edu/surl/usabilitynews/72/LineLength.asp*.

Capital letters

Setting type in capital letters calls attention to it, and not just because decades of Internet use have taught us it's the equivalent of shouting. All-caps type feels important simply by virtue of being different from the norm, but because the lack of differentiation between letterforms relative to mixed-case type makes it harder to read, all-caps type is best suited for headers and other very short text.

Some typefaces offer *small caps*, capital letters specifically designed to work in conjunction with lowercase letters at the same point size. Typographically speaking, they're meant for use as accents—for example, to typeset the "a.m." or "p.m." that follows time—but like regular caps, they can also serve as a header font.

Letterspacing

Not all typefaces are designed with the same attention to detail.[12] Well-designed fonts account for variations in space between pairs of letterforms to improve aesthetics and readability (Figure 5.13). The spacing between letters is called *kerning*, and poorly kerned type can be unattractive, distracting, and unprofessional-looking. While there are lots of adequate and even good free fonts, keep an eye on their letterspacing.

Not every font's default kerning will be perfect. CSS's letter-spacing property allows you to kern individual letter pairs, but that level of fussiness is probably best left to designers.

Letterspacing can still be a valuable tool when applied to entire words and headers. Because regular capital letters aren't usually designed to appear together in large blocks of copy—not even in headers—adding a small amount of space between each letter can help emphasize the difference between each letterform, thereby improving readability (Figure 5.14).

Figure 5.13 The capital letters A and V can be difficult to kern properly when they appear together. (a) Poorly kerned type, and (b) the font's default kerning.

---

[12]Some of our favorites are hosted on *www.fontshop.com* and *www.typekit.com*. These sites are also great to browse for learning about fonts.

Pay your bill STEP 1 OF 2

(a)

Pay your bill STEP 1 OF 2

(b)

Figure 5.14 (a) The header "step 1 of 2" uses no letterspacing, and while readable, feels cramped relative to the larger, open letterforms of the main header. (b) This version uses a small amount of letterspacing to give the step indicator text more breathing room and improve overall header readability and visual balance.

Color

Although we'll go into far more depth about color in Chapter 6, it's important to address a few simple principles about applying color to type.

Your application's color palette should include at least one type color, usually black, dark gray, or dark blue. Legibility and contrast with the background are paramount in selecting a type color. You may also need to account for how type looks when it's *reversed*—displayed in white on a tinted background—or when colored type appears on a different color background.

Black type on a white background provides plenty of contrast for readability, as well as accessibility requirements. Any type color/ background color combination you choose other than black and white needs to be tested for accessibility. Use software, online tools, or browser add-ons to test color contrast to meet accessibility guidelines (Figure 5.15), and bear in mind that increasing type size and weight can sometimes push a color combination that's on the edge of acceptability to something that works.

Effects

As CSS has improved, there's less need to use graphics editing tools to achieve effects like drop shadows on type, or type filled with gradated colors. However, these effects should be used sparingly at most anyway—they can dramatically reduce readability, particularly at small sizes, and can create visual clutter. Limit use of effects to header type that needs it to express a specific personality or aesthetic (Figures 5.16 and 5.17).

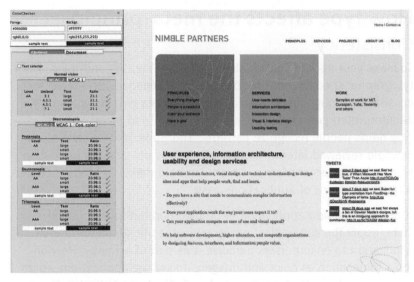

Figure 5.15 WCAG Contrast Checker is a Firefox browser add-on to check color contrast against accessibility guidelines.

Figure 5.16 SuperTracker's logo includes a blue gradient, colored outlines, and inner and outer glow effects. Although the gradient mirrors the one used in the navigation, the combination of so many effects so close together feels like overkill against the flat background.

Figure 5.17 Twitterrific's logo uses a metallic finish that helps it pop against the pale blue gradient background. Combined with the rounded-edged letterforms, the overall effect suggests a casual, fun, and geek-friendly application.

How type affects the meta-principles

Consistency

To make your application's features easier to identify and learn, keep typographic specifications for body content, headers, and other text consistent throughout an application. The cues type provides may be interpreted consciously or subconsciously, and standardizing type helps people recognize patterns. The SuperTracker case study example reviewed later in this chapter shows consistent application of type styles across platforms, which can help make switching between different versions of applications easy.

If designing a new application to be incorporated in an existing suite, apply the suitemates' typographic specifications to the new application to ensure users perceive it as part of a family. Rely on other tools, such as color and imagery, to set the applications apart *unless* use of display type is part of an individual application's personality. For example, a suite of applications that all use Arial for body text and most heads might use a different display font on some head styles to help individual applications convey personality.

You may also need to define new specifications for your application's unique requirements, but those specs should work harmoniously with the preexisting rules set out in your application's design guidelines, also known as a style guide. Rely on initial style guide specs for type size, treatment, color, and so on as the foundation for new ones.

Hierarchy

An application simply won't be successful—or at the very least, the typography won't help people discern patterns—without a hierarchy. A functional application must be able to present its feature set and communicate how to use it, and good typography is part of this success.

Contrast is the key to creating hierarchy with type, and with many of the other tools as well. It can be successfully created with size and weight alone. You can even stick to one typeface, provided it has at least three weights or styles, such as roman, bold, and italic. (In a pinch, two weights will also suffice, as long as some headers are set in all caps.)

The following examples in Figures 5.18–5.20 illustrate three possible type hierarchies using contrast. Note how changes in size, weight, style, and contrast help indicate the relative importance of each header.

STRONGEST HEAD (16pt all caps, bold, with 50px letterspacing to visually soften)

SIDEBAR HEAD OR CATEGORY HEAD   (11pt all caps, bold, 50px letterspacing)

Third Strongest Head (14pt, bold)

Slightly Strong Head (13pt, bold italic)

Text (13pt roman)

Weak Text for Bylines, Help, etc. (11pt, italic)

Figure 5.18 Typeface: Georgia.

Strongest Head (18pt black)

SIDEBAR OR CATEGORY HEAD   (11pt all caps, semibold 100px letterspacing)

Third Strongest Head (14pt, black)

Slightly Strong Head (13pt, all caps, semibold, 50px letterspacing)
or ***Slightly Strong Head*** (13pt semibold italic)

Text (13pt roman)

Weak Text for Bylines, Help, etc. (12pt, italic)

Figure 5.19 Typeface: Myriad.

STRONGEST HEAD (16pt all caps, bold, with 50px letterspacing to visually soften)

SIDEBAR HEAD or CATEGORY HEAD   (11pt all caps, bold, 50px letterspacing)

Third Strongest Head (12pt, bold)

SLIGHTLY STRONG HEAD (12pt, all caps, 50px letterspacing)

Text (13pt regular)

Weak Text for Bylines, Help, etc. (12pt, gray)

Figure 5.20 Typeface: Tahoma.

When pairing fonts from the same or different families, make sure their weights are just distinct enough to provide contrast and emphasis without distraction. For example, there may not be enough difference between a bold and a medium, and too much between a light condensed and a black extended. Two or three fonts from the same family are enough for many applications.

After establishing your type hierarchy, document it in a style guide that includes either functional code defining the different levels of type and their specs, or by providing instructions mapped to visual templates or wireframes. A visual frame of reference helps developers match type styles to the different locations and circumstances in which they appear, and allows them to apply type appropriately on every screen.

Personality

Type is a major component of an application's personality. Serif typefaces are traditionally seen as serious and business-like; sans serif ones are usually interpreted as more modern and casual. Perception of type, like the other tools, is contextual and influenced by layout and color as well as by users' frames of reference. Your application's typography should reflect the purpose of the application, the characteristics you want that application to project, and if required, the brand aspects of your parent organization. Type that runs counter to an application's purpose and personality produces an unsettling sense of disjoint; would you feel comfortable using a mobile banking application set in Comic Sans (Figure 5.21)? Trying different relationships and reviewing them with others is essential to defining a personality that communicates as intended.

Figure 5.21 Two simple menus for a mobile banking application. The one typeset in Georgia, a serif typeface, feels unexciting but reliable. The one typeset in Comic Sans feels far too casual for an application that involves managing personal finances.

Despite the range of typefaces and fonts available, it's best to stick with two or three fonts. More fonts equals more possible visual relationships to investigate and evaluate, and leads to a complex visual language that relies more on subtlety to communicate personality than a language with one or two fonts.

Defining a rationale for type

Defining a rationale for type allows you to choose the most appropriate typefaces for your application. Begin by answering these questions:

- *What's the purpose of your application?* A financial services application implies a formal look and feel; an online game portal implies an informal, visually active look and feel; and a food- and fitness-tracking application might fall somewhere in between. An application that includes lots of detailed text, such as nutritional information, will need a highly legible, readable base font; an application with little text, such as a weather application that focuses mostly on visuals, may be able to rely on a legible and clear display typeface for content.

- *Is the application part of a suite, and are there brand standards it needs to adhere to?* If so, the suite's existing standards, as well as brand rules, dictate your choice of fonts so that all new applications feel connected.

- *Who's the audience for the application?* An older audience (40 years old or higher) will need a larger default point size than a younger audience. Using an open typeface with a large x-height, like Verdana, may also improve readability for older audiences. For applications delivered in multiple languages, investigate fonts that offer a complete set of Unicode characters.

- *What personality does the application need to convey?* Bearing in mind any cultural expectations for your application based on its purpose, consider all aspects of your application's personality (Figures 5.22 and 5.23). Should it feel cheerful and inviting? No-nonsense? Trendy? Loud, or quiet? Review fonts critically against the list of adjectives from the visual design requirements that describe desired characteristics (see Chapter 3 for a sample). Every typeface has its own personality, and you may need to experiment with a few. Font websites generally allow you to typeset sample text to get an idea of how things will look before you decide to purchase or link to a font. Interpreting characteristics of fonts can be subjective. It isn't usually necessary to test font choices with users, but stakeholders and teammates should be in general agreement about desired font characteristics.

- *What platform(s) will people use to access the application?* By default, Windows-based and Mac OS–based systems support 9 typefaces across platforms: Arial, Arial Black, Comic Sans MS, Courier New, Georgia, Impact, Times New Roman, Trebuchet, and Verdana. iOS's default choices include 61 font families, while Android and Windows 8 Mobile offer far fewer. All platforms have default serif and sans serif typefaces, and website and application developers can make other typefaces available via CSS or embedding. If you're working across platforms, you may choose to stick to typefaces you know will work everywhere, or you may determine that the risk of displaying a default typeface doesn't dramatically affect your application's personality. Regardless, plan on testing your application's display across multiple devices to make sure content is readable and looks the way you expect it to look.

Figure 5.22 Reader application Pocket's typography feels clean, readable, and sophisticated.

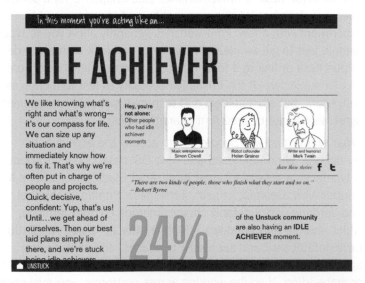

Figure 5.23 Unstuck's "solution" screens mix book weight and condensed sans serif typefaces with a handwriting font to create an approachable personality that also feels authoritative.

To develop a rationale for selecting and applying fonts in the redesign, we combined our answers to the rationale questions with an analysis of existing typography on the SuperTracker and ChooseMyPlate.gov websites.

Application purpose

SuperTracker is a food- and fitness-tracking application with the mission of helping people make better nutrition and wellness choices based on federal guidelines.

Related applications and brand standards

The SuperTracker web application relies on Arial as its primary body typeface, with Arial Black reserved for its main header. Logotypes for both SuperTracker and ChooseMyPlate.gov use Gotham. Headers on some of the ChooseMyPlate.gov website pages use Lato, a typeface very similar to Gotham (Figure 5.24). Using a header font that's visually related to

Figure 5.24 Headers for "Topics" and "Food Groups," as well as "Choose a Food Group" and all its subheads, are typeset in Lato.

the logo is one way to help type look cohesive and intentional throughout an application.

With limited ways to express personality on the small mobile phone screen, we wanted to use a more distinctive text typeface than Arial. We turned to the USDA's style guide for MyPlate. The typeface used in the MyPlate icon was Museo, a versatile semi-slab serif. The Museo family's breadth and modern style made it a good candidate to try in our redesign, but not a great candidate for text; slabs are exaggerated serifs, and would add too much visual weight to lines of text on a small screen.

Audience and personality

With obesity a nationwide issue, SuperTracker's audience could vary significantly by age, locale, and other characteristics. The personas suggested SuperTracker's personality needed to feel authoritative, but friendly. No one enjoys dieting or being told they're eating the wrong foods, but at the same time, tracking food consumption and exercise patterns is a serious step toward improving physical health, and shouldn't be treated informally.

Type had to be clean, legible, and readable at a standard body text size. It also had to scale smoothly for Betty, who would need a larger point size in her web browser than Danny and Sonia would on their mobile devices or laptops.

Platform considerations

While SuperTracker is currently a web-only application, our redesign also had to address mobile phones and tablets. Gotham, used in the logo, was only available for web use via sIFR, a Flash-based technology, and couldn't be embedded in native applications without negotiating with the font foundry. However, provided the logo remained an image, using it in an application was allowed.

For body and header text, we knew our best choice would be typefaces licensed for easy web and mobile use. Museo is available as a web font, and can be licensed for mobile applications. We needed to find a text font that met the same requirements.

Choosing and applying type

We started our type explorations with logotype designs. Beginning with simple typographic approaches that relied on combinations of font choice and weight to express SuperTracker's personality allowed us to quickly sketch out and assess multiple alternatives (Figure 5.25).

Our trial logotypes included Gotham as well as Futura and DIN, two other sans serif fonts. While we wanted to keep some of the feel of the original SuperTracker logotype, we also wanted it to convey more of Pepper's personality: the smart, technology-savvy assistant. We decided that a lighter weight of Gotham best conveyed Pepper's sophistication and helped the applications maintain a visual relationship to related sites and publications.

SUPER**TRACKER**
DIN regular and bold

super**TRACKER**
Futura bold and extra bold

SUPERtracker
DIN bold and medium

SUPERTRACKER
Gotham bold and book

Figure 5.25 SuperTracker trial logotypes.

As we moved from logotype experiments to screen layout, we also explored the idea of SuperTracker as a journal or log (Figure 5.26). This exploration was done primarily through type, and used an informal typewriter font to convey the idea. Trying it allowed us to see that the font and idea of a log felt too informal and not technically savvy enough to fit the application's personality and robust functionality.

Figure 5.26 Exploring use of a typewriter display font.

Despite the typewriter font's failure, trial layouts helped us narrow in on the feel we wanted for body and header type. We chose Museo 500, a semi-slab serif, for heads, and paired it with Meta, a slightly condensed sans serif, for the text (Figure 5.27). The pairing works because both

Lunch	Total: 484 cal	
Wheat bread, 100%	2 slices	138 cal
Cheddar cheese	1 oz	171 cal
Lettuce, green or red leaf	¼ cup	2 cal
Squash, summer (yellow or zucchini)...	1 cup, slices	76 cal
Lunch	Total: 484 cal	
Wheat bread, 100%	2 slices	138 cal
Cheddar cheese	1 oz	171 cal
Lettuce, green or red leaf	¼ cup	2 cal
Squash, summer (yellow or zucchini)...	1 cup, slices	76 cal

Figure 5.27 Museo and Meta, the header and text fonts we chose (top); Arial and Arial Bold used in the original application (bottom). Museo and Meta offer more personality than Arial without sacrificing readability.

have similar x-heights, a strong horizontal orientation to the letterforms, and blunted *terminals*, or letterform ends. Museo's slightly heavier weight also provides enough contrast to draw attention to headers without overwhelming the slimmer, lighter Meta. Finally, Meta was designed for legibility, including use at small sizes, making it a good choice for mobile device screens (Figures 5.28, 5.29, and 5.30).

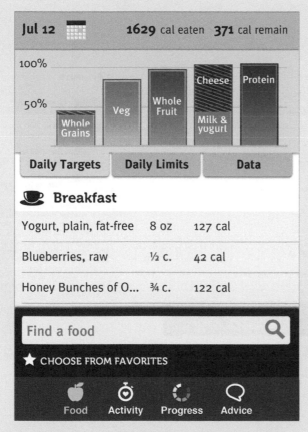

Figure 5.28 Meta and Museo in place in the refined mobile phone layout.

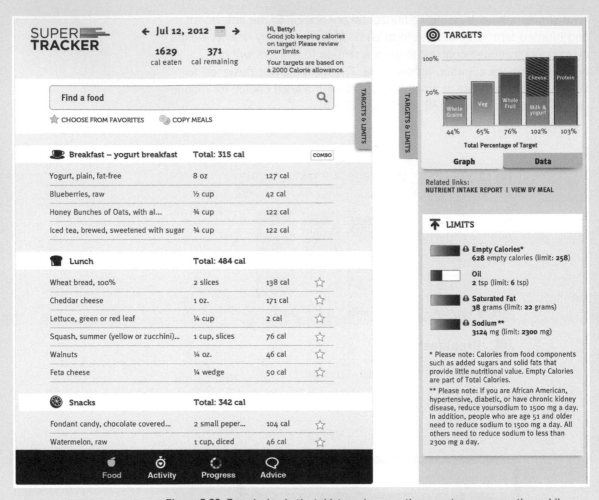

Figure 5.29 Type design in the tablet version uses the same type specs as the mobile phone version.

Our final versions of the application use two weights of Museo (500 and 700) and three of Meta (regular, medium, and bold). Variations in size, color, and weight create a consistent type hierarchy across all three delivery platforms.

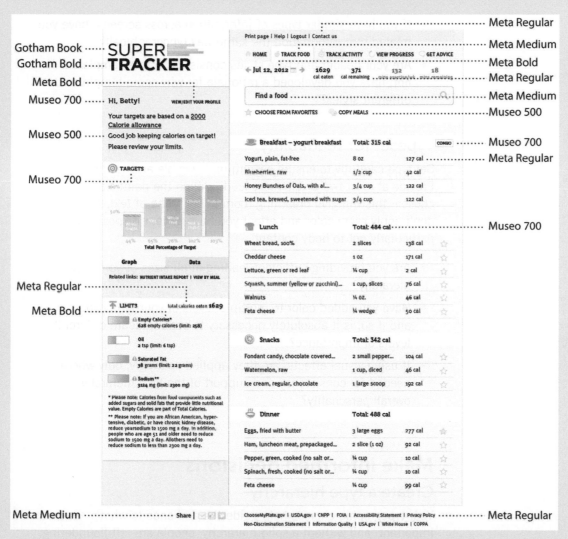

Figure 5.30 Typefaces and fonts in the web layout. While position and size of type elements change across platforms, application of font and style is consistent.

Avoid common mistakes

Use type consistently

Once people learn the particular vernacular of your application, they're going to expect the application to "speak" to them in the same way everywhere. Inconsistent application of the hierarchy is like telling people that "save" means "save data" in one location and "cancel" in another.

- If you have similar types of information across screens, have you treated that information the same way typographically?
- Are your header and type styles consistent across templates? If not, have you developed a rationale for why some templates use different styles?

Typeset for readability

Set type carefully to ensure everything is legible and readable. Provide at least two pixels more leading than the point size you've chosen; this will give breathing room to each line of text. Also, don't apply every color and effect you have at your disposal, and particularly not to body content.

- Are you providing sufficient leading at all sizes of your type hierarchy?
- Have you added color to multiple levels of your type hierarchy, and if so, is it absolutely necessary to communicate different levels of importance?
- If using visual effects, are they applied sparingly, only where needed for consistency and support of the type hierarchy and overall personality?

Make informed decisions

Create a type hierarchy

Your typographic choices help guide the audience to what's important, and without a solid hierarchy, people are left floundering. When creating the hierarchy, include variation of contrast, size, and style that clearly shows difference without distracting. We're trained to interpret bold text as important, and as a result, you may be tempted to overuse boldfaced type, simply to ensure no one misses your key messages—but emphasize everything, and nothing stands out. Boldface works for emphasis precisely because it's a contrast to the roman type that typically dominates a page.

- Can your audience tell at a glance—based on type size, contrast, and/or position—what the most and least important text is on the screen?
- Are you boldfacing and italicizing only the text that absolutely needs it to convey emphasis, and underlining or differentiating only hyperlinked text?
- Do sidebar heads and subheads feel subservient to the main page header, yet strong enough to attract some attention and contrast with text?

Limit fonts and typefaces

Unless you're an experienced designer, stick to two or three fonts when creating your hierarchy, and don't use more than two typefaces in addition to the one in the logo. As exciting as it is to have so many choices, basic typographic principles still apply. Too many fonts will create visual chaos, both if they're too similar to each other as well as if they're wildly different. Use the minimum number of fonts you need to communicate effectively.

There's no harm in sticking to reliable typefaces like Helvetica and Times New Roman. These typefaces may not have a ton of personality, but they've survived a long time because they're neutral and easy to read. Type is just one tool for conveying personality. Using plain fonts well with expressive imagery, for example, is a classic way to use type and one of many successful design strategies.

Consider these typefaces as part of your overall investigation into what type families will best suit your application. Review the questions we set out earlier, paying particular attention to how and if to express your application's personality through type. For example, weather application Dark Sky could have used any bold sans serif for a casual feel, but its designers chose Proxima Nova Extra Condensed, which feels jaunty and light despite being a condensed typeface (Figure 5.31). The application would be far less engaging with Arial or Helvetica instead.

Figure 5.31 Dark Sky's typefaces.

- How many fonts compose your type hierarchy? Can you use fewer while maintaining a strong visual hierarchy and an appropriate personality for your application?

- If using display type, are you using it at a readable size, and only where it provides needed visual punch to support your application's personality?

Elevate the ordinary

Native mobile applications can support printlike type design, providing designers with complete control over headers, body type, and interactive elements. But web-based applications are catching

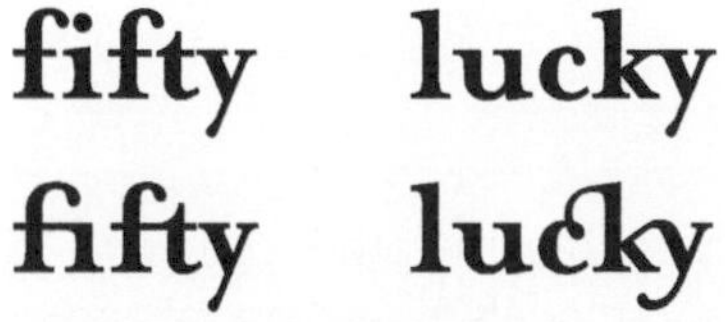

fifty lucky
fifty lucky

Figure 5.32 Ligatures are connected sets of letters. For some languages, such as German with its ß character, ligatures may be required. For others, they add visual appeal and enhance legibility by creating attractive connections between letterform elements, such as the crossbars of a lowercase f and t.

up; although CSS still doesn't provide the range of type tricks available in a page layout program, it's now possible to use it to generate typographic treatments previously restricted to print, such as pull quotes and drop caps. Web browser support for OpenType font features, such as ligatures and alternate letterform versions, is increasing, and will allow designers and developers to incorporate more sophisticated type elements (Figure 5.32).[13]

[13] Ferreira, G. (2012, June 7). OpenType Features in Web Browsers. *Typotheque*. Retrieved July 31, 2012, from *http://www.typotheque.com/articles/ opentype_features_in_web_browsers*.

Color

6

Color is one of the most misunderstood tools UI designers have. It's a powerful tool to attract the eye, as well as to help people know what to do once you have their attention. Despite this power, we see it underused—blue and gray applications, anyone?—and misused—applied randomly to create impact instead of understanding.

More than the other tools of visual interface design, color provokes emotional responses. Perhaps that's why discussions of its use are limited to brand. Used with knowledge and understanding, color is a strategic partner that helps your interface guide and direct. This chapter focuses on selecting and applying color to enhance usability and appeal.

What color can do

Color is a great tool to draw attention. Used as a highlight or accent, it helps people know where to look. Used strategically to draw the eye, it helps people know what to do (Figure 6.2). Used consistently as part of a system, it helps define a visual language so people know where they are and what to expect, and allows them to make connections between related elements, which can aid in understanding. Color can also be used to express qualities of a brand or personality to help an application stand out from competitors. The key is to know what type of attention you want to attract, what messages you want to send, and what color can do so you can use it to its full potential.

Figure 6.1 Bright, saturated colors were part of the brand and identity of the 2012 Summer Olympic Games. The eye and the brain work together to find patterns in this events results app, such as the colors of the Olympic icons. Here, badminton, basketball, and mountain biking ("Cycling – Mountain") are all magenta. However, these events are unrelated, so their icons seem randomly colored. Random use of color is a common mistake and a lost opportunity to elevate the ordinary. Color could have instead been used for patterns that aid understanding—for example, similar events, or events in the same location, could have shared colors.

A business application interface that breaks out of the gray and blue mold will likely stand out from its competitors. If it uses the bright, saturated colors of the Olympic application palette, it might be memorable when customers are deciding which application to buy—but those same colors could get tiresome for people who need to use the application every day. Communicating with color is a balancing act best achieved when context of use (where the application will be used and in what situation), physical user characteristics (e.g., age of audience), and understanding of audience culture (e.g., common meanings of certain colors) are part of defining a rationale for color.

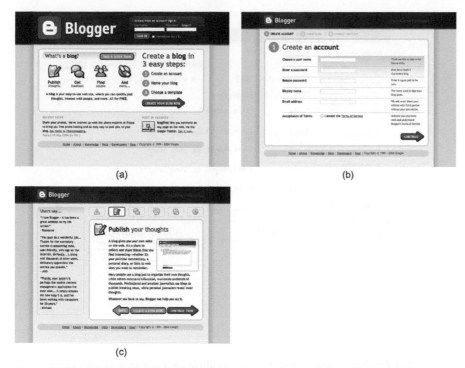

(a)   (b)

(c)

Figure 6.2 An early version of the Blogger interface used color to draw attention both to the new brand identity and to action elements on the screen. The bright orange "B" logo created visual impact. Use of orange for the primary buttons helped people know what to do.

Establish and convey hierarchy

Because of color's ability to draw the eye, it's an ideal tool to help establish and convey hierarchy (Figure 6.3). Used with layout and styling, it helps people know what to look at first, and how to make sense of what they see. This is especially important for applications with a lot of complex information. The type of color you use, amount of color, and placement of color affect hierarchy.

Saturated colors draw the eye more than dull colors (Figure 6.4), but even dull colors draw the eye if they contrast with what's around them (Figure 6.5). Small areas of saturated, bright color may draw the eye more than larger fields of a more muted color. We see best that which is directly in the center of our visual field, so if something is important but near the edge of an application, it might need to be in a contrasting color to help the eye notice it. While color can't

Figure 6.3 In this sketch, color is used in multiple ways to establish hierarchy, direct the eye, and help people know what they can do. Red is used as an accent to highlight important elements and controls. Pale orange helps the message to pop out from the background. Pale tints behind the sections on the left group the elements within, which provides order to the busy screen. The small, light yellow box in the bottom left is placed in a subordinate location, but its contrasting background helps draw attention to it.

Figure 6.4 Saturated colors (center) draw the eye more than dull colors.

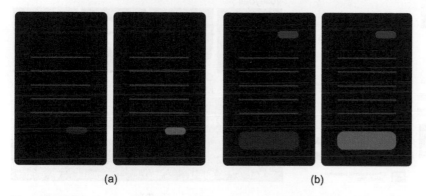

(a) (b)

Figure 6.5 (a) Dull colors draw the eye if they contrast with what's around them. (b) Small areas of saturated, bright color may draw the eye more than larger fields of a more muted color.

make someone do something, drawing the eye influences what's seen onscreen. People can only click on what they notice.

Make relationships visible

Making relationships visible reassures people by presenting what they expect. What people expect is affected by their frame of reference, or the combination of their experiences. While you can't know what's in every user's head, you can make some educated guesses to get the basics right. If a mobile application uses bright colors for sections of content, people will expect to see those bright colors used in a similar way on the web version as well (Figure 6.6).

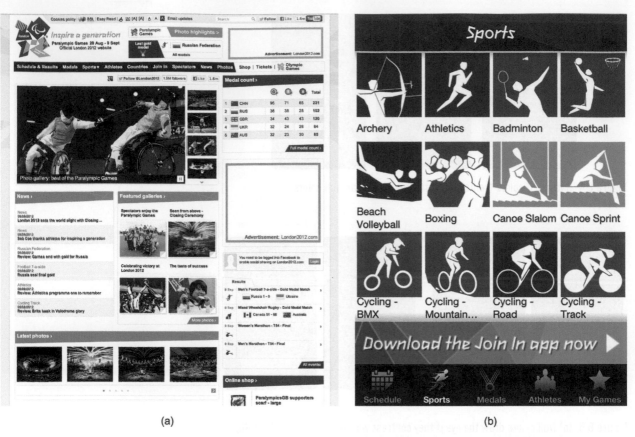

(a)   (b)

Figure 6.6 Color is a primary element that ties the London 2012 Olympic results application (b) to the website (a). The colors also relate to the logo, signage, and other communications produced for the 2012 Summer Olympic Games. The application's visual relationship to the other materials helps put it in the right context.

System relationships

When working with related applications, giving each a predominant color and using it the same way creates a pattern that tells people the applications have something in common. This is one example of color-coding, which enhances both meaning and use in application design. The reports section in Figure 6.7 uses blue as the primary color, and the account management section uses yellow. Both sections apply their respective color palettes according to the same rules. Note that color should not be the *only* cue that indicates location or status, as on its own it is not effective for color-blind or visually impaired users.

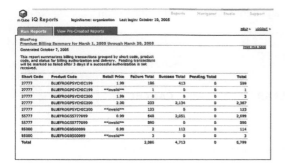

Figure 6.7 Screens from separate sections of a large application use different colors to help users know which section they are in, but each section applies colors according to the same rules.

Using the same color for elements of the same type helps people "decode" the design of a screen. For example, making the primary "Submit" button a solid color and a secondary "Cancel" button white with an outline of the primary button's color establishes a visual hierarchy system for those two types of buttons (Figure 6.8). Used consistently wherever the buttons appear, the system indicates to the user that the buttons are related but do different things.

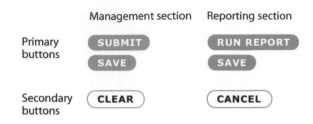

Figure 6.8 Using color to establish a visual hierarchy for buttons.

Symbolic relationships

Color helps people make associations symbolically, but these associations aren't usually strong enough to communicate a single, unambiguous message in every circumstance. Color, symbols, content, context, and culture work together to evoke relationships in people's minds. For example, black is the color that Westerners associate most with death, but use of black abounds in our digital and physical world. Similarly, Apple sells plenty of white products in China, even though it's a color associated with mourning and death there. It would be silly to avoid either color without considering the context.

Color meaning can also shift based on circumstance. Westerners associate the color red with stop signs, mistakes, and losing money, depending on the context. But in the month of December, red means merriment and is linked to Christmas. While you need to be aware of common color associations, don't rely on them to communicate on their own, or allow them to dictate color choices out of hand.

The meaning of pairs or groups of colors is less fluid. While red can take on a variety of meanings, it's hard to make red and green together look like anything other than Christmas. Saturated red, blue, and yellow are so strongly associated with primary education and young children that it's almost impossible to think of using them for other situations. When green is added, as in the suite of Google applications, the association to children is broken. To use color symbolically, you need a general awareness of color associations common in the culture you are designing for, and what associations you want people to make. Then you can use color with the other visual usability tools to communicate clearly.

Figure 6.9 The color green can be associated with nature, money, a green light, or "go," depending on context. The personal finance–tracking website Mint.com uses green as its primary color. Green, combined with the purpose of the application, the dollar sign in the logo, and the application's name, works to unambiguously associate the application interface to money and growth. All of these associations help convey the personality of the application.

Add aesthetic appeal and convey personality

Color is an excellent tool to help set tone and convey personality. Consider in Figure 6.9 how Mint.com's use of green makes its interface feel lively and alert in comparison to any blue and gray financial application. However, while color and aesthetic interpretation are subjective and contextual, there are theories of color and personality. One widely referenced theory is by Shigenobu Kobayashi, who founded the Nippon Color & Design Research Institute.[1] Kobayashi defined adjectives, such as "modern," and three colors that represent each word.

While Kobayashi's theory and others like it are worth reviewing, we do not believe that any theories of color and aesthetics should be taken and used wholesale. Tastes and interpretations change, and what's considered "modern" or "dynamic" in terms of color is not fixed.

[1] Kobayashi, S. (1992). *Color Image Scale*. Kodansha USA. Published in New York, NY.

If informal reviews of colors you're considering make you doubt their appeal, testing methods such as those described in Chapter 3 can help you determine if your colors are working for your audience as intended.

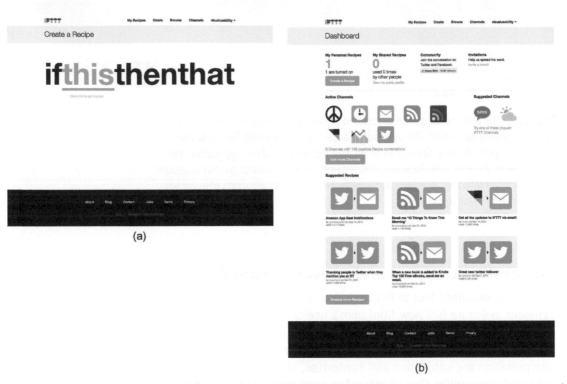

(a)

(b)

Figure 6.10 The application If This Then That uses pure, almost primary, colors. This choice helps make the application feel simple and its personality approachable, which is strategic given its purpose of enabling anyone to create simple programs.

Color and error messaging

Color isn't tied to specific interface patterns other than error messaging. Using red for errors makes sense conceptually, as an error is the right place to take advantage of contrast to attract the eye. Use of this pattern is often heavy-handed, however, and can interrupt an application's personality if it's too jarring. Too much contrast in a warning that isn't life-threatening or data-erasing can feel like a "visual spanking" (Figures 6.11, 6.12, and 6.13).

A small amount of a contrasting hue other than red can be sufficient to draw the eye. In an urgent situation, such as a hospital setting, two levels of contrast, such as a contrasting background tint and contrasting text style, may be necessary.

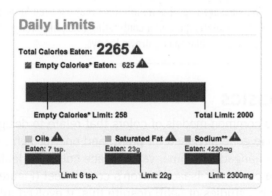

Figure 8.11 "Visual spanking" in action on SuperTracker: the chart area turns into a sea of red if users exceed their daily calorie limit.

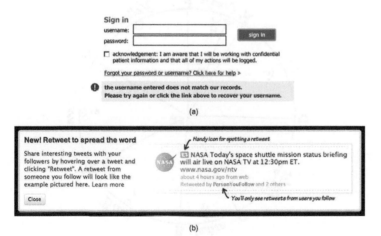

Figure 6.12 Visually polite errors and messages call appropriate attention to themselves. A small amount of red can be sufficient to draw the eye.

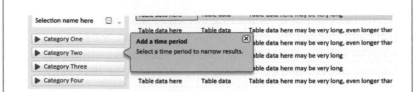

Figure 6.13 This message is part of an interface that uses red for accents and nonerror text. In this situation, use of a contrasting color, like orange, combined with styling and strategic placement, draws the eye.

Color basics

There are two common models of colors that relate to designing on the screen: one generally used for paint, and one for light. Color wheels have changed over time, yet all place colors in deliberate positions in a circle. Sir Isaac Newton's color wheel (Figure 6.14) derived from his studies of light; despite this, it evolved into a model that is still used by some artists and painters.

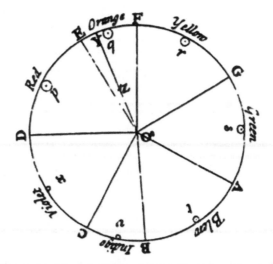

Figure 6.14 Early color wheel from Newton's *Opticks* (1704). Traditional primary colors red, yellow, and blue are placed at intervals with secondary colors orange, green, and violet/indigo between them.

The evolution of color theory has produced some confusion between light-based models and models based on mixing paints with pigments. There are terms for color popular with painters and terms used by physicists. Use of color for screens sits at the intersection of these worlds, which makes it hard to dismiss one set of terms or models in favor of the other. Confusion persists today, as there is no one model for color that accurately serves all purposes and mediums. All color models and color wheels have benefits and drawbacks. What you need to know to use color effectively requires understanding a small number of concepts at a limited depth. After the basics, understanding color comes through use and consideration. To gain expertise, as with all of the tools, we encourage you to try many combinations and observe and evaluate the results.

Traditional color model

People learn early in life about red, yellow, and blue (RYB), and associate these colors with the term *primary*. Children learn about mixing them to create *secondary* colors—green, orange, and purple. The model of placing these colors in circular form—primaries with secondaries between them—derived from Isaac Newton's experiments with light.[2] This RYB, or traditional, model is a *subtractive* color model, or model based on starting with a white surface and mixing paints, dyes, or inks to come between the eye and the light (Figure 6.15).

Figure 6.15 This version of a traditional color wheel based on the model by Johannes Itten (*The Art of Color*, 1961) is popular with designers.

[2]Colors were arranged in a circle before Newton; however, those circles included black and white. Briggs, D. (2012, April 12). *The Dimensions of Colour*. Retrieved Sept. 4, 2012, from *http://www.huevaluechroma.com/011.php.*

This model doesn't work for every circumstance. The notion of red, yellow, and blue as the primary colors from which all colors can be mixed does not hold up in the case of mixing colors with paints. However, the model serves as a simple, useful reference for contrasting complementary colors, which are discussed in depth later in the chapter.

Red, green, blue model

In the model for mixing colored light, red, green, and blue (RGB) are the primary colors. In this type of color system, called *additive*, the primaries, when mixed, create white (Figure 6.16). All discernible hues on screens are created from combinations of these primaries.

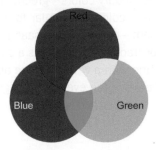

Figure 6.16 Adding red, blue, and green light creates white, while the intersections create the cyan, magenta, and yellow elements of the subtractive color model.

Hue and saturation

Hue refers to the property that allows something we see to be described as a distinct color. Hues are saturated colors seen in the spectrum (red, orange, yellow, green, cyan, blue, and violet) and nonspectral colors (magenta, purples).[3] *Saturation* is the relative purity of a color compared to gray.[4]

Saturated colors draw the eye due to their brightness and intensity. Using colors that are different hues but similar in saturation is one way to effectively create contrast, such as the colors in the Olympics results application, or those on a traffic light (Figures 6.17 and 6.18).

---

[3] Briggs, D. (2012, April 12). *The Dimensions of Colour*. Retrieved Sept. 6, 2012, from *http://www.huevaluechroma.com/011.php*.

[4] Dondis, D. A. *A Primer of Visual Literacy*, p. 51.

The light's red, green, and yellow-orange all draw the eye but are quite different in hue. The effect when used in equal amounts is active and intense.

Figure 6.17 Saturated hues, like those used on a traffic light, are distinct and contrast with one another.

Figure 6.18 A palette of sharply saturated hues like those used in the 2012 Olympics application creates an exciting interface.

Figure 6.19 A saturated color with a less saturated, or muted, color also creates contrast, but is less intense.

Value, brightness, and tone

Value, used in terms of the color of objects, is relative lightness or darkness. It applies to shades of gray, hues, and *tones*. Value can be visualized as a scale going from white to black. Light–dark relationships are a type of contrast achieved with value, with black and white creating the greatest amount of contrast. Use of a light tint and a dark shade of the same hue (e.g., a light red and a dark red) is a subtle way to create contrast (Figure 6.19).

Brightness is the relative amount of light, and is a scale without limit. We use *lighter* and *darker* to refer to the brightness of what we see on screen.

Tone refers to the color of an object that has been modified to be less saturated. Tones come in all values. Though its use in color comes from mixing pigments, we include tone here for the purpose of clarification, and to introduce some of the possible variations of a hue, as shown in Figure 6.20. The concept of creating variations of a color—by lightening (tints), darkening (shades), or otherwise muting (with gray or other colors that neutralize intensity)—is relevant. Tones can be created using the primary colors of screen display—red, green, and blue. Creating shades, tints, and tones onscreen from a hue creates monochromatic colors. It is one way to create colors that harmonize with one another; for example, all tones created from a red hue share a visual relationship.

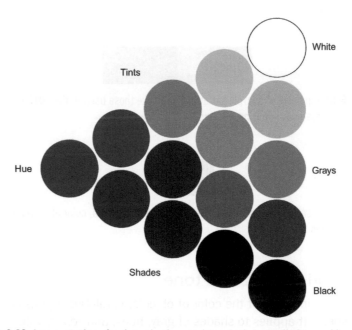

Figure 6.20 Interpretation of painters' colors and terminology applied to working with color on screen.[5] Tints have the effect of adding white to a hue. Shades have the effect of adding black. Tones are hues that have been "broken" by adding the effect of black and white, yet still relate to a particular hue. The three colors in the center of the triangle are tones.

Figure 6.21 Use of a light tint and a dark shade of the same hue is a subtle way to create contrast.

[5] Illustration based on photograph at http://www.wetcanvas.com/forums/showthread.php?t=543997&page=2, retrieved September 12, 2012.

Contrasting colors

Contrast is the key to creating hierarchy and drawing the eye. The degree of contrast also helps establish personality and mood. There are several ways to use color to create contrast, three of which we've already discussed: hue, saturation, and light–dark. Color teacher Johannes Itten outlined four additional types of color contrast in his book *The Art of Color*, used as a guide by designers since its publication in 1961: cold–warm, complementary, simultaneous, and extension. All are timeless, and used in all mediums of art and design.

Warm–cool contrast

Warm generally refers to colors that are yellow, red, and orange in hue, while *cool* refers to colors that are green, blue, and violet in hue (Figure 6.22).

Figure 6.22 Colors thought to be warm (top) and cool (bottom).

Figure 6.23 A warm color, red, shifts to a cool color, violet.

Half the colors in a traditional color wheel are warm, and the other half cool. The colors on the "line"—yellow-greens, red-violets, and some violets—can act as warm or cool, depending on what colors they are paired with (Figure 6.24).

Juxtaposing warm and cool hues creates contrast. Painters and designers use color "temperature" to help suggest depth in the two-dimensional plane of a canvas or screen. Warm colors, depending on usage, can have the effect of coming forward; comparatively, cool colors can have the effect of receding. A big, saturated, red button on a pale green-blue background can feel like it's "popping out," or giving dimension to a flat surface.

Figure 6.24 The same color (left) appears warm when seen with a cooler hue (violet), and cool when seen with a warmer hue (red).

Painters know that any color can feel warm or cool, depending on the composition of pigments that make up the color and its juxtaposition with other colors. Orange can be relatively cool if it has a hint of blue mixed in and is next to a warmer hue.

Tips for warm–cool contrast

- Warm–cool contrast works with two saturated hues such as blue and orange, with two muted tones, and with one muted tone and one saturated tone. Explore color combinations onscreen with a free color tool like *http://kuler.adobe.com*, or with paper and markers or pencils to find relationships that convey the personality you want.

- If you have a warm hue and a neutral color, try adding a little cool color to the neutral to shift its temperature and create warm–cool contrast, and vice versa (Figure 6.25).

- Warm–cool contrast does not need to be obvious to the eye to have an effect. Adding blue to a gray to make it cooler will affect how that cool gray interacts with other colors.

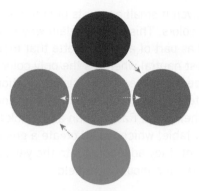

Figure 6.25 Shifting a neutral color (center) to cool (left gray) or warm (right gray) adds vibrancy to color pairs by changing how the neutral interacts with same and opposite temperature colors.

Complementary contrast

Complementary contrast uses pairs of colors across from each other on the traditional color wheel to create vibrancy and luminosity. *Complementary* doesn't mean that the colors make an attractive pair; whether they are perceived as attractive is subjective. It means that when the colors are placed next to each other and are of equal value and saturation, each will cause the other to appear their most vibrant, compared to when seen alone or paired with other colors (Figure 6.26).

Figure 6.26 Traditional complementary color pairs. Complementary doesn't mean that the colors are pleasing, but rather that each item in the pair, when viewed together, makes the other appear at its most pure or true hue. Simultaneous contrast is an effect that makes the edge of two colors appear to vibrate where they meet. This effect is most pronounced in pairs on complementary colors. Delacroix, Van Gogh, and Monet are a few of many painters who relied on complementary pairs to add vibrancy to their paintings to great result.

This effect is true even if small amounts of complementary colors are added to other colors. This helps explain why red can be too intense when used as part of a color palette that includes greens, but can seem almost neutral when it's the only color used in large areas of an interface, as in the Epicurious application in Figure 3.10. Impressionist painters relied on complementary colors to achieve effects of light in their work. Rather than add black to create a shadow on a yellow table, which would create a greenish hue when working with oil paint, they added violet to the yellow used for the table, which created a luminous, dark field.

We use the principles of complementary color to create the appearance of luminosity through color selection and juxtaposition, even though we work with combinations of red, green, and blue rather than red, yellow, and blue. (See the final color images of the SuperTracker application and explanation of color choices later in this chapter.) Using complementary color principles when designing for screens is not an uncommon approach; for example, use of blue and orange abounds on websites and applications, as well as in advertising and in film.

Creating contrast and luminosity with complementary colors is complicated somewhat by the different color wheels and models. Artists and designers learn the complementaries identified by Michel Chevreul (see sidebar "Complementary colors and color models" later in this chapter) and depicted by Itten. We use the traditional complementary pairs as a starting point and source for variations, relying on the contrasting property of warm–cool relationships in addition to complementary pairings to guide our color selections (Figure 6.27).

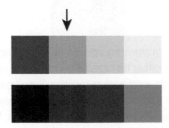

Figure 6.27 Approximation of an early version of Blogger's color palette. The palette uses several types of contrast described in this chapter: complementary contrast, light–dark contrast, warm–cool contrast, and contrast of extension. The addition of a muted tone (indicated) that has been "broken" with a cool color contrasts with, but also complements, the orange as well as the blues.

Tips for creating complementary contrast

- Using the most saturated hues of the complements in juxtaposition creates strong contrast that makes the eye vibrate between the two colors. The effect is like drinking too much caffeine. It should only be done with awareness and caution.

- Using muted hues of complements will also produce complementary contrast.

- Using a saturated color and a muted version of its complement is a third way to create contrast with complementary pairs.

Contrast of extension

Not all colors are equal. For example, in a yellow/purple pairing, yellow is light and purple is dark. They're also unequal in terms of saturation used straight from the wheel. To visually balance a purple hue, only a small amount of yellow is needed.

This also affects orange/blue pairings to a lesser degree; Johann von Goethe calculated that orange equaling about one-third the amount of blue is necessary to create visual equity.[6] However, red and green hues are equally intense, so when using green as the lead color in an interface design, should you use an equal amount of red? Not unless you want to create maximum contrast. Contrast of extension is included here to help you be aware of the amount of each color you use and the degree of contrast that results (Figure 6.28).

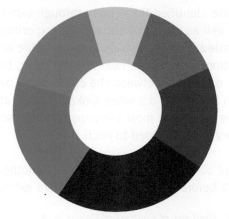

Figure 6.28 Traditional color wheel with proportions of colors altered to balance the visual weight of each hue.[6]

[6] Image based on Itten's "circle of harmonious extension." Itten, J. *The Art of Color*, p. 104.

Tips for balancing contrast

- Unless you are using color to create a particularly strong, expressive statement, balance the use of saturated hues with muted, neutral tones. Early Blogger interface designs (see Figure 6.2) do this well.

- If using a single saturated hue with white and black, make sure you have white space to give the eye a chance to rest, and get maximum impact from the contrast of the color.

- If using a saturated hue, apply it strategically to draw the eye to the most important element, and then use less of it (or a tint or shade of it) to draw the eye to a limited number of other elements.

Complementary colors and color models

The concept of complementary colors is significant for artists and designers in any medium. Michel Chevreul, a French chemist employed by the Gobelins textile factory from 1824 to 1883, stated that "Red is complementary to Green, and *vice versa*; That Orange is complementary to Blue, and *vice versa*; That Greenish Yellow is complementary to Violet, and *vice versa*; That Indigo is complementary to Orange Yellow, and *vice versa*."[7] He identified these pairs through experiments with light, as well as extensive ink and dye experiments. Chevreul recorded that when strips of equal value and intensity of different colors were placed next to each other, the eye perceived the difference between the colors to be more profound than they really are when looked at separately.[8] He noted that this effect was most pronounced when some of each complementary color is added to each pair.[9]

The reaction of complementary colors to one another was used by artists before Chevreul and even more extensively

[7] Chevreul, M. E. *The Laws of Contrast of Colour*, p. 8.
[8] Chevreul, M. E. *The Laws of Contrast of Colour*, p. 4.
[9] Chevreul, M. E. *The Laws of Contrast of Colour*, p. 9.

afterward to increase intensity and the effect of luminosity with color. Chevreul's research was undertaken with the purpose of discovering why fabrics appeared pleasing or not. His studies led him to believe that the dyes of the fabrics were not to blame when colors seemed off, but rather that the juxtaposition of colors of fabrics and the effect of viewing successive bolts of different colors affected how they are perceived.[10] The importance of his work is the effect it's had and continues to have on artists, and on informing use of color for maximum results in any medium.

Another color expert, Albert H. Munsell, extended Chevreul's work (and that of others) and created a comprehensive system for identifying and representing color. Munsell used his system to create a wheel of perceptually equal differences between hues. In his system, yellow is across from blue, violet is across from yellow-green, and red is across from blue-green. This model throws off the traditional complementary pairings. Munsell's work is similar to the hue, saturation, and brightness (HSB) wheel[11] created for monitor display in 1978. The HSB wheel further skews Chevreul's complementaries, with yellow across from bright blue, red across from cyan, and yellow-green across from magenta.

With all this variation, it's hard to know which model to use to create complementary contrast. We rely on the traditional complementary pairs shown in Figures 6.15 and 6.26, which have proven successful both in fine arts and in visual design.

[10] Chevreul, M. E. *The Laws of Contrast of Colour*, pp. 32–33.

[11] The HSB/HLS Color Model—Color Models—Technical Guides (2000). *Cell Biology and Anatomy—University of South Carolina School of Medicine*. Retrieved Oct. 10, 2012, from *http://dba.med.sc.edu/price/irf/ Adobe_tg/models/hsb.html*.

Defining a rationale for color

Working first without color and images and using plain typography, as shown in the case study in Chapter 4, we can directly see, manipulate, and establish appropriate hierarchy through placement, scale, and light–dark contrast. If we've used patterns from internally or externally related applications, starting with black and white makes it easier to evaluate if the patterns work in harmony with the other elements. We work iteratively with color as we refine all aspects of the interface.

Working with color often starts with a requirement, like a corporate color or set of colors. With a single required color, a palette is defined to complement or contrast with the required color, depending on the application's desired personality. With a set of required colors, roles need to be established so there is a logic for how to use them.

When no color requirements exist, one approach is to select sets of one or more colors that embody the desired application personality, assign each color a role, and try them out, refining the layout as needed. You can also start by selecting a saturated color to be the accent color, the role of which is to draw the eye, and choose other colors to help the accent color do its job. There's no right or wrong way to begin with color, as long as your color decisions are grounded in what you know about the people using the application, and you have knowledge of what color can do and how it works to achieve the meta-principles.

Know your requirements and constraints

An application design may need to address corporate or federal requirements, or cultural or competitor conventions. (Refer to Figure 3.20 to review where you may need to look for requirements that affect color selection.) Questions to ask include:

- Are there existing colors in brand standards or related applications that must be used?
- Are there user characteristics or cultural interpretations that affect color choice?
- How do accessibility standards affect color choice and use in your application?

Know what personality characteristics you want to convey

Color is an essential part of personality. Choose one or two lead colors that communicate the personality you want, and a few shades, tints, or accents to support the lead colors.

- Create a list of attributes the application should convey and think about how color can support them. Feely boards, described on page 90, are a good tool for helping stakeholders identify important design characteristics, including color.

Identify the "star" of the screen

The "star" of the screen is the most important element or elements. In complex applications, there's often more than one star, which means using color and the other tools to draw the eye to the elements, as in the Blogger screens. Use black-and-white layouts, which focus on features and their hierarchy, to identify the star or stars.

- Determine what's essential to the purpose of the screen. Which element needs to be seen first?

- Determine which elements play supporting roles. Your personas are a source for determining sequence and flow.

- Assign a color that fits the requirements to the star element or elements as a starting point, and see how adding color affects the black-and-white layout.

- Analyze the other elements. How much contrast does there need to be between the star and other elements?

- Try variations out on a few rough screens. Experimenting, adjusting, and refining are part of an iterative design process.

Identify additional color needs

To create a useful palette, most interfaces need black, dark gray, or dark blue for text; two or three hues; and tints and shades of those hues. One lead hue should be fairly neutral, or used as a neutral, as it will be the primary color for nontext elements. This is where the question of how much contrast comes in.

- Do you need small accents of a bright, eye-catching color to draw attention to lots of small controls?

- Work with a color template, such as the one in Figure 6.29, and fill in what you know.

- Work with a tool like kuler.adobe.com to see different color combinations based on a key color. Resist the temptation to use a "canned" palette as-is. Canned palettes are good starting points,

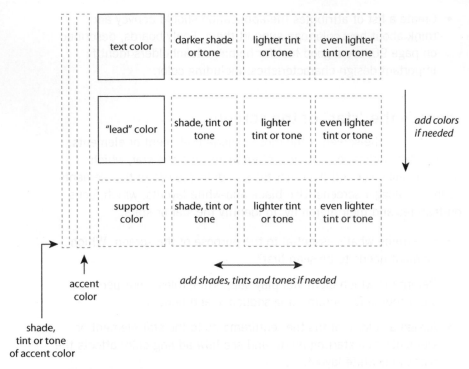

	text color	darker shade or tone	lighter tint or tone	even lighter tint or tone
	"lead" color	shade, tint or tone	lighter tint or tone	even lighter tint or tone
	support color	shade, tint or tone	lighter tint or tone	even lighter tint or tone

add colors if needed

accent color

add shades, tints and tones if needed

shade, tint or tone of accent color

Figure 6.29 Our color palette template. At a minimum, a useful palette needs three colors: a text color, a lead color, and a shade or tint of the lead or text color. Accent colors must work with all colors in the palette, and are only used in small amounts.

but will likely need to be tweaked to apply to a well-thought-out layout, requirements, and rationale.

- Test assumptions. See Chapter 3 for suggested qualitative testing methods.

- Think of the palette as part of the process that will *begin* at launch and need to be refined throughout the life of the application.

The requirements, constraints, and personality characteristics are the "bones" of your color rationale. The rest of the palette grows from there. In this section, we walk through the rationale and decisions for using color in the redesign of SuperTracker.

We chose colors for SuperTracker based on three requirements:

- The need for the application to feel approachable for the users in our personas: Betty, Danny, and Sonia.
- The need to maintain a visual relationship to the MyPlate program.
- Federal accessibility standards.

From the personality standpoint, we needed to choose colors that would help express Pepper—our concept of a smart, technology-savvy assistant—in an encouraging way. We also needed to make the interface appear related to other materials within the USDA's existing MyPlate initiative so that consumers familiar with one would feel comfortable with the other. From a brand perspective, familiarity is a desirable characteristic.

The existing SuperTracker application color-coded daily food totals based on the corresponding colors in the MyPlate palette (Figures 6.30 and 6.31). We thought this was a smart approach, and one that should continue. Used consistently, the color coding relates the application to the parent initiative and serves as a visual cue that helps users decode charts more efficiently.

Tying the application visually to MyPlate initiatives meant either using a color from that palette to play the lead, or choosing a new lead color that would work with the MyPlate palette. Given that there are already five to seven hues in the MyPlate palette, we had limited choices for a hue that would be distinct from the others while playing well with them.

We decided to try a dark blue based on the one used in the existing SuperTracker logo (Figure 6.32). We could see from the existing website how dark blue worked with the MyPlate colors, and could be fairly certain that it would not be objectionable or unexpected for Betty, Danny, and Sonia.

The third requirement for selecting color had to do with accessibility. As a government initiative, the application must adhere to Section 508 standards for accessibility, including use of color. The dark blue would be appropriate for text as long as we maintained enough contrast between the text and the background.

With criteria and a "cast" of colors, we needed to think about what roles our cast members should play, and whether we had more roles to fill.

Fruit Group Red

	CMYK	RGB	HEX
	C: 5 M: 100 Y: 100 K: 30	R: 169 G: 19 B: 23	A91317
	C: 5 M: 100 Y: 100 K: 10	R: 206 G: 27 B: 34	CE1B22
	C: 0 M: 65 Y: 15 K: 0	R: 242 G: 124 B: 156	F27C9C

Protein Group Purple

	CMYK	RGB	HEX
	C: 70 M: 80 Y: 0 K: 40	R: 70 G: 49 B: 110	46316E
	C: 70 M: 80 Y: 0 K: 20	R: 87 G: 65 B: 135	574187
	C: 40 M: 50 Y: 0 K: 0	R: 157 G: 133 B: 190	9D85BE

Vegetable Group Green

	CMYK	RGB	HEX
	C: 90 M: 5 Y: 100 K: 25	R: 0 G: 32 B: 61	00843D
	C: 85 M: 5 Y: 100 K: 0	R: 0 G: 167 B: 76	00A74C
	C: 30 M: 0 Y: 100 K: 0	R: 191 G: 215 B: 48	BFD730

Dairy Group Blue

	CMYK	RGB	HEX
	C: 75 M: 40 Y: 0 K: 20	R: 51 G: 112 B: 167	3370A7
	C: 75 M: 40 Y: 0 K: 0	R: 61 G: 133 B: 198	3D85C6
	C: 50 M: 15 Y: 0 K: 0	R: 120 G: 182 B: 228	78B6E4

Grain Group Orange

	CMYK	RGB	HEX
	C: 0 M: 65 Y: 100 K: 35	R: 171 G: 84 B: 16	AB5410
	C: 0 M: 65 Y: 100 K: 15	R: 211 G: 105 B: 27	D3691B
	C: 10 M: 35 Y: 50 K: 0	R: 227 G: 172 B: 131	E3AC83

Figure 6.30 The MyPlate style guide includes a color palette for food groups.

	CMYK	RGB	HEX
	C: 30 M: 0 Y: 100 K: 0	R: 191 G: 215 B: 48	BFD730
	C: 0 M: 30 Y: 100 K: 0	R: 253 G: 185 B: 19	FDB913
	C: 85 M: 0 Y: 0 K: 0	R: 0 G: 182 B: 241	00B6F1
	C: 0 M: 100 Y: 0 K: 0	R: 236 G: 0 B: 140	EC008C
	C: 0 M: 0 Y: 0 K: 0	R: 255 G: 255 B: 255	FFFFFF

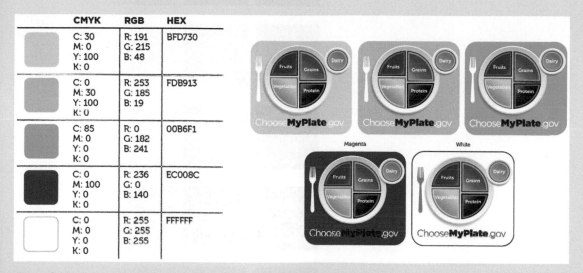

Figure 6.31 Additional palette for accent colors used in the logo's placemats.

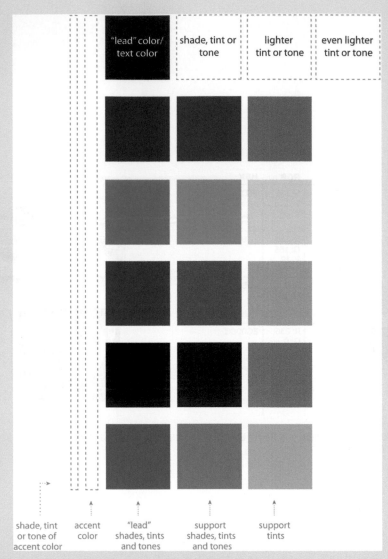

Figure 6.32 Color palette template in progress, filled in with the dark blue from the existing application and the colors from the MyPlate food group palette.

Working with color

We began by trying colors for the logo, because the logo sets the tone for the personality in consumer-facing applications. We took two approaches to color: the first used only blues, similar to the existing logo, and the second incorporated colors from the MyPlate palettes (Figure 6.33).

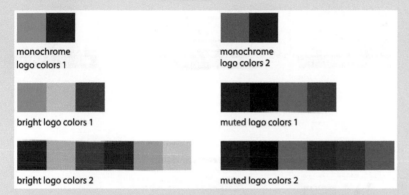

Figure 6.33 Color explorations for the logo included trying monochrome palettes intended to work with colors from the style guide, bright palettes based on the saturated hues of the MyPlate palettes, and less dramatic palettes based on the muted hues of the MyPlate food group palette. We added gray or dark blue to all palettes to have a legible, dark, neutral color for the logotype.

Rather than make a color decision based on the logo sketches and what we imagined Betty, Danny, and Sonia would prefer, we put the color decision aside until we had more data—that is, until we added the logos and palettes to a representative layout. We avoided common color mistakes and made informed decisions by trying color ideas in layouts before making a choice.

We started with the mobile layout. We tried representing our "smart, data-driven assistant" personality, Pepper, with a background image of fresh, green vegetables. Combining the image with the data and one of the logo ideas, we could see this approach wouldn't be successful (Figure 6.34). It didn't look smart and organized, two characteristics we were aiming for. From a color standpoint, having a strong color in the background created too much contrast of hue—there were just

Figure 6.34 First color attempt for the mobile layout. This design showed us that there were too many hues to be able to detect color patterns. We could also see that the logo's bright colors didn't complement the muted colors from the palette.

too many colors—used in ways that made it hard to identify patterns. This experiment made it clear that we needed to use a more neutral background (Figure 6.35).

Adding to the effect of too much color, the sample logo's bright colors weren't pleasant alongside the more muted shades of the palette used in the chart. Even though the muted colors were shades of the bright ones, their relationship was neither apparent nor attractive. Mixing the palette's bright and muted hues didn't work in the layout, and we were

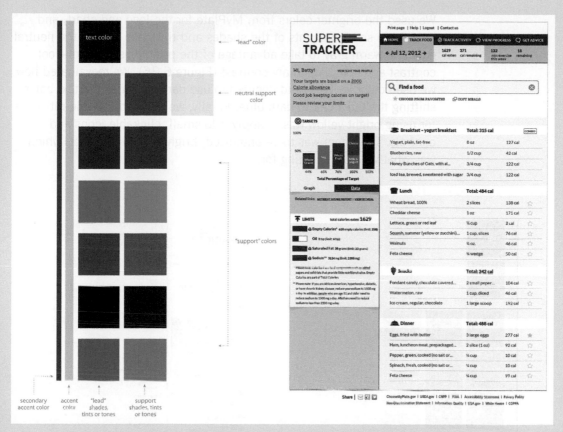

Figure 6.35 For the second round, we added a neutral gray to help define the structure of the layout. We used the muted colors from the palette for this version of the logo and the graph. While much more legible compared to the previous round, the overall effect was drab.

fairly certain that the issues we saw in the mobile sketch would carry over to the web and tablet versions as well.

To increase our understanding of the breadth of what we were designing, we switched from applying color to the mobile layout to the web layout. We reviewed the characteristics we were looking for, and began with a solid, pale, muted background to make the food log as legible as possible while adding elements and attributes conveying personality.

We used the brighter colors from MyPlate for the logo and chart, and brought in small amounts of the shades and tints. We shifted the neutral gray to a warm gray to take advantage of the principles of warm–cool contrast and complementary contrast (Figure 6.36). We reevaluated how we used color for type, and decided to use dark brown as the text color, shifting the link color to dark blue. Finally, we decided that the rationale for using bright yellow was to apply it to small, clickable icons and controls. The effect was more organized, brighter, and snappier, which was what we were shooting for.

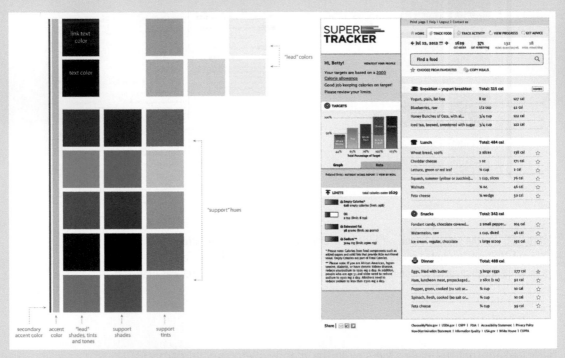

Figure 6.36 We shifted the neutral gray to a warm gray to brighten the design, lightened the pale blue, and added small amounts of the brighter food group palette colors to the logo and graph.

Color and the meta-principles
Consistency

Color is applied consistently in each version of the redesign, with the exception of the "Find a food" area (Figure 6.37). The change in color is due to different layouts and screen sizes.

Color decisions need to be documented to answer questions about color that might arise throughout the life of the application. Include the hexadecimal or RGB color codes for your color palette, and mark up a sample layout to show where each color is used. Documenting your rationale informs people about why decisions were made, which can help when changes arise.

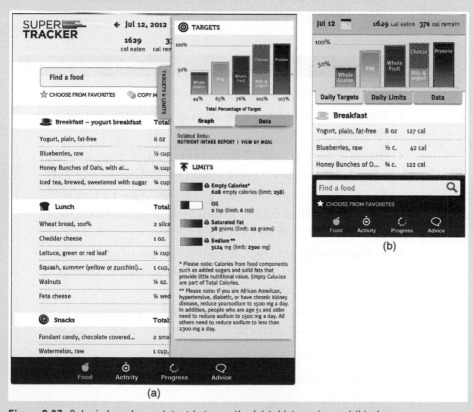

Figure 6.37 Color is largely consistent between the (a) tablet version and (b) phone version.

Here's an example of how our rationale for color decisions could be documented:

Goals for color

- The color palette for the redesigned SuperTracker ties the application to existing MyPlate initiatives.
- Color use and coding of food groups are consistent across MyPlate communications.
- The color palette supports a professional layout with bright accents that enhance the meaning of the content, add personality, and draw the eye appropriately to functionality.
- Application of colors as intended is in accordance with accessibility guidelines.

Use of color

- Dark blue is used as the link text color.
- Tints of the dark blue define areas of the screen and are used for rules.
- Brown is the text color. Tints of brown define areas of the screen and are used for less important text.
- The hues of the MyPlate food groups are used for charts and the logo, in accordance with their assigned food group documented in the MyPlate style guide.
- Yellow is an accent color. Accent colors are used in small quantities to draw the eye to clickable elements, such as controls and clickable icons.
- Bright red is the secondary accent color. It is necessary to call attention to small, important elements that are not clickable.

Maintaining consistency

As the SuperTracker example shows, defining a palette is an iterative process. If an element needs to be added, and none of the existing colors or rules applies, the palette will need to continue to evolve.

Palettes and rules are thought of as final when documented in a style guide. While every attempt is made to define colors and rules in advance, the reality is that applications evolve, and the point of the palette, rules, and style guide is to guide evolution intentionally and appropriately. If the style guide is viewed as final but doesn't address a new element or situation, it can be mistakenly deemed out-of-date and disregarded. Style guides that include a rationale are the starting point for making changes. They are living documents with rules and guidelines that are updated and maintained.

Hierarchy

Color supports the hierarchy decisions made in layout and helps define sections of the SuperTracker interface on all platforms. A visible structure is necessary to organize the different types of information and keep screens looking approachable.

For example, the lack of tinting—literal white space—draws the eye to the "Find a food" area at the top of the web and tablet versions. Also, the chart's bright colors, combined with its position at the top of the phone version, make the charts more prominent there than on the tablet and web. We felt this position and treatment supported the scenario of seeing where you stand at a glance while on the go, but only testing would show whether our assumptions were correct, or whether the charts should be revealed on demand instead.

Personality

The use of blue and brown for text and to delineate the structure of the screens provides a businesslike tone that underpins the design. This supports conveying the personality of a super-smart, organized assistant with the latest data at his or her fingertips. Blue and brown are neutral, and don't sway the design as female or male. Using bright hues with tints and shades provides a spark of contrast that keeps the interface feeling peppy, while limiting the use of the hues keeps it from feeling domineering.

Avoid common mistakes

Not enough contrast

Lack of contrast affects two main aspects of application design: legibility of type and lack of hierarchy. Color should be used to make it easy to read any and all text on the screen. Check legibility and contrast of text colors and background colors with Vischeck (*http://www.vischeck.com*) or other color accessibility tools.

Hierarchy isn't created or communicated with color alone; however, color plays a strong role in drawing the eye and directing it. Squinting at or zooming out of an interface layout during design and testing it to find out if people know where to go and what to do help you know if you have enough contrast.

Questions to consider:

- Have your colors passed accessibility tests?
- Have you used color to draw the eye to the most important elements or areas first?
- Do user tests indicate any areas of confusion that might be addressed by increasing color contrast?

Too much contrast

If an interface has too much contrast, people will have a hard time settling their eyes on important areas and elements; such interfaces can also "vibrate." This results from using color too similarly in too many places, as well as colors that clash and distract from the content. There should be just enough contrast to indicate differences unless color is being used to make a personality statement in which distraction or strong visual impact is the goal.

- Does your design have places for the eye to rest?
- Do user tests indicate any areas of confusion that might be addressed by decreasing color contrast?

Too many colors

Using too many different hues may create too much contrast, and make it hard for users to know where to look. There are many successful designs that use a lot of hues, however, because the hues are applied in a clearly systematic way.

- If you have more than three hues, are your rules for how to apply the colors simple and clear?
- Does the use of many hues add to the meaning of your content?

Not enough color

Using only one color without using tints, tones, or shades is unlikely to make an application appealing or memorable. In general, the rule of thumb is to use at least one color in addition to a text color, and at least one tint, tone, or shade of the text or supporting colors. Exceptions to this rule apply if part of the personality is conveyed through use of a one- or two-color palette.

- Do you have one color in addition to a text color, plus at least a tint, tone, or shade of the text or supporting color?

Use of color as the only means of differentiation

Relying only on color to differentiate will not help color-blind or visually impaired users. If color is indicating a difference, make sure that difference is discernible to color-blind/visually impaired users by checking it with an accessibility tool. Always provide an additional cue if your use of color does not pass the test.

- Have you checked your design with an accessibility tool?
- If color is the only way some items can be distinguished, how can you integrate other visual treatments, such as type weight or style, to help color-blind and visually impaired users interact with your application?

Color applied randomly, not systematically

Color is an excellent tool for helping people notice things. If it's applied randomly—without thought to if or how it is drawing the eye—it can mislead, as users unsuccessfully or incorrectly assign meaning to a random use of color.

- Do you have a rationale for how color is used?
- Is your rationale in keeping with the characteristics of contrast and people's natural tendency to look for patterns?
- Are rules based on your rationale applied consistently throughout the application?

Make informed decisions

Making informed decisions with color has to do with understanding, anticipating, and planning. Understanding comes from knowing how your users interpret certain colors and color combinations. Test designs with representative users to determine whether your color choices and rationale are sound. Ask questions that get at how participants interpret color in your application. Find out if the relationships you're representing with color come across to participants and help them identify the important elements onscreen.

Anticipating means looking ahead to business factors that may affect content and features. It also applies to checking color use for contrast during the design process so that you know if users will be able to see your text.

Finally, planning involves including anticipated changes in the design process; for example, if color coding, selecting more colors than you think you need so that you're ready to add sections, products, or categories.

- Do you know how user groups interpret your color choices and use?
- Are there changes you can anticipate that might affect the use of color in your application?
- Do you have a plan for dealing with likely changes?
- Have you tested color use with a color-checking tool (we can't emphasize this enough!) to be sure your choices are legible?

Elevate the ordinary

Thoughtful use of color can help differentiate your application from competitors, as it does for the Solar application shown in Figure 6.38 in the crowded weather application marketplace.

Recall Mullet and Sano's framework for principles of style, discussed in Chapter 3:

- Distinctiveness
- Integrity
- Comprehensiveness
- Appropriateness

Figure 6.38 The Solar iOS weather application relies on color to help communicate temperature.

Distinctiveness needs to go hand in hand with appropriateness and integrity. We could have differentiated our redesigned SuperTracker from its competitors with a less conservative approach to color, but we felt that it was more important for this particular application to have wide appeal. Using color appropriately is one way for an interface design to demonstrate integrity.

Questions to ask to address color and style include:

- Does your color palette help your application stand out from competitive or similar applications?
- Are you using color to help people and not just to attract attention?
- Do you have enough colors, hues, and shades to address the range that color needs to communicate?
- Do your colors and your use of them help connect people to related experiences in digital, print, and the physical world?
- Do your colors and your use of them help express the desired personality characteristics in a way that your audience understands?

Imagery

People expect to see different types of imagery depending on the type of application they're using. In an analytics application, people expect to see tables and charts. When walking around looking for businesses nearby, people expect a map and hope to see photos that help them recognize their surroundings. When evaluating applications to install, people expect to see screenshots that provide a sense of using the application.

Imagery is a great tool for answering questions, such as what something looks like. Appropriate images also communicate softer messages, such as helping someone feel more engaged or decide whether an application is right for them. Use of imagery is a great opportunity to elevate the ordinary and delight people with expression that supports an application's content.

Images are not just icing on a cake, however. They add information, such as the way an author's comment avatar expresses something about the author himself, and are integral to using, getting information from, and enjoying applications.

Applications use many kinds of imagery: photos, illustrations, charts, icons, animation, video, maps, screenshots, infographics, logos, and patterns. Imagery is a type of content, except when used as a pattern or texture. It communicates information, not just something *about* the information (Figures 7.1 and 7.2).

In consumer applications, imagery is essential to appeal, communication, and use (Figure 7.3). The question is not whether to use imagery, but rather what kinds to use, and how. In business or technical applications, the range of appropriate image types can be limited. A logo, icons, charts, and patterns may be all there is to work with. Avoiding common mistakes and making informed decisions can help business and technical applications communicate data *and* qualities of the brand. Icons and styled controls can help

Figure 7.1 Applications can combine multiple types of imagery. Converse's Design Your Own application combines product photos, illustrated controls, live previews, animation, patterns, and textures to help people use the application and feel inspired to make a purchase. The casual, sketchy style conveys the brand's personality.

make navigation and function clear while expressing personality that differentiates your application from competitors.

As with the other visual usability tools, using imagery successfully requires knowing what people expect, and providing it in a way that makes sense and appeals to them. Understanding what roles images can play, and knowing about different types of imagery and their characteristics, allows you to make informed choices and decisions about your design.

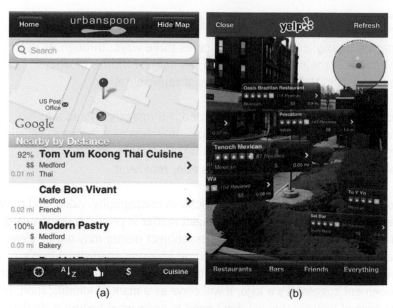

(a)   (b)

Figure 7.2 (a) Urbanspoon's restaurant locator combines your location on a map with a list of nearby restaurants; it's efficient, but provides only an abstract sense of place. Yelp offers a similar locator tool, but provides quick access to Monocle (b), which uses augmented reality to virtually overlay restaurant names, ratings, and directions on an image of your current location.

Figure 7.3 Trefis' interactive stock-trading charts use animation and a unique diagram style to convey information and differentiate the application from competitors.

Communicating with images

Imagery in applications communicates three ways: through its use, or its *role* in the interface; through the *subject matter* of what's depicted; and through the *qualities* of representation.

Role is the reason imagery is included. All imagery should support communication by drawing attention, providing explanations, showing detail, expressing personality, inviting interaction, or reinforcing patterns. If imagery doesn't have a role, remove it.

Subject matter is what imagery depicts. In photography, video, and maps used in functional applications, subject matter is pretty straightforward. In expressive logos or textural images, subject matter may not be clear, leaving people to rely on role to interpret imagery: an abstract logo's meaning may be ambiguous, but if the image's characteristics, size, and placement suggest it's a logo, it will serve as a mark of identification. In the case of textures, people don't need to know what texture is depicted, as long as it subtly communicates a desired quality.

An image's *qualities* need not be noticeable for it to be successful. For example, if an e-commerce website's product photos are sharp, consistently well lit, and treated with the same background, they'll work effectively. Imagery that's blurry, inconsistent, poorly lit, or too prominent for the subject matter is distracting, and compromises sending effective messages.

When deciding whether to use imagery, the key question is, "What do we want to convey?" Decisions about imagery, like those about layout, type, and color, need to be grounded in overall communication goals, benefits to the user, and personas or contexts of use. Matching goals to types of imagery that achieve your objectives gives the images a role to play in the interface.

Drawing attention

Images draw the eye for a variety of reasons. One is speed of understanding: we quickly derive meaning from images if what they show is easily recognizable. We're also drawn by contrast, and images often contrast with other elements, such as text. Novelty appeals to us for similar reasons: we're attracted to images we haven't seen before.

Figure 7.4 These whimsical messages on Converse's Design Your Own application take advantage of familiar symbols, novelty of execution, and animation, which draw the eye in a fun way that also expresses the brand style.

Finally, when combined with motion, imagery attracts us even if we're not interested in the subject matter. Humans are "wired" to look at moving elements in our field of vision.

Providing explanations and showing detail

Images are great for presenting examples and details. Illustrations of processes, functions, or individual items; photos of products, people, or places; and charts of data or diagrams help make information clear (Figure 7.5).

Representing content

In some applications, charts, photos, video, animations, and so on *are* the content, raising questions about subject matter and qualities. You need to decide what type of imagery best communicates your messages, as well as what size, position, spacing, alignment, and overall layout support those messages (Figure 7.6).

Keep in mind that each type of imagery is a subspecialty of its own, and after evaluating which to use, you may need a professional to

Figure 7.5 The title of a recipe tells you what it is, but the photo of the finished dish, and icons that show at a glance if people like the recipe, give you a better sense of whether you'd like to make it.

(a)   (b)

Figure 7.6 (a) Photography on Kiva versus (b) video on Kickstarter is an example of making decisions about image types. Size and presentation are similar: the photo augments the text content, and the video provides content not available otherwise. If Kiva presented its funding cases with video, would they be even more successful?

create the imagery. In many cases, such as a product demo video or a data visualization, this specialist will be part of the decision about what to represent, and will know how best to use the medium to communicate the message.

Expressing feeling, brand, or style

Expressive qualities help us care about and enjoy what we see. Personal, emotional associations help us feel connected and engage us.

In the examples in Figures 7.7, 7.8, and 7.9, the "soft" information the images communicate is both strategic—it helps the applications differentiate themselves—and tactical—each presents a unique

Figure 7.7 This illustration in the Clothia browser application is purely expressive, yet strategic as well. It represents qualities of the brand—new, unique, fashionable, creative, exclusive—and serves to attract users who find it appealing. The illustration doesn't try to attract everyone.

Figure 7.8 MailChimp's cheerful mascot looks fun, but is working hard. The illustration helps make the job of creating email campaigns feel lighthearted rather than dull.

(a) (b) (c)

Figure 7.9 Each of these photo application logos expresses a different personality, and tells us something about the applications they represent. (a) SmugMug is simple and fun for anyone. (b) Flickr is too cool for an "e"—if you don't get it, it's not for you. (c) Instagram is nostalgic, both in terms of the images it helps create and its focus on sharing.

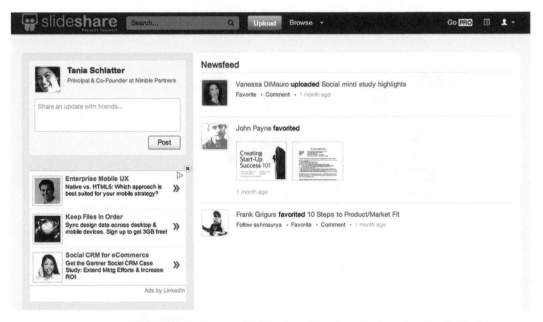

Figure 7.10 Avatars identify friends in Slideshare. Seeing what friends like takes advantage of our desire to feel connected and makes people more likely to pay attention and possibly click.

visual image and suggests different emotional associations. These associations help people know if the application is right for them.

Inviting interaction

Any image's subject matter can provoke an emotional response. Once people are emotionally engaged, they're more receptive to persuasive messages that involve taking action (Figure 7.10).

Figure 7.11 Decisions about what style of control to use should be conscious and based on visual prominence and personality. Converse's website uses image textures to create expressive, highly stylized navigation buttons. This unusual approach looks usable enough in context and helps communicate brand attributes—casual, hip, not bound by convention. The trade-off of potentially compromised usability is part of making a strategic decision. Based on the audience for the website, it's one that almost certainly paid off.

Images may also be incorporated in controls, such as buttons and form elements that people interact with to perform tasks. (We discuss controls in more detail in Chapter 8.) The visual treatment of images as controls influences whether a control feels interactive, and communicates qualities of the brand (Figure 7.11).

Reinforcing similarities and differences

Use of imagery helps people detect patterns and make associations by revealing similarities. As with color, treating images consistently indicates they refer to the same type of things.

At the same time, inconsistent image use or treatment can help people see why something is different. In the project summaries in Figure 7.12, the similar shapes of the "New" and "Staff pick" flags indicate their information is related, but their unique colors and icons indicate a difference. If each flag were the same shape and color, changing the small icon alone would make it hard to determine the difference between the flags.

Figure 7.12 Although each project on Catapult.org has a different photo and set of icons, their similar treatment and placement indicates they're related types of information. This consistent use of images helps people group and understand what they see.

Types of imagery and uses

Knowing the range of image types, their characteristics, their typical uses, and dos and don'ts will help you make decisions about choosing appropriate imagery.

Photography

Primary characteristics

Realism. Photography provides detail depending on the subject matter and qualities of the photo. Everything shown in a photo communicates, so it's important that what's depicted (e.g., the background) is intentional. Qualities such as cropping and lighting can affect meaning and interpretation of the subject matter. Photography is the best choice if the details of a real thing matter (Figure 7.13).

Figure 7.13 At first glance, these two product photos look similar. (a) The mixer photo on the Target website doesn't have a drop shadow or show anything other than what comes with the product. (b) The waffle iron photo on the Walmart website adds a shadow and food. It shows less of the product, and adds context. As a rule of thumb, show the product as clearly as possible, without editorial embellishments, unless you know that users expect and want a different approach.

When to use it

- Anytime realism matters.
- Anytime people are considering visiting a place, such as choosing a vacation condo rental or planning a trip to a museum.
- Anytime people are considering a purchase, whether a T-shirt or a streaming movie.
- If people are researching personal services, such as choosing a doctor or a hairdresser.

Details

- Size affects impact. Photos that show detail but are too small are frustrating. Photos that are too large may distract from the content.
- Color treatment (natural or manipulated). Using a duotone effect may undermine realism, or may add an expressive quality. Interpretation of an effect depends on what people expect; that is, whether they're relying on the photo to provide absolute detail, or just the gist of something.
- Lighting has a huge effect on mood and tone. Consider the lighting in your images, and if it's supporting the application's purpose and goals.
- Posed stock photos of people that don't look realistic should be avoided.
- Settings can be just as expressive as subject matter. Martha Stewart differentiates her recipes and crafts through photography that communicates the qualities of her brand. The photos—not just their subject matter—look special because every visible aspect in the frame helps set the mood.
- The shape of a photo adds to how it communicates. Photos in a circle feel informal (and can be a pain to auto-generate). Shape can also be a tool for grouping image types; iTunes uses squares for music, rectangles for movies, and rounded-cornered rectangles for promotional graphics.
- The minimum required image resolution changes from platform to platform, and changes further when considering standard-resolution displays versus high-resolution ones, such as Apple's Retina displays. Keeping two copies of images—one high-resolution version

and one regular one—to serve based on different device types is one common solution until there's convergence on a new display resolution standard.

- Studies show that generic images on informational websites don't attract the eye.[1] One of these studies also found that on a website with investment information, photos of people looking at the camera didn't create an impression of trust.[2] Even though both websites tested were informational rather than functional, these studies suggest that photography isn't useful unless it's specific in its subject matter and directly related to text content.

Video

Primary characteristics

Motion and realism. Video can help people understand complex processes, situations, and concepts more quickly than text descriptions and still images (Figure 7.14). Video can bridge distances, such as watching a video of someone presenting at a conference versus seeing slides of the presentation. Video's capability for sound makes it a powerful tool for communicating aurally as well; a video's content and sound quality communicate as much as what's shown.

When to use it

- When explaining a process.
- When describing details better revealed through motion; for example, Zappo's provides videos that show how shoes look while someone is walking.

[1] Ruel, L., and Paul, N. (2007, Mar. 13). Eyetracking Points the Way to Effective News Article Design. Online Journalism Review | Knight Digital Media Center. Retrieved Oct. 26, 2012, from *http://www.ojr.org/ojr/stories/070312ruel/*; Tullis, T., Siegel, M., and Sun, E. (2009). Are People Drawn to Faces on Webpages? Paper presented at the Proceedings of the 27th International Conference on Human Factors in Computing Systems, Extended Abstracts, Boston, MA.
[2] Tullis, T., Siegel, M., and Sun, E. (2009). Are People Drawn to Faces on Webpages? Paper presented at the Proceedings of the 27th International Conference on Human Factors in Computing Systems, Extended Abstracts, Boston, MA.

Figure 7.14 Cooking application Hello, Cupcake! uses video to demonstrate cupcake construction and decoration techniques.

Details

- Bigger isn't necessarily better. Video can add to understanding even when shown at a relatively small size, as it helps people get the gist of a process with more clarity than a still image.

- Quality matters. If you have an application for professional use, amateur-quality video may do more harm than good.

Illustration

Primary characteristics

Abstraction, exaggeration, simplification, imagination. Illustration can show things that are known but hard to see, such as scientific behaviors. It's a primary tool for describing ideas and concepts, and is a great tool for persuasion.

When to use it

- When showing concepts or things that are real, an abstraction helps communicate clearly. For example, illustrations of processes we can't easily see, like photosynthesis, or the systems of the body.
- When showing ideas, such as new product concepts.
- When expressing intangible qualities, such as the Clothia illustration (see Figure 7.7).
- When exaggeration helps communicate, such as evoking a mood that a photo or video can't capture.

Details

- Illustration is expressive by nature. Selecting a style that appropriately represents what you want to your audience is crucial.
- As an expressive medium, illustration styles go in and out of fashion. Think about the lifespan of your illustration in advance, and select a style with lifespan and trends in mind.

Animation
Primary characteristics

There are two types of animation relevant for application imagery. One presents content and uses abstraction and motion to communicate details and personality. The other involves motion of interface elements onscreen to reveal information, provide feedback, and reinforce relationships, and is discussed in Chapter 8.

When to use it

- When reviewing concepts where the gist of a message is more important than specific details, such as the animations in the Structures application in Figure 7.15.

Figure 7.15 The Structures application uses illustration and animation to explain principles visually.

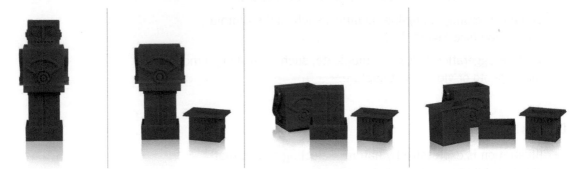

Figure 7.16 An animated GIF on thinkgeek.com shows how the "Robocup" measuring cups come apart. Without the images, buyers wouldn't know how the robot could also be measuring cups. Four still images could do the job, but seeing them animated is both fun and in keeping with ThinkGeek's brand and personality.

- When communicating with diverse cultures where clarity and understanding are important, but details might distract or not translate.

- When personality is important, and motion adds to conveying personality effectively.

- When an alternate communication style is needed—for example, if a still image won't adequately show details, or when novelty is needed to grab attention, such as in Figure 7.16.

Details

- There are many styles of animation: cartoon, claymation, 3D renderings, etc. Selecting the style that expresses what you want to your audience and fits your personality is crucial.

- Because of its expressive nature, styles of animation go in and out of fashion. Think about the lifespan of your animation in advance, and select a style with lifespan and trends in mind.

- Careful use of animation can make interactions feel clear and special. Gratuitous use of animation feels gimmicky. Positive answers to these questions should help you decide if animation is a good choice:
  - Would adding animation help people understand the concept you want to explain?
  - Would adding animation convey personality in a nondistracting way?
  - Would the animation load instantly?
  - Would the animation be appreciated on the third or fourth viewing? What about the tenth viewing?

Logos

Primary characteristics

Logos are often abstract, and communicate symbolically as "flags" for an organization or product. They need to be memorable, and must work at very small and very large sizes (Figures 7.17 and 7.18).

When to use them

- On a product. Every product needs a logo (also known as a *mark*) that identifies the product in a simple, expressive, notable way.

- To represent a product. When shopping for applications, icons are a key part of communicating the essence of the application. They also need to stand out on a crowded mobile device screen.

- On a branded service. Applications blur the line between product and service. Both need logos to help people identify them.

- When a product or service is part of a parent organization, consider using the parent organization's logo. Ask yourself whether the parent logo adds meaning through association, as well as whether it's distracting or confusing.

Details

- The term *logo* is commonly used to refer to a symbol that represents a product, service, or organization; a name set in a typeface that refers to a product, service, or organization;

Figure 7.17 The Amazon.com logo can be abbreviated, augmented, and abstracted without losing meaning or the successful ability to refer to the company it represents.

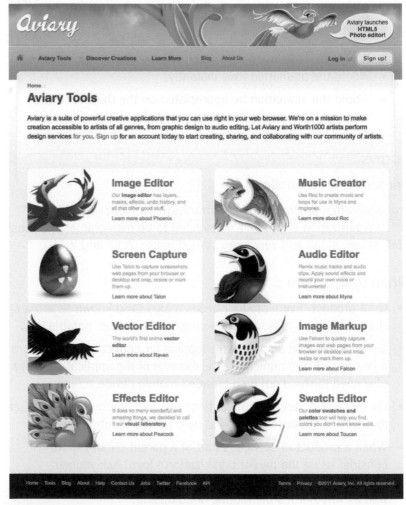

Figure 7.18 Aviary's applications each have an illustrated logo. The logos are unique and attractive, and can be combined with the parent logotype. However, they are also visually complex, which can be distracting in an interface and make it hard to reduce them to a small area. While each logo is clearly part of a family, the individual logos don't relate to their products in an obvious way. As such, it is hard to know at a glance which logo goes with which product.

or both. However, the correct term for a logo that only uses type (no symbol) is *logotype.*

- Logos can include letters and words.
- A logo is *not* a brand. It's a symbol that communicates something about a brand.
- Logos should suggest an idea, feeling, principle, or description related to the product, service, or organization they represent.
- Like illustrations and animations, logos are expressive and communicate style. Logos should be designed for a minimum of five years of use, and ideally the lifetime of the product or service. As such, logos need to be designed to avoid trendiness. The expressive qualities of a logo should be classic, utilizing symmetry, a highly organized arrangement, and clean (simple) forms.
- Logos that lend themselves to a variety of uses are flexible and more likely to serve for a long time.

Icons

Primary characteristics

Simplicity, abstraction. An icon is a simplified picture of a thing. It needs to look enough like what it represents to be understandable and to be used in place of a word or more detailed image.

When to use them

- When you can represent something with a simple picture in place of words, and you want to add variety for visual interest.
- When standards call for an icon, such as an application store or start screen.

Details

- Icons can be a single color or multicolored.
- Icons are simplified pictures. Defining features may be exaggerated to help the icons communicate what they are.
- To be successful, icons need to communicate clearly to their audience. If an icon's meaning could be ambiguous, use a word alongside it.

- Designing an icon to represent an application is very different from designing icons that appear within applications to represent tasks and concepts. Application icons should be memorable and unique; icons for use within applications should be familiar and obvious. Before designing an application icon, be sure to check device standards.

- Icons used in applications are typically created in sets or families. An icon set is two or more icons used to communicate the same type of information, such as actions a user can take, or categories of information.

- Icons in a set need similar styles. For example, if one icon uses shading or curved corners, all others in that set should be treated the same way (Figure 7.19).

- Different icon sets in a single application can have different styling, but should have something in common so they look related.

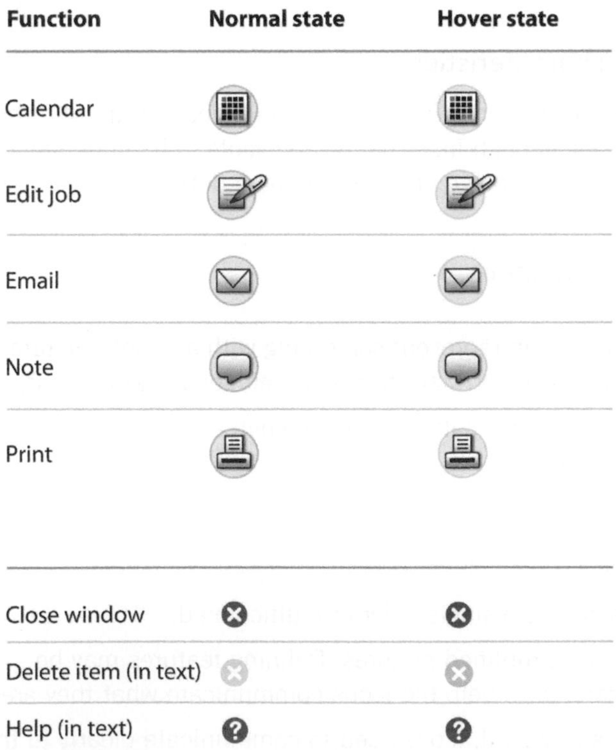

Function	Normal state	Hover state
Calendar		
Edit job		
Email		
Note		
Print		
Close window		
Delete item (in text)		
Help (in text)		

Figure 7.19 Two sets of icons from the same application use different styles but have color and shape in common.

Symbols

Primary characteristics

A symbol stands for an object, action, or idea, but unlike icons, symbols don't need to *look* like what they represent. For example, flags are symbols for countries, and arrows and shapes can be symbols with contextual meanings, such as a hexagon representing "stop" and a triangle representing "yield." Letters of the alphabet and numbers are symbols.

When to use them

- When you want to communicate something universally understood by your audience (Figure 7.20).
- When common symbols exist for the concept you want to represent—for example, a triangle in a circle is frequently used to start playing a video.

Details

- The meaning of a symbol can be different depending on context and use. A five-pointed star is our symbol for large balls of plasma in space, but used next to an item in a list, a star can indicate preference or importance.

(a) (b) (c)

Figure 7.20 In America, a red cross is the symbol for the American Red Cross disaster relief agency. In Europe, a green cross is the symbol for a pharmacy, such as this pharmacy sign in Spain.[3]

[3] NOLA Red Cross photo (*http://flic.kr/p/x2QrE*) is © 2006 by Elaine Vigneault and made available under an Attribution 2.0 Generic (CC BY 2.0) license. Pharmacy Sign photo (*http://flic.kr/p/6gRBdn*) is © 2009 Andres Rueda and made available under an Attribution 2.0 Generic (CC BY 2.0) license.

- The meaning of symbols is assigned by the cultures of the people who use them. As such, meanings can change; they aren't fixed.
- Symbols work best when they communicate a single idea. Avoid combining symbols to create new meanings, unless you're intentionally defining a new visual language that people will expect to learn.
- Color can affect the meaning and interpretation of a symbol, such as a red cross versus a green cross.

Data visualizations

Primary characteristics

Data visualizations can be dynamic—connected to databases and updated automatically—or static. Data is commonly represented in the form of charts and graphs to reveal patterns and show status. Words, numbers, symbols, shapes, lines, color, layout, and sometimes photographs combine to help people make sense of abstract representations of transactions, occurrences, or behaviors (Figure 7.21).

To design successful visualizations, you need to understand the data and its significance. Then you can decide what form it should take to express the meaning, and apply visual usability principles to help people make sense of it.

Specialists analyze data and design representations to communicate meaning. While successful data visualizations can be designed using visual usability principles and standard graphing software, some data visualizations are projects and applications in themselves, created by teams of specialists using custom software.

When to use

- When you have factual or quantitative data that can be represented visually to enhance understanding.
- When comparing multiple sets of data to quickly understand their differences.

Details

- Using standard forms of data visualizations, such as bar charts, pie charts, and line graphs, means that people will not have to decipher unfamiliar formats.

Figure 7.21 The variety of data presentation types—bar charts, tables, flags, and maps—makes this MailChimp email report look engaging. The familiarity of the chart types and amount of white space makes the report look approachable, while limited use of color helps blue and red accents pop out.

- Representations of data in less well-known or unfamiliar formats may use a unique or unexpected visual language people will need to learn to read (Figure 7.22).

- Different forms show different things. Select the type of chart or graph that fits the data and purpose. Know what you need to show—for example, relationships, parts of a whole, change over time, or hierarchy—and select a format that fits.

- Design charts and graphs to have some visual characteristics in common with the visual style of your application. You'll need to

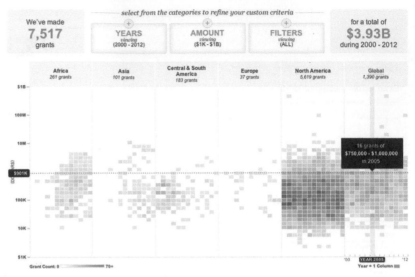

Figure 7.22 People may need a minute to figure out how to use and read this custom interactive chart on the William and Flora Hewlett Foundation website that combines bubble plot, heat matrix, and timeline formats. Once they get it, the controls are easy to use and remember, and the display of information is clear.

decide how much you want them to match or stand out, and select and manipulate the tools accordingly for appropriate contrast.

- Each element in a chart or graph should add to its meaning and aid interpretation. Eliminate all unnecessary elements. This may mean eliminating "standard" elements, such as rules (lines) that fall behind a graph but don't help people see the trend.

- The principles of layout, color, and type apply to the design of charts and graphs: align content and text consistently; depending on desired visual emphasis, use colors that contrast or blend with the rest of the colors in your application; and use the same fonts as the rest of the application unless there's a good reason for contrast (Figure 7.23).

- Colors should be used in charts and graphs to:

  - Convey meaning—be especially conscious of the use of red and green, as they imply quality of performance.

  - Differentiate content types—pie chart colors should be unique, but don't add colors just for the sake of it. If there's no cognitive reason to differentiate with color, don't.

  - Highlight meaningful areas that people should notice.

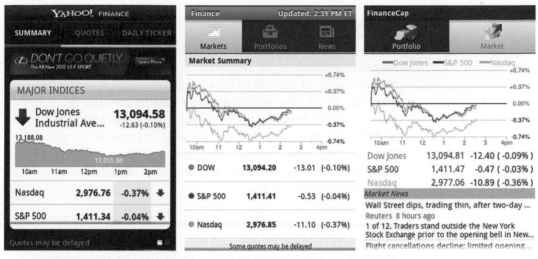

Figure 7.23 These three finance applications communicate the same information. (a) Yahoo! Finance is clear, but generic. The arrow indicator is unnecessary, considering the use of color and plus/minus symbols to indicate status, nor does it need the "Major Indices" header. (b) Google Finance uses Google's primary color palette to identify the three markets. Bringing in parent brand colors enhances the information and helps us know this is a Google application. The three colors in the chart give a clear picture of overall status, and icons for the sections of the application are subtly treated so as not to distract from the data. (c) FinanceCap's chart uses the same colors as Google, but the unnecessary key, large type, and tight spacing make it harder to read, and the colorful icons draw the eye away from the data.

- Continue to convey appropriate personality—don't throw your palette out the window when choosing colors for charts and graphs. The colors you use to convey information and data must be part of the overall application palette. If applicable, they can be stronger (more saturated) versions of colors in your palette, but they shouldn't clash.

- Be wary of visual metaphors and using illustrations in chart and graph design. Using a tachometer-style chart isn't good design unless you're designing data that has to do with speed or rotations per minute.

- Don't use gradations or other treatments when a solid color or plain treatment would convey the same meaning.

- Don't use three-dimensional graphics when two-dimensional ones will do. Keep the visual focus on the data.

- Design dynamic charts and graphs based on a representative amount and type of data to make sure styles work with live data.

- Using a variety of graphs and charts helps keep the presentation of the data interesting, as long as the forms are also effective.

Infographics

Information graphics, or *infographics,* are illustrations that may also include aspects of data visualizations and interactive graphics. When infographics are pure illustration, they're static graphics designed based on someone's interpretation of data, and often include limited content to provide context (Figure 7.24). More complex infographics incorporate dynamic visualizations based on a data set, and may include motion or interactivity (Figure 7.25).

Because infographics are a form of illustration, those same characteristics, tips for use, and details apply to them. However, when introducing motion or interactivity, the tips for interactive graphics apply as well.

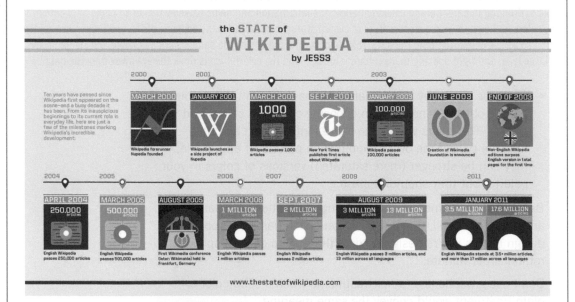

Figure 7.24 The State of Wikipedia is a static infographic outlining Wikipedia's growth and important milestones between 2000 and 2011.[4]

[4] State of Wikipedia image is © 2011 JESS3 and made available under a Creative Commons Attribution-ShareAlike license.

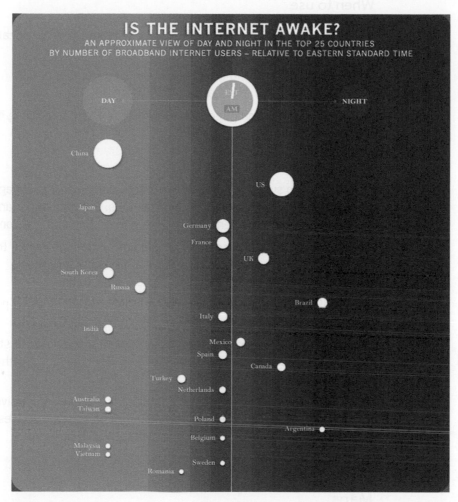

Figure 7.25 Artist Bård Edlund uses motion and simple shapes to demonstrate how worldwide Internet usage changes over the course of a day. As the clock in the center ticks forward, circles representing each country shift back and forth between day and night.

Interactive graphics

Primary characteristics

Interactive graphics can be applications on their own or be embedded within applications. They may contain multiple forms of images, such as photography, video, and illustration, and need to incorporate principles of successful image design as well as design and presentation of appropriate controls.

When to use

- When configuring something, like the custom Converse sneakers (see Figure 7.1).
- In teaching tools and educational games, where input and feedback are key to engagement.
- In demos and simulations, to allow people to try something out.

Details

- The trick to successful interactive graphics is balancing engaging content with necessary interaction controls. Both are important, but visually complex content can make it hard to find and use controls.
- Use standard, styled controls in interactive graphics, since the graphic itself is likely to be unfamiliar to users, and seeing familiar controls will help people know what to do.
- Highly visual feedback is crucial in interactive graphics. If people don't see feedback, they assume the graphic isn't working.
- Some interactive graphic interfaces present a sequence of steps, which can be a good way to help people navigate and use the graphic.
- The ability to return to the default state is crucial. Interactive graphics are an opportunity to manipulate things and see results. Users must be able to easily clear what they've done and try again.

Maps

Primary characteristics

Maps based on data represent real places. They can be abstract or realistic, or a combination of both. They rely on illustration, photography, text, and other symbols to communicate (Figure 7.26).

When to use

- When people need to make their way to a destination or visualize how locations relate to one another.
- When providing a visual reference for a location would add meaning, recognition, or context.

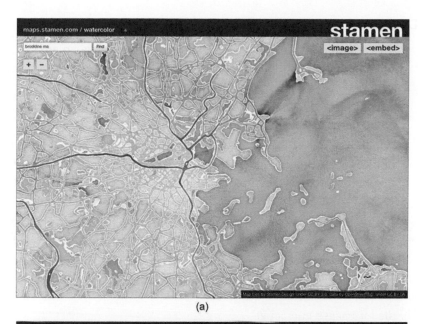

(a)

(b)

Figure 7.26 These maps use texture and contrast to push and play with what's expected and necessary to communicate geographic data successfully. Considering role, subject matter, qualities, and context of use will help you determine if unexpected images or treatments are appropriate for your application and users.[5]

[5] Map tiles by Stamen Design, under CC BY 3.0. Data by OpenStreetMap, under CC BY SA.

Details

- The design of maps, like that of data visualizations, is an area of design specialty unto itself.

- Unless your audience is familiar with or expects a particular type of map, or styling a map is important to convey brand characteristics, any map software or API will do.

- When selecting a map application, consider how the map's default appearance will look with the rest of your interface and content. If all applications have comparable functionality, select the one that looks most aesthetically related to your interface.

- Refine the presentation of your map to visually integrate with your UI: change default fonts and colors that are *not* part of the actual map image to your fonts and colors. Do not change colors and fonts on the maps themselves, unless you're making an artistic statement that's more important than accurate use.

Patterns, textures, backgrounds, and gradations

Primary characteristics

Used successfully, these visual effects support content and brand, adding personality without upstaging content.

- *Patterns* are typically repeated areas of an image. Repeating patterns can have the effect of creating a texture (Figure 7.27).

- *Textures* are image effects that change the surface of the screen (Figure 7.28).

- *Gradations* are fields of one or more colors that vary in shade to give the illusion of depth. Gradations are a type of texture.

- *Backgrounds* may be any type of image or solid color that appear behind content (Figure 7.29). They create depth as well.

When to use

- When the content of a pattern or texture adds meaning to your content.

- When you want to affect mood.

- When you want to convey a sense of space or depth.

- To differentiate sections of content.

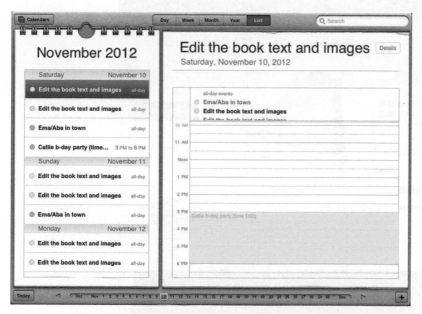

Figure 7.27 The iPad Calendar application's background mimics a leather and paper calendar. While this makes the application feel familiar, the combination of realism and computer fonts (not handwriting) is odd.

- When the effect will help communicate personality and brand.
- When looking for ways to connect visual design across platforms and mediums.

Details

- Always test type that will appear on a background for legibility and contrast.
- The simpler the pattern or background, the less distracting it will be.
- Patterns and backgrounds are most successful when they convey conceptual rather than literal qualities. This is a subtle but important distinction. Apple uses photographic textures to make Calendar appear as a *specific type* of tangible calendar. Converse uses photographic textures to *suggest* materials, such as the cloth and cardboard textures in their Design Your Own application. These images are accents to add personality, not to make the interface look like it's made out of cardboard and canvas.

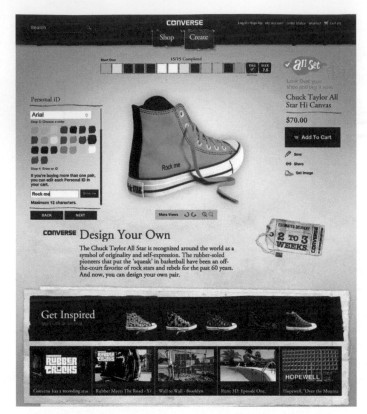

Figure 7.28 Textures used in the backgrounds and color swatches of Converse's Design Your Own application add realism and personality that help convey the brand without being too literal.

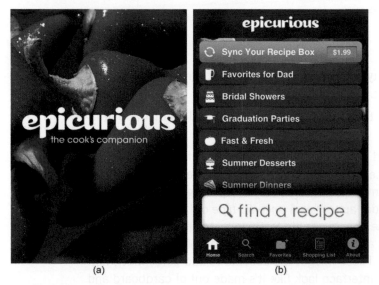

(a)   (b)

Figure 7.29 The background photo used in the Epicurious application adds visual interest and depth. Use of a semi-transparent color field in between the background photo, type, and icons ensures they're legible.

Skeuomorphs: Visual metaphors

Skeuomorphs are decorative elements designed to reference a real object, like the flame-shape of a light bulb designed for a chandelier.[6] In interface design, they're graphic images, movements, and sounds of real, tangible things used in an application interface to make something seem realistic and familiar, such as a page curl or lines and holes suggesting a paper notebook. Early in the history of the Apple user interface, skeuomorphs were used to style some features, like the clock that could be represented with hands, and HyperCard's text-entry area (Figure 7.30). At the time, working with a graphical interface was new, and use of skeuomorphs helped people quickly grasp how screen-based functions were similar to tangible ones.

Skeuomorphs are still prevalent in interfaces, including Apple's, but today reactions are often negative and subjective, pointing

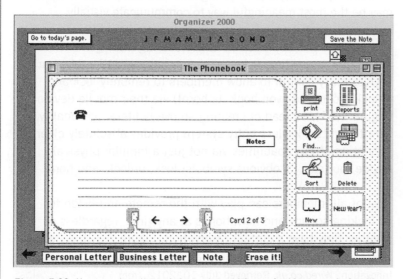

Figure 7.30 Hypercard replicated the real-world form of address cards familiar to users at the time.

[6]Skeuomorphs. (2012, July 19). Wikipedia. Retrieved July 9, 2012, from *http://en.wikipedia.org/wiki/Skeuomorph#Physical_skeuomorphs*.

out that skeuomorphs can stifle more creative approaches to interface design.[7]

Simplicity versus abstraction

The aesthetic principle of simplicity often relies on distilling forms to abstract, basic visual elements to communicate quickly and universally. Skeuomorphs are literal representations of real things, and as such convey highly specific visual information, which goes against the principle of simplicity. In *Primer of Visual Literacy,* Dondis A. Donis states, "The more representational the visual information, the more specific its reference; the more abstract, the more general and all-encompassing it is. Abstraction, visually, is simplification toward a more intense and distilled meaning."[8]

Interpretation of visual representation is contextual and subjective. In some situations, such as the introduction of a new feature or interaction, or designing for young children, using skeuomorphs may be the most meaningful way to communicate visually.

Zipcar takes this approach in its car-sharing management application, providing a skeuomorphic representation of a car's keyless entry control to allow members to remotely lock and unlock a car (and even honk its horn!) via their mobile device (Figure 7.31). Instead of creating an overly literal personality, here the virtual keyless entry system provides absolutely clear indication of its capabilities via not just a familiar physical device, but also its obvious symbols: lock, unlock, and horn.

Best of all, members can play with the remote and listen to its locking sounds and horn honks at any time, regardless of whether they have a current reservation (Figure 7.32). A "voice

[7] Thompson, C. (2012, Feb. 7). Clive Thompson: Retro Design Is Crippling Innovation. *Wired.co.uk.* Retrieved July 10, 2012, from *http://www.wired.co.uk/magazine/archive/2012/03/ideas-bank/ clive-thompson*; and Hobbs, T. (2012, May 30). Can We Please Move Past Apple's Silly, Faux-Real UIs? *Co.Design.* Retrieved July 10, 2012, from *http://www.fastcodesign.com/1669879/ can-we-please-move-past-apples-silly-faux-real-uis.*
[8] Donis, D. A. *Primer of Visual Literacy*, p. 74.

Figure 7.31 Zipcar's virtual keyfob.

Figure 7.32 Zipcar members without a current reservation may still play with the keyfob.

of the system" alert tells members they can "make fun sounds anyway," which helps people understand how the control works while reinforcing Zipcar's playful personality.

Simplicity and abstraction, when successful, are more likely to be aesthetically pleasing than the subjective, expressive nature of some skeuomorphic representations. Some of the best interfaces and images we've seen successfully abstract familiar characteristics, creating a distinctive and pleasing new visual language as a result (Figure 7.35). The Solar mobile weather application shown in Figure 6.38 is one example; by representing temperature with color and gradation, Solar creates visual abstractions that describe how temperature feels.

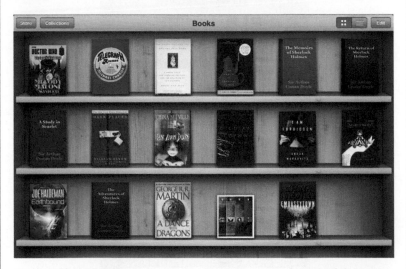

Figure 7.33 Apple's iBooks application. This hyper-realistic image of the wood bookshelf is too visually prominent for a background image that doesn't add meaningful information.

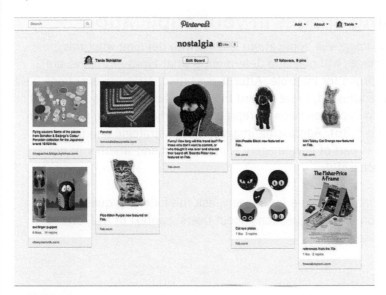

Figure 7.34 Pinterest allows users ("pinners") to create "pinboards"; however, the interface doesn't contain any visual references to tangible pinboards or corkboards. Naming is enough to put the metaphor in mind and suggest the act of using pins to attach images to a surface.

Figure 7.35 Trees, Cabs & Crime visualization by Stamen Design. By reducing objects—trees and cabs—and occurrences—crime—to color-coded dots, Stamen uses abstraction to create a new and beautiful way to see what happens in a city.[9]

[9] Map tiles by Stamen Design, under CC BY 3.0. Data by OpenStreetMap, under CC BY SA.

Using images in your application

Using images in applications begins with defining what role the images will play and determining what types of images are appropriate for that role. After these broad, strategic questions have been addressed, move toward more specific, tactical questions about what to depict and how to represent the images in the application (Figure 7.36). Addressing images at both strategic and tactical levels is part of how imagery is interpreted and whether or not it's successful.

To define a rationale for imagery, ask the following questions in addition to basic questions about users, context of use, and business goals.

Strategic

- What's the purpose of the application?
- What content will it include?
- What do users expect to see depicted?
- What role will the imagery play?
- How important is it to differentiate your application with imagery?

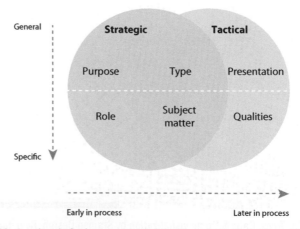

Figure 7.36 A rationale for imagery needs to address both strategic and tactical issues. Early on, strategic questions might include whether icons will help people decide what to click on, or whether photos or video best showcase product features. Later, more tactical questions address specifics about the imagery, such as whether people understand what an icon means, or whether a video's lighting favors a product.

Strategic/tactical

- What are the qualities of the personality?
- What types of imagery will help communicate the content? The personality?
- What should the imagery represent?

Tactical

- How should the imagery be presented? Where should it go?
- What are the qualities of the images? Are they large, small, detailed, simple, representations, abstract, contrasting, supporting, etc.?

Looking at the existing SuperTracker application, we identified several ways images were being used. This simple analysis helped us know what users might expect to see in a redesign, and qualify the current use of images to determine what was successful and where opportunities existed.

On the SuperTracker start screen (Figure 7.37), images are used to:

1. Identify the application via logotype (SuperTracker).
2. Relate the application to the MyPlate initiative.
3. Convey statistics or graphing (via a background pattern).
4. Show that the application is for families.
5. Contrast with the text (grocery bag, meal on a plate).
6. Reference measuring weight, creating and checking off goals, and gathering data for reports.

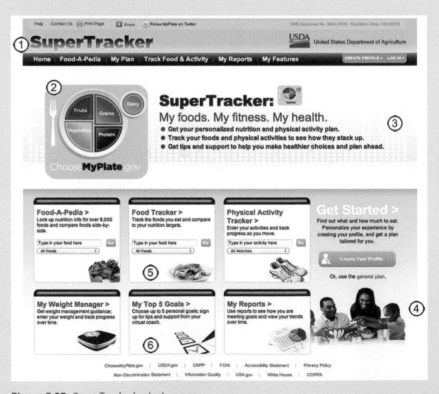

Figure 7.37 SuperTracker's start screen.

In the Food Tracker screen (Figure 7.38), images are used to:

1. Show status and progress via charts.
2. Help actions stand out by using icons in buttons.
3. Control functionality (arrows in the date selection area).
4. Provide visual interest (gradations).

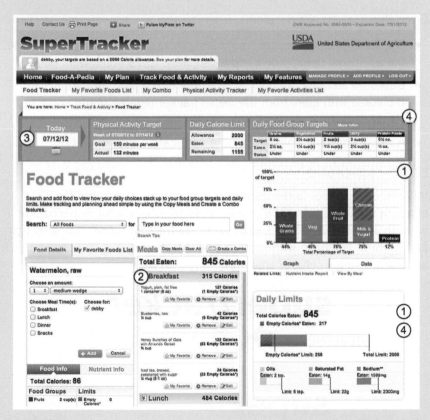

Figure 7.38

Qualifying images—moving from "what is" to "what could be"

The simple inventory and analysis showed that there were few images in the tracking areas of the application. Other than the logos, all images in those sections related directly to content and functionality, and even the visual tie to ChooseMyPlate.gov was lost once away from the start page. We found that the image types in use—gradation in the logotype and MyPlate logo, stock photos, graphic pattern in the background, and gradations in headers and buttons—didn't work together to convey a personality.

Given this analysis, we decided:

- The stock photos were communicating more detail than necessary, and the additional detail didn't add personality. Icons would work better.

- Based on test use, we decided that the charts were important, and if colored with hues from the SuperTracker palette, could serve as a visual tie to MyPlate programs.

- A new logo would help convey the application's personality.

Logo exploration

Initially, as a symbol to represent the application, we wanted the redesign of the logo shown in Figure 7.39 to convey what SuperTracker is—a tool for tracking food and activity. For the first round, one direction took a literal approach with icons, while the other took a more symbolic approach, using a sneaker sole print.

SuperTracker

Figure 7.39 The SuperTracker logo is a logotype.

Figure 7.40 The first-round logo redesigns tried to convey the essence of tracking food and activity.

We dropped the idea of using icons in the logo after this round because we anticipated using icons in the interface, and wanted the logo to contrast in terms of image style (Figure 7.41).

The third round of logo designs started back at the drawing board (Figure 7.42). We revisited and refined the goal for the logo—to express the sophisticated and tech-savvy "Pepper" personality and tie the applications to the MyPlate identity. We realized we could use imagery in the interface rather than the logo to convey food and activity tracking.

Figure 7.41 The second-round logo ideas focused on alternate ways to integrate food and activity with the type. While the apple in the "p" was working, the sneaker tracks looked ghostly.

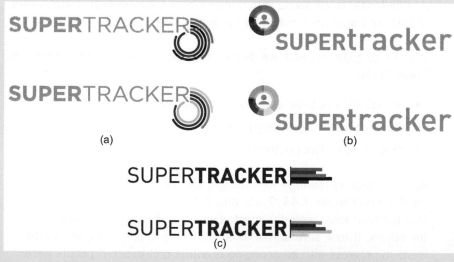

Figure 7.42 All three third-round logos achieved the new goals in different ways. (a) This logo was stylish, but too much so; we wanted the application to feel like a resource. (b) This logo was a little too cute. (c) This logo looked sophisticated and useful with the contrast between the dark type and the bright colors.

Figure 7.43 The final version of the logo.

Our final version of the logo works stacked vertically or horizontally (Figure 7.43). The logo doesn't explicitly convey tracking food and activity, but relies on the subtle cue of the colors and shading in the chart to reference the MyPlate logo.

Icon exploration

Based on the wireframes, we knew icons could add visual interest to the list of foods eaten without taking much space. We also knew they would be more expressive than words to label meal types and amounts when adding foods. Icons styled with curves would contrast with straight lines of text, and were an opportunity to express personality.

With these goals in mind, we defined the role of icons in our redesigned SuperTracker:

- Attract the eye to actions and important data.
- Convey personality through slight expression.
- Provide attractive controls for inputting data.

After the second round of logo design, we started to explore different meal icons (Figures 7.44, 7.45, and 7.46). This exercise showed us that the food icons were the most obvious, and had more character than the others. It took several rounds to get to the final set. We tested the icons in progress with an anonymous online poll to see if people were comfortable with the icons, and in particular to see if vegetarians and vegans would be offended by the depiction of an icon that showed meat.

breakfast
lunch
snack
dinner
1
2
3
4
AM
PM
PM
PM

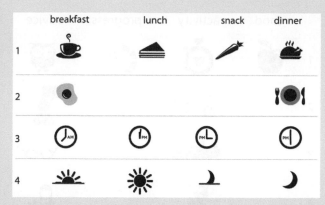

Figure 7.44 The initial round of meal icons explored different ways to represent meal types.

breakfast
lunch
snack
dinner

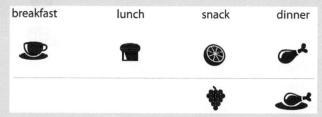

Figure 7.45 Refinement of meal icons focused on subject matter and consistent style.

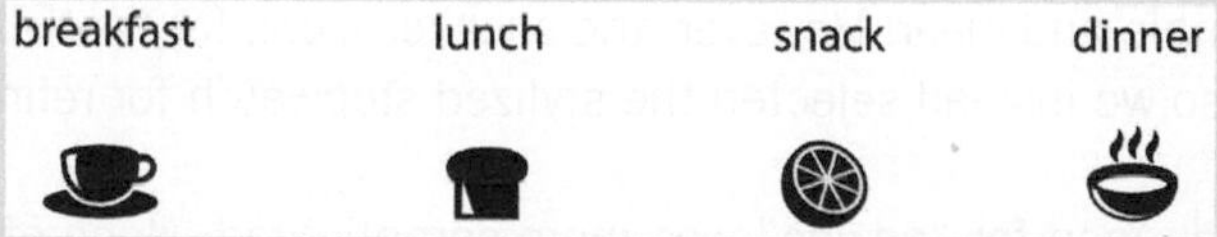
breakfast
lunch
snack
dinner

Figure 7.46 Meal icons with final subject matter and visual qualities.

As we refined the icons, we dove into the details of subject matter. We tried fruit for the snack icon, a more appealing choice than a carrot. We also tried a leg of poultry instead of a whole bird, which seemed too special for everyday meals, and took the curl of steam off the cup to make the icons look more like a family. (We considered using one of the dinner bowl's steam curls on the cup, but then the icons looked too similar.)

Figure 7.47 Icon design for the application sections.

While designing the logo and food icons, we also designed icons for each section (Figure 7.47). Some icon ideas were more obvious than others— for example, the apple for "food" and the circular segments for "progress" seemed simple and clear. However, the sneaker icons for "activity" were less clear, so we instead selected the stylized stopwatch for refinement.

Designing an icon for "advice" was more complicated. None of the initial options both fit the personality we were looking for and communicated as simply and clearly as the apple.

Chart exploration

As discussed in Chapter 6, we started exploring design through the mobile layout. We briefly considered using a food groups chart that referenced the MyPlate logo, but weren't sure if the guidelines allowed for this kind of approach. Even if they had, this approach looked more confusing and less straightforward than a traditional bar chart (Figure 7.48).

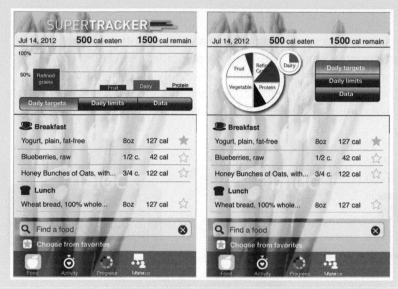

Figure 7.48 Image use in the first round.

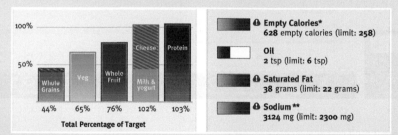

Figure 7.49 The final charts use familiar, straightforward formats. Although information design experts Edward Tufte and Stephen Few don't recommend using gradations in chart bars, we felt that they had more benefits than drawbacks. The gradations add needed visual interest in keeping with Pepper's personality and make a connection to related materials without detracting from chart legibility.

Based on the personas and test use, we defined these roles for the chart (Figure 7.49):

- Convey at-a-glance information about how well the user meets daily food group targets.

- Serve as a visual reference to the ChooseMyPlate.gov parent site and MyPlate initiative.

Images across screens

The final phone screens show icons as well as button treatments and chart design (Figure 7.50). We took particular care with icon design, an integral part of the interface's personality and functionality. The flat, one-color design helps icons blend into the interface, yet provides enough contrast with the text to add visual interest.

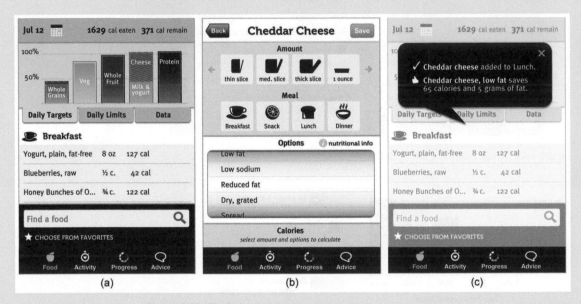

Figure 7.50 Final phone screens.

Imagery and the meta-principles
Consistency

For the SuperTracker redesign, images are used as consistently
as possible across platforms, but differences in screen size and
conventions forced some variations. One is that the logo doesn't
appear on all screens of the phone version; it would use up too much
space without adding comparable value. Another difference is the
position and visual hierarchy of the navigation icons, which follow
platform conventions for placement.

Some of the icons are clickable or tappable, and some are not. The
meal icon is decorative on the food-tracking screen, and interactive
on the food selection screen shown in Figure 7.50b. Being completely
consistent in color use to indicate interactivity would compromise the
visual design and create a confusing visual hierarchy (Figure 7.51).
Using other interaction cues from our design, such as pairing the
icons with tappable blue text, a round-cornered box, and a familiar
scrolling control, allows the icons to feel interactive.

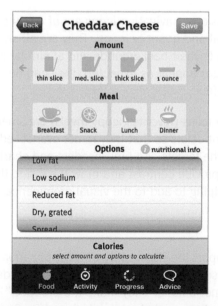

Figure 7.51 If we were completely consistent with how we treated tappable images,
the icons on the screen to add a food would be yellow. While yellow icons are consistent
with one of our rules—yellow icons are clickable—too many yellow items appear to
shout for attention. They're visually "loud," which cancels out yellow's purpose as an
accent to draw the eye.

In a visual interface with a lot of screens and elements, some inconsistency may be necessary to keep all the elements and the overall design in balance—aesthetically pleasing and usable. Rather than define a rule that all clickable icons must be yellow, we defined rules for different sets of icons—for example, the icons in the navigation bar are governed by a rule that they're white by default and yellow when highlighted. Breaking up rules for display and behavior helps in two ways: the bright yellow highlight shows users at a glance where they are in the application, and the limited use of yellow as an accent color draws appropriate attention to all yellow icons.

Hierarchy

Other than the logo, our SuperTracker redesign contains six sets of images. One is the target and limits charts, and the rest are groups of icons. On the go, the charts will often be most important, as they support the scenario of checking calorie intake status in the context of making a decision about what to eat. In all versions, position, shading, treatment, and color help communicate the charts' priority compared to other images.

In the mobile versions, navigation icons are of equal importance with the clickable meal and quantity icons. They are all shown at similar levels of contrast to their backgrounds and at similar sizes. Because the navigation logos appear as expected, they can be smaller than the icons in the interface.

Status and action icons (favorites, copy meals) are small, but are presented in bright colors so that they're not overlooked. Finally, icons that accompany the targets and limit headers and charts are mostly decorative. They provide contrast and draw the eye to the data in those sections while helping to add to the visual prominence of the charts.

Personality

Images must support the personality of an application. In balancing expression and use, it's important to remember that details matter. "The details are not details. They make the product," Charles Eames said.[10] The icons, logo, and chart we designed for SuperTracker aren't very expressive on their own; they work together with the other tools to communicate personality.

[10]Caplan, R. *Connections: The Work of Charles and Ray Eames.* p. 15.

Figure 7.52 Providing feedback in a large speech bubble helps convey the "voice of the system." Pepper, the personality for our redesign, is no-nonsense, yet helpful.

One additional way we contribute to SuperTracker's personality is to use images to support feedback. After adding a food item, Pepper gives her feedback in a speech bubble and makes recommendations (Figure 7.52). Using the large version of the "advice" icon to convey feedback helps users feel that they're interacting with a system that has a subtle, no-nonsense personality. Many seemingly small decisions like this one, made with all the tools, work together to convey Pepper's personality attributes.

Avoid common mistakes

The descriptions of each image type include some common mistakes to be avoided. The following recommendations are general and apply to all image types.

Don't use meaningless images

All images must have a purpose and play a role that you can articulate and defend.

Apply the "Goldilocks" rule to image quantity

Depending on content and context, an application without images will likely lack appeal, and may lack visual hierarchy. An application that uses too many images without enough context will send visual noise, which interferes with clear communication. An application with useful images that express personality without interference will feel "just right."

Present images clearly

Present images so that they can be seen clearly by providing:

- Sufficient contrast against the background.
- Sufficient contrast to clearly show the content.

- Appropriate sizing based on the level of detail.
- The right image resolution.

Present only essential information in an image

Each image should clearly communicate its message. Using only pixels that add information helps make sure image meaning is clear.

Design images of the same type consistently

If you include photography or video, shoot it all with the same visual style. Make sure all icons and symbols look like a family—that they share visual characteristics.

Present images of the same type consistently

All images sharing the same role should be presented the same way. Define rules and templates for how to present each type of image group, including rules for any necessary differentiation. For example, all product images should be the same size and displayed the same way in a layout, but featured images should be noticeably larger than nonfeatured ones.

Include a caption or supporting information unless the image's meaning is obvious

Images have multiple meanings. If your images are explaining something or are application content, include a caption.

Make informed decisions

Be aware of cultural conventions and if they affect interpretation of your images

Informally test images with a handful of representative users before launch, or before finalizing illustration styles and shooting all of your photography and videos.

Be aware of trends in image styles and content, and their connotations

Image style communicates just as much as image content. Show people in your target audience samples of the image style you plan to use to make sure it appeals to them. Think about how long your images need to last before deciding to adopt a trendy or expressive style.

Don't allow default chart design to overshadow content and dictate personality

When selecting a graphing or chart design toolkit, select the most plain and customizable option. Gradations on their own don't give an application personality.

Define rules and standards for imagery

Don't degrade your application with a hodgepodge of image types, roles, and styles. Set a rule for the appearance and use of every type of image in your application, include your rationale, and make sure everyone involved in the interface design is aware of the rules and follows them. Being a "logo cop" or having one on your team may be annoying, but it's necessary to establish and maintain a professional interface.

Elevate the ordinary

Image as interface

Opportunities to use images as interface controls increase with technological advances, such as with the applications shown in Figures 7.53 and 7.54. We discuss direct data manipulation controls in more detail in Chapter 8.

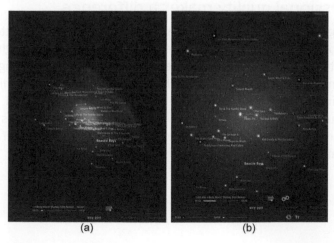

(a)   (b)

Figure 7.53 Tablet application Planetary uses a solar system metaphor to represent and interact with your music collection.

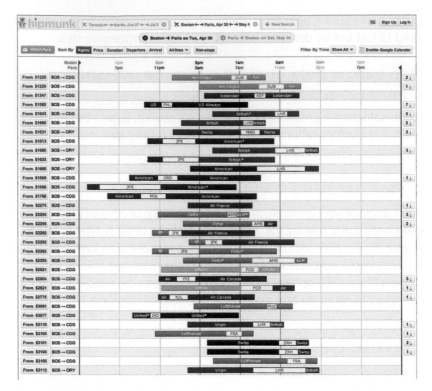

Figure 7.54 Flight search tool Hipmunk returns results in an interactive data visualization.

Professional quality makes a difference

Working with a professional adds value when image quality matters to the bottom line. If you work with a professional, think through your rationale for images in advance to know what you're looking for. Don't assume the designer or photographer will read your mind. At a minimum, be clear about how the images will be used and what purpose they will play, and be prepared to share adjectives that convey how you want people to interpret the images in your application.

Controls and Affordances

What makes functional applications work is their use of interface controls—everything from clickable buttons to custom-designed tools—that allow people to interact with data via a screen. The visual design of a control can strongly affect whether people understand what it is, what it does, and how to use it.

In application design, *affordances* are the properties people perceive about interface controls—whether buttons feel clickable, sliders draggable, and icons tappable. Controls and their affordances straddle the line between user experience and visual design. This chapter focuses on making decisions about how controls look as part of designing a visually usable application.

An affordance is an *implication*: an interface control implies behaviors based on a person's impressions of it. The control's shape, symbols (e.g., a down arrow or plus sign), color, shading, position, motion, and other visual cues, along with context, affect how people interpret what they see and what they think the control will do. Is a blue "Delete" button acceptable, or will people understand its purpose more quickly if it's red, to indicate a very serious action?

These implications form what Don Norman refers to as *signals* in his book *The Design of Everyday Things*. Signals help people know what to do, and they need to be designed.

> *Affordances can signal how an object can be moved, what it will support, and whether anything will fit into its crevices, over it, or under it. Where do we grab it, which parts move, and which parts are fixed? Affordances suggest the range of possibilities, constraints limit the number of alternatives. The thoughtful use of affordances and constraints together in design lets a user determine readily the proper course of action, even in a novel situation.[1]*

[1] Norman, D. *The Design of Everyday Things*, p. 88.

Every signal users see is a clue about how to interact with an application. Sending misleading signals through inaccurate or unclear design treatments makes it that much harder for people to correctly interpret what they perceive. Half the battle to create clear affordances is choosing the correct control and actions; the other half is applying the meta-principles and visual design tools to foreshadow a control's actions. This combination adds up to affordances that are visually usable—that signal at a glance what they do.

Using design to reveal affordances

Because controls are the means for interaction, it's crucial that users understand what they see. Starting with familiar patterns is the best way to do this. Once you select your controls, applying them requires attention to detail, but it's straightforward work. It requires awareness of the library of controls, discipline to use controls consistently, and flexibility if the addition of a new feature means that the library or the use of controls needs to change.

It's more of a challenge to accurately communicate hierarchy through placement and use of controls. While other applications can be used as a reference for where to place controls, it's likely that your control layout will need to be considered uniquely in the context of your content. If you want to elevate the ordinary, extend this consideration to evaluate familiar patterns once you have them in place. Look for opportunities to improve on the expected, informed by your personas, and visual usability principles.[2]

Paying attention to details will help your design stand out. Designing controls is worth the effort to infuse personality throughout an application. We'll survey common controls to help you know what works and where to start.

Types of controls and affordances

The controls and affordances in functional applications fall into three categories:

- *Navigation controls* such as tabs, scrollbars, and dropdown menus that suggest movement from place to place within an application.

[2]The shift we made in controls shown in Figure 4.18 of the SuperTracker case study is one example of applying familiar patterns, evaluating them, and shifting controls to improve appeal and use.

- *Data manipulation controls*, such as form fields and submission buttons that suggest ways for people to select and manage information.
- *Information display controls*, such as accordions and overlays that suggest revealing information on demand.

Interface controls may overlap between categories because their affordances are useful for a variety of purposes and contexts.

The following examples give a sense of how the meta-principles and tools can be applied effectively (or not!) to different types of controls, and recommend points to keep in mind as you do the same to your application.

Navigation controls

Although people understand the most basic online navigation controls, such as hyperlinks and tabbed categories of information, visual treatments, along with use of language (e.g., "next"), still make the difference between navigation that's findable, and navigation people have to struggle to locate and use.

Navigation controls include:

- Image-based links, such as clickable/tappable icons
- Tabs
- Internal scrollbars or carousels to browse navigable items
- Stepped process indicators

Like any other visual element, these controls must be considered within the overall screen hierarchy. Placement must be balanced against location of functional controls and other screen elements so that all items accurately represent their status in the hierarchy. The best way to do this is to quickly try options and evaluate how well the different relationships work.

Links

Communicating links is about contrast and expectation. In text paragraphs, hyperlinks need to stand out from the rest of the text. They should be high contrast relative to the text color, and ideally underlined to help differentiate them.

Lists of navigation links are different, because lists stand out already. Depending on context, people expect list items to be clickable. Links in a list do not need to be underlined provided they appear in locations where users expect to find them, such as the side or top of a screen, and are differentiated from text in some way.

Alternatives to underlining links in a list include:

- Highlighting list item on rollover
- Underlining on rollover
- Changing link color on rollover
- Always displaying links in a different color from the main text color (Figure 8.1)

Page(s): ◀◀ previous **1** 2 3 .... 8 9 10 next ▶▶

Figure 8.1 In this pagination example, color makes unavailable options recede, while the selected option is boldfaced. Underlining links here is unnecessary; they could create visual clutter in a list of numbers, and people understand a pagination control will include active links. Arrow icons reinforce the concept of moving forward to the next page. Numbers underline on rollover, and though mobile device users won't see that additional feedback, use of well-understood paradigms makes these controls easy to interpret no matter the platform.

Internal scrollbars

Like many default controls, system scrollbars are often overdesigned. While their shading is great for suggesting depth, it can also be too visually prominent, overwhelming an interface. In the case of internal scrollbars, the goal is to help users see and interact with the contents of the scrolling area, but balancing visibility between controls and content is a challenge. How much design do you actually need to make a control and its affordances obvious?

Scrollbars used for subsections of the screen need a high-contrast, clear representation of a scrollbar with up/down arrows and a scrubber, the grabbable portion of a scrollbar (Figure 8.2). Altering the look and feel can be vital to supporting personality; if you've styled every other control on the screen, a browser-default scrollbar could clash with your design, like a pair of scuffed-up sneakers worn with a high-fashion gown. At the same time, you must provide enough visual cues at a large enough size for people to recognize

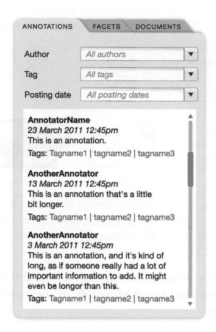

Figure 8.2 This well-designed internal scrolling control uses a high-contrast scrubber with a pale scrollbar so people know what element to grab, and provides up and down arrows as additional cues to the scrolling affordance.

the redesigned control for what it is and use it successfully. A small, muted scrubber that floats between two tiny, pale triangles isn't enough information for people to perceive the affordance.

Navigational buttons and icons

Any number of visual treatments can apply to navigational buttons and icons, depending on the desired personality: rounded corners, gradients and highlights to indicate depth, shades of color, integration of icons *within* buttons, and so on. (See Chapter 7 for a more detailed discussion of icons.) Regardless of the approach you take, the colors of your buttons should be part of your overall palette, possibly based on tints of your primary colors, or the full-strength version of your accent colors (see Chapter 6 for more on color). Color choices should be consistent throughout your application, with a limited set of link and button colors and styles to make it easier for people to understand what's interactive and what isn't.

Grouping buttons will help simplify the interface, but only works if the buttons do similar things and are presented in the same way. If

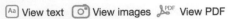

Figure 8.3 Only icons sure to be understood by your audience can stand alone. Accompanying text confirms user expectations of what will happen when they click on each area.

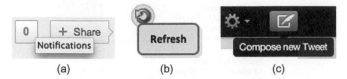

(a) (b) (c)

Figure 8.4 Tooltips provide another way to confirm the purpose of an icon. (a) Browser default styles are fine in most circumstances, but (b, c) custom tooltips offer another opportunity to infuse personality into a design.

one button performs a very different action than the others, it may need to be differentiated to set expectations instead of providing an unwelcome surprise.

Stepped progress indicators

Stepped progress indicators should use color, typography, and other visual treatments to identify not just the active area, but also the inactive ones so that people know what steps they have completed (Figure 8.5). If users may revisit previous steps, consider highlighting them on rollover or tap so users get confirmation that their interaction expectations are correct.

Figure 8.5 RedEnvelope's progress bar uses color, contrast, and symbols to clearly track previous, current, and next steps in the checkout process.

Pattern libraries

One common way to ensure that an application provides consistent and appropriate controls and affordances is to use *pattern libraries*, collections of typical design problems and solutions that include suggested controls and sets of interactions. Because these solutions recur frequently in digital applications, users recognize them, providing external consistency and making your application simpler for users to grasp.

Patterns do not generally address visual design, concentrating instead on the controls and affordances expected to perform an action, as well as the feedback to provide along the way. How interface elements and any confirming feedback are presented is up to you, and applying the wrong design to the right pattern can still result in a poor user experience for your audience.

When researching solutions with pattern libraries, it's important to keep in mind that there are often multiple good ways to solve a problem, and only testing can reveal which method best suits your audience (or whether your audience has no significant preference). Testing may also reveal where your implementation and/or visual design is impeding usability through insufficient visual contrast, poor placement, confusing hierarchy, or other issues.

As you design and develop your application, create your own library of patterns if users must perform similar tasks throughout, and document it in your style guide. As more features are added onto the application, refer back to your set of patterns as the foundation for any new functionality, extending control features and affordances where needed, and adding new ones when absolutely necessary.

Data manipulation controls

For functional applications, this is a broad but critical category, since virtually every type of application, from e-commerce to banking to travel and more, relies on controls that allow users to locate information, make selections, and complete purchase, registration, and other types of transactions. Regardless of whether the transactions involved are simple or complex, the controls must be styled to effectively foreshadow their capabilities: typeahead fields need to provide visual highlights to confirm selections, sliders need bars that feel grabbable so people know what to move, and draggable elements need visible "invitations" to cue where users can drop an item.

Controls for data identification, manipulation, and transactions include:

- Radio buttons
- Checkbox- or dropdown-based search results filters
- Multiple-select boxes
- Configurable lists allowing users to move items from one to the other
- Sliders
- Typeahead fields
- Calendar pickers
- Color pickers

Form elements

Form elements, including buttons, are the most common controls used to manipulate data, and have a nominally well-understood set of affordances: input fields suggest typing, radio buttons and checkboxes suggest clicking, and dropdowns suggest clicking (or tapping) and pulling. Because of this, visual design of these elements should concentrate on making them match the website's style and personality.

JetBlue's web-based flight search interface demonstrates one good way to apply visual design to reveal controls and affordances. The flight booker's orange highlights on the radio buttons and form submission tie into how color and type are used throughout the application. Subtle interior gradients and exterior shadows on the dropdowns provide depth to form elements and act as an invitation to click.

The flight booking tool also uses symbols and icons to emphasize form elements and their affordances (Figure 8.6). Downward-pointing arrows in the location boxes, recent search list, and dropdowns imply a selection interface will appear below once the user starts typing or clicking. Right-facing arrows imply forward motion—information

Figure 8.6 JetBlue.com's flight-search interface.

visible on another screen. And calendar icons foreshadow selecting a date via a calendar widget, as well as subtly cue the concept of depart and return dates by presenting a solid blue "date" in slightly different locations for each icon.

Size and contrast are also valuable tools in making form elements and their affordances clear. If This Then That applies bright colors and oversized type to its UI controls to carry through the friendly, almost whimsical, personality. Their invitation screen consists of two fields and a giant blue submission button (Figure 8.7). Even if the button weren't clearly marked "Invite," it would draw attention because its size, color, and shape look inviting.

Android's default picker interface shows how to effectively use contrast in formlike controls to reveal interaction points and highlight important information (Figure 8.8). Solid gray arrows stand out from their darker background, their directions clearly indicating that tapping will move content up or down. Unselected values appear in the same gray color as the arrows, but appear to recede due to their thin line weights. This helps draw attention to the selected values, which appear in high-contrast white. Finally, brightly colored rules help confirm the choice of selected values, literally blocking them off from unselected ones.

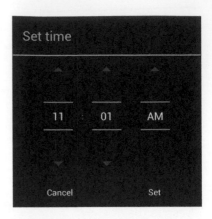

Figure 8.7 ifttt.com's invitation form.

Figure 8.8 Android's default picker interface.

The music identification application Shazam uses size, contrast, and motion to draw attention to its primary interface element—one giant, black-and-white button on a pale blue background (Figure 8.9).

Figure 8.9 Shazam's main screen. The symbol on the button is Shazam's logo, a stylized S that suggests continuous motion without actually moving at all.

The glossy highlights and subtle dimensionality of the button make it feel clickable, but true confirmation of its purpose comes only from the text: "Touch to Shazam." Ideally, explanatory text shouldn't be necessary to clarify a UI element's purpose, but using short, clear text on or next to buttons is a common and effective technique for ensuring people understand exactly what effect clicking or tapping something will have.

Although the instructions serve not just to confirm the button's affordance, but also to reinforce application branding, a simple motion treatment could have made the button feel more clickable— for example, transitions on the white border that subtly expand it, adding a glowing halo that pulses into red and then returns to its original state. This transition is in fact in use on Shazam's navigational icon (Figure 8.10), but not on the main button itself. Despite the main icon's unmissable placement, the glow and motion below it are distracting and can draw the eye lower on the screen, away from the primary task.

Figure 8.10 Shazam's navigational icon.

Shazam uses motion more effectively once the button is pressed, shrinking it and surrounding it with a gray arc that sweeps into a circle as the application listens to a song (Figure 8.11). Turning the button into a feedback mechanism strengthens the relationship between the button and its purpose, and provides clear evidence of task progress. (The text provides additional confirmation, but the visual feedback is so unmistakable that the text is superfluous.)

Figure 8.11 As Shazam listens to a song, a gray arc denoting progress sweeps around the logo.

One task; many controls and affordances

A single, straightforward flow, such as locating a recipe for eggplant and adding its ingredients to a shopping list, can involve many of these controls, as well as navigation. When sketching a sequence, consider how many controls are put in front of people. Thinking about controls abstractly can help you look at them with a different perspective, which may open up opportunities to simplify.

The Epicurious application's search screen shown in Figure 8.12 takes familiar design patterns—a carousel, links, and a search bar—and layers custom design on top of them to create a consistent and visually quiet style that remains noticeable and clear.

The carousel at the top grabs attention with simple icons, and its directional arrows at right and left imply a scrolling action. Scrolling icons with a finger, we quickly discover eggplant doesn't have an icon; we resort to the search bar, which suggests

Figure 8.12 Epicurious' search screen.

its purpose and affordance through a magnifying glass icon and small type reading "Enter keywords." After typing "eggplant," the action button below dynamically updates to indicate the number of recipe results, which encourages tapping to see more.

A "view recipe" navigational control is one of the largest items on the next screen, shown in Figure 8.13. The button's size, shading, and size of its type make it feel as important as the recipe title and photo, and because the button looks similar to the previous screen's results button, we expect it to be tappable. Notably, although tapping on titles or photos to see more is a common action on mobile devices, doing so here does nothing. While the design doesn't explicitly suggest that either area is tappable, it also doesn't take advantage of user expectations of typical platform affordances.

The plus-sign icon on the recipe screen, also visible in Figure 8.13, implies through its symbol that tapping it will allow us to do something more to the recipe (Figure 8.14). Unfortunately, the symbol is the only indication that the icon is an interactive control, and it's unclear what its affordances might be other than potentially adding one thing to another.

Figure 8.13 A search result includes a large "view recipe" navigational control.

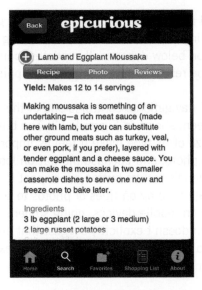

Figure 8.14 The plus-sign icon suggests interactivity, but not the control's purpose.

Tapping the icon reveals an iOS action sheet with a set of clearly labeled buttons (Figure 8.15). While the action sheet's behaviors are obvious, it's jarring and inconsistent to suddenly present users with a generic system design instead of one that meshes with the application's personality.

Figure 8.15 iOS action sheet.

The recipe is added to the shopping list, but now we'd like to see the ingredients. Here, with the recipe name and photo the most likely potential interaction points for viewing ingredients, the application does take advantage of user expectation of platform affordances, and displays more after tapping the recipe name (Figure 8.16).

Figure 8.16 Epicurious' shopping list.

Finally, we reach the shopping list screen (Figure 8.17). Checkboxes imply we'll be able to tap them to indicate we've purchased an item, and once we do, the name of the ingredient is grayed back, providing additional feedback that our purchased item is no longer a priority.

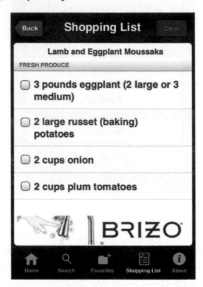

Figure 8.17 The populated shopping list.

Six major sets of controls later, we've added our recipe to the list and viewed its list of ingredients. Could we have done it in significantly fewer steps, or with fewer interaction points? In this case, probably not, but always keep streamlining in mind when adding controls to your screens. Carefully balance feature requirements, visual design, and user expectations to ensure your final screens aren't weighed down by too many controls, or the wrong ones entirely.

Direct data manipulation

On handheld mobile devices, where space is at a premium, directly manipulating the data itself is sometimes a better approach than providing separate UI controls. However, because removing an interface layer can make it harder for users to identify points of interaction, the visual treatment of data needs to reveal affordances as clearly as possible.

Tap

Tapping is one of the most basic interactions on a mobile device, replacing mouse scrolls and clicks with finger-based selection. It's a simple affordance, but the interface must present items that look likely to be interactive or tappable for people to feel confident about what to do.

For example, in the iOS Photos application, after tapping a sharing icon, users are presented with a grid of their photos, a large header reading "Select photos," and grayed-back action buttons (Figure 8.18). On a desktop interface, the user would probably select photos with a mouse, so here the obvious choice is to tap to select, and the interface reinforces this behavior with a checkmark icon to confirm each selection, as well as activated buttons.

Figure 8.18 iOS' photo-selection interface.

Drag and drop

Drag and drop is another common direct data manipulation affordance. To drag and drop successfully, users must understand where their draggable items can be dropped. A drop target need not be visually complex to be successful; jQuery's default drop feedback uses a simple color shift of text and background color (Figure 8.19).

Figure 8.19 Default drag-and-drop hover behavior demonstrated on jQuery's user interface resources website, *www.ui.jquery.com*.

For some applications, this straightforward treatment may be all that's necessary. But applications with different purposes or more robust personalities may need something more visually complex to mesh with their look and feel, as well as provide the right cues to each affordance.

For example, iOS finger-painting application Inspire Pro allows users to create a palette of frequently used paint colors. Like some real-world painter's palettes, Inspire Pro's palette includes visible depressions where an artist would place paint colors (Figure 8.20).

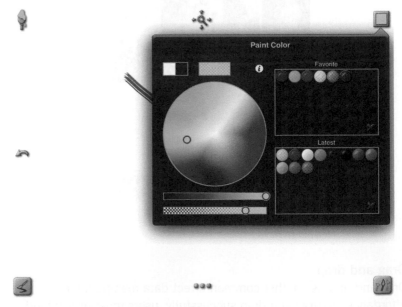

Figure 8.20 Painting application Inspire Pro allows users to create their own palette of colors.

Figure 8.21 Tapping the rectangular block and dragging it toward the Favorite area creates a circle of the selected color.

How would you expect to select a new color and add it to your palette? The obvious first step is to drag the selection dot on the color wheel to find the right color (Figure 8.21). This then updates a rectangular block above the wheel to confirm the selection. Since moving the selection dot provides clear feedback about its purpose by changing the color in the rectangle, this implies the selection dot isn't the tool for adding colors to the palette—but the rectangular block displaying the selection might be.

Tapping the block and dragging it toward the palette creates a circle of the selected color, outlined with a solid white border (Figure 8.22). Drag the dot on top of an empty space on the palette, and the white border begins to pulse and glow, confirming that the palette is the correct place to drop the color and save it.

Figure 8.22 As the user drags a new color into the Favorite area, the colored circle glows to indicate a drop target.

Sliders

Sliders allow users to narrow a range of values, and may include one or more movable grab bars to mark specific endpoints. Because they mirror real-world, physical controls, their affordances should be easily understandable, but visual design can work for or against this goal.

Flight-search tools are a common type of application making heavy use of sliders. Kayak.com's sliders, even the ones that have only one endpoint, are clear and simple to use (Figure 8.23).

These slider handles use a thin gray border to provide the illusion of depth—of something resting on top of the bar below. They also

Figure 8.23 Kayak.com's sliders.

incorporate thin vertical lines that add texture to help them feel grabbable, and pointed ends to indicate the selected range. As the user moves the handle, feedback appears directly above the slider, right where the user is looking and would expect to find confirmation of his or her choice.

By contrast, Google Flights' sliders, while visually consistent with the look and feel of the website (as well as other Google tools), aren't as clear, as shown in Figure 8.24.

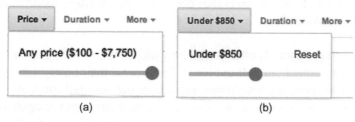

Figure 8.24 Google Flights' sliders.

What's wrong?

- The slider barely looks like a slider—it looks like a horizontal thermometer, a widget typically used to measure progress.

- Even if users do recognize the element as a slider, they can't confirm they're correct without rolling over the ball, which darkens in color and gets a cursor change to a left–right arrow.

- The slider endpoints are unmarked. Once users move the slider handle, they lose information about the low and high ends of the ranges.

- In the version of Google Flights we initially reviewed, Google provided slider feedback by updating its text to read "Under" a specific price point. However, the most important feedback, an updated list of flights, appeared elsewhere on the screen, and wasn't always visible without making a dramatic change to the price range.

Google has since updated its Flights tool to move the updated list of flights directly below the sliders, putting feedback right where the user expects to find it. Although the other slider design flaws persist, this feedback change is a significant improvement.

Information display controls

This category is related to revealing and hiding information. The principle of progressive disclosure, discussed in Chapter 4, frequently relies on controls to manage information display. Such controls include:

- Accordions
- Tabs that display information in a single section rather than refreshing a screen
- Links, buttons, or icons that open or close overlays, tooltips, or dialog windows

These sorts of controls often work like switches that are flipped on to display content, and off to hide it. They reveal their binary nature through symbols, like plus/minus signs or arrowhead indicators in accordions, or through sharing the signals associated with navigation affordances—cursor shifts when passing over a help icon that will launch an overlay, or the mental mapping of screen-based tabs to file folders or book tabs that can be flipped through. Only iOS-style popovers take a different approach, relying on the user to understand that tapping on the background will dismiss them, but even that assumption is based on the most basic, learned affordance in tablet interfaces: that tapping on the screen indicates what's important to you.

Accordions

Accordions frequently use pairs of symbols to signal their ability to show or hide information, such as plus and minus signs or triangles pointing in different directions (Figures 8.25, 8.26, and 8.27).

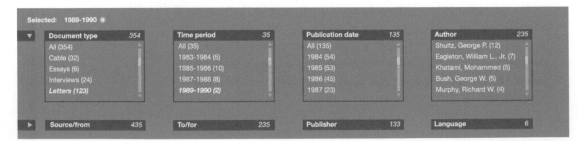

Figure 8.25 Users may choose to show or hide sets of search filters. Directional arrows shown to the left of header sets suggest this affordance. The show/hide feature is not essential to use, so the subtle treatment is appropriate.

Figure 8.26 These accordions from an application's job search form use plus and minus symbols in a contrasting color to signal their respective open/close behavior.

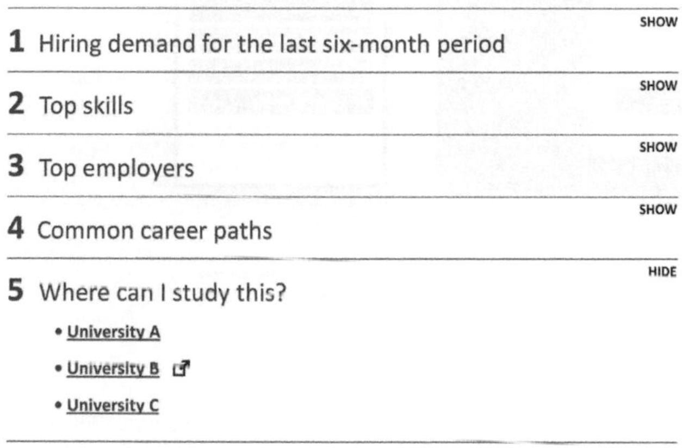

Figure 8.27 Depending on an application's audience, a different approach to revealing an accordion's affordance may be helpful. The audience for this application includes people with limited computer expertise. Thus, the accordions, each of which contains important information about a career, are numbered to encourage people to view each one. Rather than using an icon to control content display, accordions include "show" and "hide" text to clearly direct people.

Although an accordion need not include any symbols to be functional, or can include symbols alone, the combination of symbol and navigational text provides a stronger cue to the affordance.

Overlays

Because overlays involve displaying an entirely new content area on the page, foreshadowing them through visual design can be tricky; you must rely on an icon or explanatory text to cue that there's something more to see (Figure 8.28). The good news is that certain icons, such as question marks, are such commonplace tools for signaling specific types of information that users expect something to happen when they click, tap, or roll over the icons. While the audience may not expect that an onscreen overlay will be the delivery medium, they at least won't be surprised to see something change.

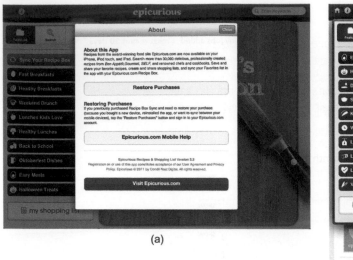
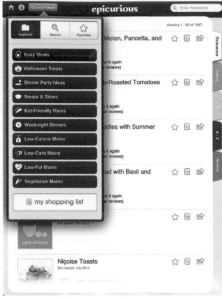

(a)

(b)

Figure 8.28 Tapping the "i" icon at the upper left of the Epicurious menu bar launches a modal dialog with information about the application. In vertical orientation, the menu bar includes a "Control Panel" button that loads an iOS popover.

Figure 8.29 Twitterrific loads an account info popover when the user taps on an icon shaped like a head.

User experience guidelines for the major mobile platforms discuss overlays primarily in terms of the circumstances in which designers and developers should use them, and provide little guidance about how to communicate to the user that a popover, multipane layout, or flyout—all terms for the same concept!—will appear once a certain icon, button, or screen element is tapped (Figure 8.29). Without a standard rule for how to communicate this affordance, applications don't signal overlay capability consistently.

Normally, a lack of consistency in how controls communicate their purpose is a fatal flaw. However, launching an overlay is a *nondestructive* action—merely the display of additional information and tools not otherwise available, and ideally not disruptive to the tasks in the parent window—so what's more important is that there be a consistent way to communicate how to *dismiss* the overlay. For nonmodal popovers, the solution is simply to tap elsewhere. For modal dialogs, a prominent "close" button or icon will do the trick.

For example, a job-search application we designed includes a common help feature: displaying an overlay when a user clicks on a help icon. This overlay includes a close box, symbolized by an X, to allow users to dismiss the overlay after they've finished reading the text (Figure 8.30).

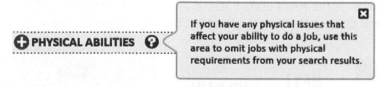

Figure 8.30 A friendly help overlay in a job-search application.

The look and feel of the help overlay are meant to connote friendly but authoritative advice: a tinted yellow background with black type grabs attention, but the gentle curves of the arrowhead and the rounded edges of the X in the close box literally soften the message.

Although the close box is not strictly necessary—we could have designed the overlay to appear on rollover of the help icon, and disappear when the user rolls off the icon—we based our rationale for adding it on several reasons:

- On screens with many help icons, the act of moving a mouse could trigger multiple overlays quickly, causing visual confusion.

- The content in the overlays may sometimes be long or complex, and users may need time to absorb it. It shouldn't disappear before they're ready.

- Requiring an explicit click on the help icon is ultimately a more mobile-friendly solution, since mobile device users will need to tap the icon instead of rolling over it to view content.

These decisions were made based on our understanding of the user scenarios and context of use for the application. Different scenarios and contexts might have resulted in different decisions.

Sliding drawers

Drawers may slide vertically or horizontally, and act much like an accordion in that they open and close to reveal information. However, unlike slim, narrow accordions, which serve essentially as clickable headers, a drawer may display more information simply by virtue of its larger real estate.

Weather application Dark Sky uses a sliding drawer to show the full day's rain forecast (Figure 8.31). A combination of content and visuals suggests the current rain forecast area is a sliding drawer: the words "Full Day" appear embossed in a depression bordered by grabbable handles. In the event users mistakenly assume they should pull the drawer downward to see the forecast, Dark Sky slows the drawer's

(a)   (b)   (c)

Figure 8.31 Weather application Dark Sky uses a sliding drawer.

Figure 8.32 JetBlue's application menu in (left) default position, (center) slid halfway up, (right) all the way up.

motion to discourage this interaction; at the same time, it displays a hint of the content below so people understand there's something to view. Releasing the incorrectly slid drawer snaps it back into place.

Similarly, the JetBlue application uses a drawer to display its key features, and a simple but effective combination of design elements and motion to confirm affordance expectations. When the menu is in its default position (Figure 8.32a), which hides some of its options, an upward-pointing arrow with emphasis lines below it suggests that the menu bar should be grabbed and pulled up to reveal more. As the user slides the bar up, the arrow begins to shift position, rotating clockwise (Figure 8.32b) until the options are fully revealed. The arrow and its emphasis lines now point downward to indicate how to hide the menu area (Figure 8.32c).

Integrating motion to reveal affordances

Visual design incorporates not just colors, type, images, and their position and use on a screen; it also includes how interface elements move. Motion enhances use by drawing attention to elements and showing changes of state, both of which provide confirmation of success and progress through a task. Movement affects personality, and should be selected to work with the tone you are conveying;

for example, in applications with playful personalities, unexpected animations can be delightful. The examples that follow, while hardly an exhaustive list of the ways motion can be applied to reveal points of interaction and their affordances, provide food for thought about integrating motion into a visual design.

Rollovers

The simplest rollovers create the sense of onscreen motion with transitions between on and off states, no different than a flipbook with two pages. Since the "flipping" happens so quickly, we perceive the state change as motion.

Rollovers are typically used to confirm a possible selection. Default link rollover behavior changes its color (Figures 8.33 and 8.34). In form dropdowns, rolling over a menu option highlights it. Similarly, rollovers have the visual effect of animating buttons and icons, confirming a user is hovering over a point of interaction.

Figure 8.33 "Cancel" buttons fill with color on rollover.

Figure 8.34 Tumblr icons subtly shift above the baseline on rollover (here shown with the "Text" option), giving the impression of bouncing up and down as the user passes a mouse across them.

CSS3 transitions allow for even more sophisticated rollovers, integrating time-based motion, border and color changes, size changes, and other effects (Figure 8.35). These effects can also be applied to elements in other states, such as when a user clicks or taps into a form element, giving it focus.

Finally, while rollovers are one of the most common ways to provide basic feedback identifying interaction points, they unfortunately don't work on mobile devices without a tap to enable them. Keep this in mind when designing your application—controls will have to rely on other criteria, such as color, placement, and text, to signal their interactivity.

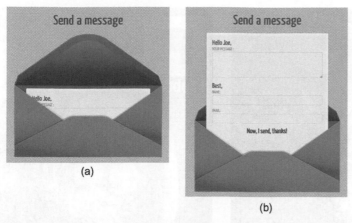

Figure 8.35 A demo contact form at *http://pehaa.com/2011/07/create-a-unique-contact-form-with-css3-transitions/* uses CSS3 transitions to slide smoothly out of the envelope when a user rolls over the form.

Flipping parts of the screen

Flipping parts of the screen allows you to reveal additional information within the same real estate (Figure 8.36). Although iOS includes a screen flip as part of its basic set of UI behaviors (it's used to display preference settings), applications on multiple platforms use the same technique to show content without fully refreshing the screen.

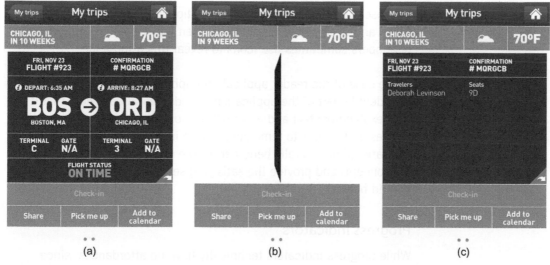

Figure 8.36 (a) The JetBlue application includes a triangular shape and curved arrow icon at the lower right of the flight information area to suggest there's more to view, and that it might involve a page flip. (b) A transition rotates the entire screen until the additional information is shown (c).

(a)   (b)

Figure 8.37 (a) Flipboard bends the image onscreen as the user flips it to the left (b).

Because the mechanism for a screen flip—a swipe or touch—does not in and of itself suggest that a screen flip will occur, designers and developers sometimes use icons to reveal this affordance.

In the case of the reader application Flipboard, screen-flipping is such an indelible part of the application's fundamental behaviors that it uses explanatory text and a symbol only on its main screen; after that, it relies on the user to remember how to interact with it (figure 8.37). Animations that literally bend part of the screen as it flips reinforce the concept, and provide the satisfying sensation of paging through a printed book or magazine.

Progress indicators

While progress indicators technically have no affordances, since they allow you to do nothing other than observe them at work, they do provide critical feedback confirming that a task is running, and sometimes how long it is likely to take.

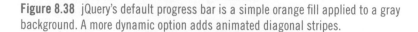

Figure 8.38 jQuery's default progress bar is a simple orange fill applied to a gray background. A more dynamic option adds animated diagonal stripes.

Figure 8.39 Dark Sky takes a similar approach as it loads local weather data, moving diagonal stripes toward the upper left of the screen.

From a visual design perspective, progress indicators provide a good opportunity to introduce some personality into what can otherwise be the very boring task of sitting and waiting. Although there's nothing wrong with a simple rotating circle or horizontal bar that slowly fills with color, particularly in an application with a businesslike purpose and visual style, even the simple application of a texture can add a little bit of pop to an otherwise staid design (Figures 8.38 and 8.39).

For applications that can handle a lot more personality, progress indicators can reinforce that personality through clever visuals. Hipmunk, a flight- and hotel-search website whose design features a chipmunk illustration, continues this same graphic approach in its progress indicator (Figure 8.40).

While the user waits for the content to load, the chipmunk tilts its body back and forth, as if pretending to be an airplane. A literally cartoonish approach won't work for every application, but here it

Figure 8.40 Hipmunk's animated chipmunk supports the site's personality.

adds a sense of whimsy to the screen, and makes waiting for flight information seem less tedious.

Controls, affordances, and the meta-principles

Consistency

Once you've determined which controls and affordances support the primary interactions in your application, you need to use the same controls and affordances everywhere those interactions apply. A small set of controls with expected, well-understood behaviors limits what people have to learn about your application, making it easier to use. No one expects to re-order items in a list with number boxes on one screen, drag and drop on another, and arrows on a third—or worse, to be presented with several similar-looking controls that do completely different things. Sending mixed signals to your audience is as bad as sending no signals at all.

Similarly, the look and feel of controls should not shift from screen to screen. Dropdowns should appear the same everywhere. Buttons with the same purpose, or at the same hierarchy level, should be treated the same way. Icons for application actions should use the same visual style. Every point of interaction in an application is another verb within your visual language, and irregular verbs can be hard to learn.

Inconsistency

Sometimes, inconsistency is the best way to accurately represent importance and difference. For example, the "Clear All" button in SuperTracker, shown in Figure 8.41 along with "Copy Meals" and "Create a Combo," is visually consistent with SuperTracker's button style. However, unlike the other two buttons, "Clear All" performs a destructive action. Treating it exactly the same way as two buttons supporting features that allow users to track what they've eaten is potentially dangerous; it sets up a visual language in which the words for "stop" and "go" are the same. The only reason users aren't punished for accidentally clicking a button that looks exactly the same as the one beside it is that "Clear All" triggers a dialog box asking the user to confirm the deletion.

Treating the button *inconsistently* would improve usability. Changing one of the visual characteristics, like button or text color, and separating the "Clear All" button slightly from the group would differentiate it appropriately.

Figure 8.41 Treating the "Clear All" button inconsistently from the other two would reinforce the difference between its purpose and that of its neighbors.

Hierarchy

For functional applications, controls and their affordances support the primary reasons people use such applications in the first place: they're searching for information, buying clothing, tracking food intake, and so on. A visual hierarchy must reinforce the importance of these primary actions—it's why Google's home page is a single search box on a largely blank screen instead of a long list of instructions about how to use advanced search or sign up for a Gmail account.

As we know from Chapters 2 and 4, the size and placement of UI controls on the screen directly affect a user's perception of not just which items are important, but also how the items relate to one another. You may know that a "Submit" button affords clicking to save your registration information, but if the screen layout doesn't clarify which form elements the button applies to, it's impossible to click that button with complete confidence that it will do what you expect.

Similarly, controls grouped together will be interpreted as acting on the same task or set of tasks, while onscreen placement of groups dictates which ones are perceived as most important. For example, although the "Clear All" button in Figure 8.41 was poorly designed, grouping it with "Copy Meals" and "Create a Combo" made sense, because all three items are related to managing meals. The overall placement of the group is less successful, however; cramming the buttons near large headers (see Figure 8.42 later) makes them harder to find on a densely packed screen, and gives them too much prominence.

Finally, controls with information display affordances, such as accordions, can support a hierarchy by hiding less important information and revealing it on demand. Use scenarios (described in Chapter 3) to determine what's most important to your audience and how they expect to proceed through your application. Then make sure that the screen design—including control size, placement, grouping, and other visual treatments—reinforces what people came there to do, as well as their expectations of how they'll be able to do it.

Personality

At times, interface controls feel like the orphan children of application visual design. Until the rise of JavaScript frameworks like jQuery that included skinned UI controls, web developers had limited control over the look and feel of HTML-based form elements, and what control they did have sometimes didn't work reliably across browsers. Even now, with sophisticated mobile operating systems available, default UI elements can look clunky and unrefined.

It's important that people recognize a control and what it does at a glance. Applying the visual design meta-principles and tools to an application while ignoring its functional controls is like going out half-dressed. As we showed earlier in this chapter, all aspects of a control and its affordances—from what color it is, to how it's highlighted if there's an error, to the smoothness of the way a screen flips over to reveal new information—must work together to support the personality.

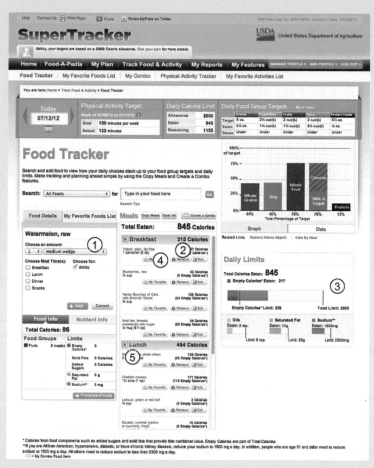

Figure 8.42 SuperTracker's food-tracking screen.

We analyzed controls on SuperTracker's food-tracking screen to see what was working and what could be improved (Figure 8.42). We based our analysis on:

- Usability heuristics
- Visual design heuristics, including our assessment of interface consistency, hierarchy, and personality
- Knowledge of competitive and similar interfaces
- Common interface patterns
- Likely scenarios of use

1. The food search filter dropdown doesn't accurately represent the way most people will locate items within a database of thousands of foods. If presented at all, it should not be presented at the same size and level of importance as the search box itself.

2. Tracking food, the most important task, has so many other elements surrounding that it doesn't feel as important as it is.

3. The food group chart and the tabs that control its display are too large relative to the food-tracking area, and feel too prominent.

4. "Copy Meals," a valuable tool for people who eat the same food items on a regular basis, is squeezed between a header and two other buttons. Paradoxically, the entire button group's location actually makes it feel more important than it is, simply because the buttons are so large and so closely spaced next to major headers.

5. Action buttons within each food item area ("My Favorite," "Remove," "Edit") are too big relative to the information they affect.

Our redesigned SuperTracker screens address each of these issues (Figure 8.43), make the application more approachable, and give people a better idea of which controls affect which content.

1. On the web and tablet versions, treatment of "Find a food" draws attention to itself, reinforcing that locating food items to track is SuperTracker's primary task. Putting the bar at the bottom of the phone version accomplishes the same goal, because its placement makes it easier for device users to activate it with the touch of a thumb.

2. The "Copy Meals" button, previously hidden as a small, gray button, is presented more prominently on the web and tablet versions, along with an icon that suggests duplication. On the phone version, which has less real estate available and must only present the most important features, "Copy Meals" would be available by tapping the name of a meal or a food item.

3. With "remove" and "edit" options moved to a detail screen available with a click or tap on a food item (not shown), the star icon used on the original SuperTracker's tiny "Favorites" button can now be presented on its own next to each food item, and displayed as empty. Clicking or tapping it feels like the only possible interaction one

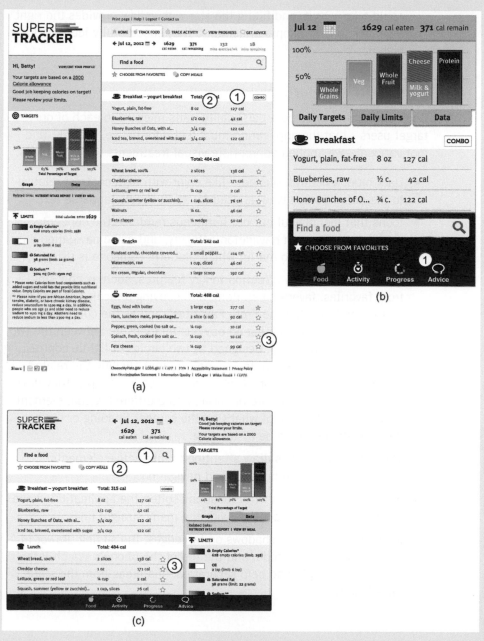

Figure 8.43 Redesigned SuperTracker screens for (a) web, (b) phone, (c) tablet.

could take with it, and filling the star with yellow provides the right feedback to help people understand they successfully identified a favorite.

Personality in SuperTracker

Keeping in mind three core personality traits relevant to each of our target users—that the application must feel informative, friendly, and motivational—we applied appropriate visual treatments to our controls.

- Dark blue, a neutral, business-like color with high contrast relative to the default black type, is used for all clickable/tappable text.

- Icons that feel playful but not humorous reinforce the concepts associated with each navigation category, and make navigation easy to find at a glance no matter which platform someone is using.

- Similarly, icons draw attention to key features, such as choosing from favorites, favoriting an item, and copying a meal. The star icon is used both on "Choose From Favorites" and as the control for favoriting an item, creating an obvious relationship between the two. The "Copy Meals" icon, designed as two circles of lightly contrasting color, provides additional foreshadowing that clicking the related text will copy information. These icons are styled simply; they draw attention because they are pictorial, and a different visual element from much of the rest of what's on the screen. Shading or more detailed styling would be distracting.

- The color yellow helps draw attention to interactive elements: favorite icons, action buttons, and navigation.

- Round edges in a number of locations soften the application, make it feel friendlier, and contrast with the many straight lines.

- Judicious use of drop shadows on tab edges, the sliding drawer in the tablet's vertical mode, and the top of the phone's search interface provide depth and help separate action areas from the static ones below.

Avoid common mistakes

Interactive areas should feel interactive, and read-only ones should not

Although people are used to filling out forms online, it's easy for them to lose track of where they are in a long form, especially if they use keyboard shortcuts to move from field to field. Providing instant visual feedback as users enters data help them quickly identify where they are and what they can do on the form.

- As people type in active fields, highlight the fields with a border, tint, or combination of both.

- Use the same graphic style for all buttons, icons, and other points of interaction in your application so that people learn that part of your visual language.

- Don't treat read-only elements the same way as interactive ones. People will assume they can manipulate controls unless they receive clear signals that something is different. Simply hiding a form field's border is usually enough to provide cues that a read-only field cannot be manipulated.

Provide feedback

Your visual design approach should account for system feedback— where it's placed, how it looks, and when it appears. No matter how carefully you've designed a control to foreshadow its affordances, no one can be confident their interaction worked without feedback.

- Put feedback where the user is looking, ideally near the control itself. If multiple controls must be manipulated to perform a task, make the feedback part of the results display.

- Use rollovers on links, buttons, icons, and other points of interaction. On mobile devices, rely on other visual forms of feedback, such as changing a button's color as it's pressed.

Apply design to form controls

If you've applied the meta-principles and tools to the rest of your application, don't leave UI controls undesigned, which makes the application feel half-finished. Simple treatments based on CSS, JavaScript libraries, or minimal customization of mobile device controls are often enough to integrate controls into your application's overall visual design and personality (Figure 8.44). More complex treatments can wait until you're ready to elevate the ordinary.

- Form field design need not be complicated; if anything, fields should be designed for readability and usability. Consider minimal treatments such as using a thin border around text inputs, or applying a splash of color to buttons in both inactive and active states.

- For the next step in design treatments, look into JavaScript frameworks, such as jQuery or extJS, that allow customization of checkboxes, radio buttons, dropdowns, and other elements difficult to style consistently with CSS alone. On mobile devices, create custom styles for your controls.

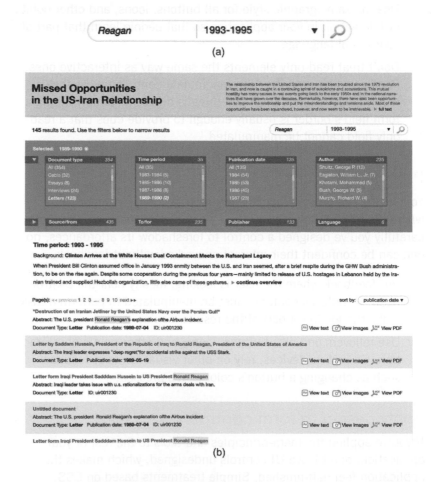

(a)

(b)

Figure 8.44 (a) A curved search box provides visual contrast to the squared corners of the search filters and zebra-striped results shown in (b). The integrated timespan filter is called out with a down arrow to suggest it's a dropdown.

Make informed decisions

Start with expected patterns

Design patterns represent the ways people expect to interact with objects on a screen.

- Rely on common design patterns to solve most design problems, at least at first.

- If you have a problem that can't be addressed with a design pattern, look to the most closely related patterns to see how they might be modified to serve your purposes. This provides you with a solid foundation to design from, and your audience with hints about how they might be able to interact with your application.

- Choose treatments for controls carefully, and test novel approaches to see if people understand them.

Elevate the ordinary

Improve flow and visual appeal with appropriately customized controls

Unique visuals for your controls can support your application's personality by pushing it beyond what people expect. The Epicurious search screen (see Figure 8.12) and our redesigned food entry screens (see Figure 8.43) both include customized controls to help flow and express personality. See also Figure 8.45.

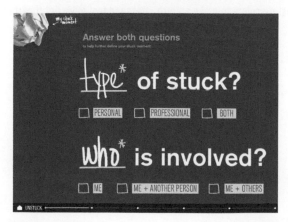

Figure 8.45 iOS application Unstuck gives its checkboxes a hand-drawn treatment, but their roughly square shape still clearly represents what they are. Form input fields that dispense with the full border in favor of an underline and handwritten help text contribute to the application's informal personality.

Take advantage of feedback to express personality

Feedback is another opportunity to express an application's personality, particularly if that personality includes a sense of humor.

- Seek out places to add special feedback that reinforces your application's personality, particularly error and alert messaging. Tools such as illustration and messages that have an appropriate tone of voice can be especially effective (Figure 8.46).

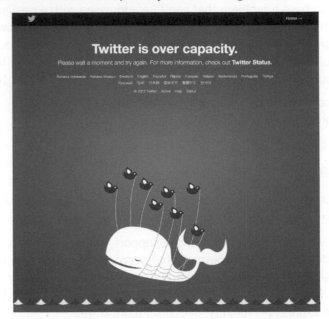

Figure 8.46 Twitter's classic, cheerful "fail whale" illustration uses its bird mark and bright, contrasting colors to make an error message feel more lighthearted.

Summary: Interface Design as Visual Conversation

Throughout this book, we've discussed application design in terms of creating a visual language: developing grammar through consistency and hierarchy, then vocabulary through personality and the tools used to express all three meta-principles. Designing this language involves an iterative question-and-answer process, as designers and developers ask questions, explore possibilities, raise new questions, and work together to resolve them. Having a rationale for decisions is crucial for realizing the purpose of the interface and keeping the design and everyone involved on track.

The meta-principles help you know what questions to ask and put you on the right path to answer them. The tools help you know what you can do and how to do it. What does placement of an element in relation to other ones imply? What if its size or position changes? Would these changes match treatments for similar situations and elements, and do the changes affect the hierarchy? Rather than making abstract or theoretical decisions about your interface design approach, let your rationale guide you and evolve as you try different possibilities to evaluate what's working and what isn't.

The SuperTracker case study demonstrates our internal conversations, and the rationale that grew and changed as we incorporated requirements, assessed our designs against our frameworks, and determined which visual choices were successful. At each step, we began with a direction that evolved as we put it into action. The process of manipulating elements and their characteristics is core to the act of designing. Asked by students if he thought a solution or approach was a good idea, renowned Swiss designer Armin Hofmann would shrug and say, "Try it."

Designing based on internal conversations alone will only take you so far. A true conversation includes the user, whose frame of reference and patterns of behavior must also inform the design. The ultimate goal of your conversations is not just to develop your visual language, but to ensure your users understand the messages you're communicating in that language, and that they hear the messages they expect.

We hope this book has helped you start design conversations of your own, avoid common mistakes, make informed decisions, and elevate the ordinary. Anyone can design and develop a functional application. But with a little effort, knowledge, and a lot of experimentation, anyone can design an application that's also helpful and satisfying— visually usable.

Recommended Resources

Interaction, interface, and user experience design

Cooper, A., Reimann, R., Cronin, D., & Cooper, A. (2007). *About face 3: The essentials of interaction design*. Indianapolis: Wiley.

Goodwin, K., (2009). *Designing for the digital age: How to create human-centered products and services*. Indianapolis: Wiley.

Johnson, J. (2010). *Designing with the mind in mind: Simple guide to understanding user interface design rules*. Amsterdam: Morgan Kaufmann/Elsevier.

Krug, S. (2006). *Don't make me think!: A common sense approach to web usability*. Berkeley, CA: New Riders Publishing.

Norman, D. A. (2002). *The design of everyday things*. New York: Basic Books.

Wroblewski, L. (2011). *Mobile first*. New York: A Book Apart.

Personality

Norman, D. A. (2004). *Emotional design: Why we love (or Hate) everyday things*. New York: Basic Books.

Rand, P. (2000). *A designer's art*. New Haven, CT: Yale University Press.

Wheeler, A. (2009). *Designing brand identities: An essential guide for the whole branding team*. Hoboken: Wiley.

Layout

Marcotte, E. (2011). *Responsive web design*. New York: A Book Apart.

Vinh, K. (2011). *Ordering disorder: Grid principles for web design*. Berkeley, CA: New Riders Publishing.

Type

Bringhurst, R. (2008). *The elements of typographic style: Version 3.2.*. Point Roberts, WA: Hartley & Marks Publishers.

Google Fonts

http://www.google.com/webfonts

Thinking with Type
http://www.thinkingwithtype.com

Typecast
http://typecast.com

Typekit
http://typekit.com

Typetester
http://www.typetester.org

Color

Itten, J., & Birren, F. (1970). *The elements of color: A treatise on the color system of Johannes Itten, based on his book The Art of Color.* New York: Van Nostrand Reinhold Co.

Colors on the Web's Color Contrast Analyzer
http://www.colorsontheweb.com/colorcontrast.asp

Kuler
https://kuler.adobe.com

The Paciello Group's Colour Contrast Analyser
http://www.paciellogroup.com/resources/contrast-analyser.html

WCAG Contrast Checker browser add-on
https://addons.mozilla.org/en-us/firefox/addon/wcag-contrast-checker/

Imagery

Few, S. (2009). *Now you see it: Simple visualization techniques for quantitative analysis.* Oakland, CA: Analytics Press.

Tufte, E. R. (1997). *Visual explanations: Images and quantities, evidence and narrative.* Cheshire, CT: Graphics Press.

Tufte, E. R. (2001). *The visual display of quantitative information.* Cheshire, CT: Graphics Press.

Controls and Affordances

Norman, D. A. (2002). *The design of everyday things*. New York: Basic Books.

Tidwell, J. (2005). *Designing interfaces*. Beijing: O'Reilly.

UI Patterns

http://ui-patterns.com

Yahoo! Design Pattern Library

http://developer.yahoo.com/ypatterns/

Bibliography

Beyer, H., & Holtzblatt, K. (1997). *Contextual design: Defining customer-centered systems (interactive technologies)*. San Francisco: Morgan Kaufmann.

Briggs, D. (2012). *The dimensions of colour*. Retrieved September 4 & 6, 2012 from <*http://www.huevaluechroma.com*>.

Bringhurst, R. (2008). *The elements of typographic style: Version 3.2*. Point Roberts, WA: Hartley & Marks Publishers.

Caplan, R. (1977). *Connections: The work of Charles and Ray Eames*. Los Angeles: Frederick S. Wight Art Gallery. University of California, Los Angeles.

Chevreul, M. (1861). *The laws of contrast of colour*. Translated by J. Spanton. London: Routledge, Warne, & Routledge. Retrieved September 4, 2012 from <*http://books.google.com/books/about/The_laws_of_contrast_of_colour_tr_by_J_S.html?id=KmEDAAAAQAAJ*>.

Cooper, A., Reimann, R., & Cronin, D. (2007). *About face 3: The essentials of interaction design*. Indianapolis: Wiley.

Dondis, D. A. (1973). *A primer of visual literacy*. Cambridge, MA: MIT Press.

Few, S. (2006). *Information dashboard design: The effective visual communication of data*. Beijing: O'Reilly.

Hofmann, A. (1965). *Graphic design manual: Principles and practice*. New York: Van Nostrand Reinhold Co.

Itten, J. (1961). *The art of color: The subjective experience and objective rationale of color*. New York: Van Nostrand Reinhold Co. (1973 ed.).

Itten, J., & Birren, F. (1970). *The elements of color: A treatise on the color system of Johannes Itten, based on his book The Art of Color*. New York: Van Nostrand Reinhold Co.

Johnson, J. (2010). *Designing with the mind in mind: Simple guide to understanding user interface design rules*. Amsterdam: Morgan Kaufmann/Elsevier.

Kobayashi, S. (1992). *Color image scale*. New York, NY: Kodansha USA.

Krug, S. (2006). *Don't make me think: A common sense approach to web usability*. Berkeley, CA: New Riders.

Lidwell, W., Holden, K., & Butler, J. (2010). *Universal principles of design*. Beverly, MA: Rockport Publishers.

Marcus, A. (1992). *Graphic design for electronic documents and user interfaces*. New York: ACM Press.

Mullet, K., & Sano, D. (1994). *Designing visual interfaces*. Englewood Cliffs, NJ: Prentice-Hall.

Norman, D. A. (2002). *The design of everyday things*. New York: Basic Books.

Norman, D. A. (2004). *Emotional design: Why we love (or hate) everyday things*. New York: Basic Books.

Rand, P. (1985). *Paul Rand: A designer's art*. New Haven and London: Yale University Press.

Roque, G. (2011). *Chevreul's color theory and its consequences for artists*. Great Britain: The Colour Group. Retrieved September 4, 2012 from *<http://www.colour.org.uk/Chevreuls%20Law%20F%web%20good.pdf>*.

Ware, C. (2008). *Visual thinking for design*. Burlington, MA: Morgan Kaufmann.

Weaver, W. (1963) *Recent Contributions to the Mathematical Theory of Communication*, published as the Introduction to Shannon, C. and Weaver, W. (1963) *The Mathematical Theory of Communication*. Urbana and Chicago: University of Illinois Press.

Index

Note: Page numbers followed by "*b*" and "*f*" refer to boxes and figures respectively.

Printed and bound by CPI Group (UK) Ltd, Croydon, CR0 4YY

03/10/2024

01040325-0007